CRACOW LANDSCAPE MONOGRAPHS

3

INSTITUTE OF ARCHAEOLOGY
JAGIELLONIAN UNIVERSITY IN KRAKÓW

INSTITUTE OF LANDSCAPE ARCHITECTURE
CRACOW UNIVERSITY OF TECHNOLOGY

CRACOW LANDSCAPE MONOGRAPHS 3

**Landscape as impulsion for culture:
research, perception & protection**

PROBLEMS OF PROTECTION & SHARING

Kraków 2016

CRACOW LANDSCAPE MONOGRAPHS
VOL. 3

REVIEWER
Agata Zachariasz

VOLUME EDITORS
Piotr Kołodziejczyk
Beata Kwiatkowska-Kopka

COVER DESIGN
Katarzyna Kołodziejczyk

PROOFREADING
Piotr Kołodziejczyk
Izabela Sykta
Beata Kwiatkowska-Kopka

TEXT DESIGN
Elżbieta Fidler-Źrałka

ISSN 2451-1692
ISBN 978-83-942469-6-9

Publishers:

Institute of Archeology
Jagiellonian University in Kraków
Gołębia 11 str., 31-007 Kraków, Poland
www.clc.edu.pl

Institute of Landscape Architecture
Cracow University of Technology
Warszawska 24 str., 31-155 Kraków, Poland
www.architektura-krajobrazu.pk.edu.pl

CONTENTS

PROTECTION, VALORISATION AND MANAGEMENT OF CULTURAL LANDSCAPES IN POLAND

Katarzyna Pałubska
Presidium of ICOMOS-Poland, University of Life Sciences in Lublin

The split between natural and cultural environment is the most vital threat to the appropriate protection and valuation of landscape, particularly in light of the well-known U Thant's report (1962), which emphasised the importance of comprehensive approach to the environment - inclusive of its biotic, abiotic and man-made components.

In order to understand the principles governing cultural landscape, it is fundamental that its influence upon the environment is properly recognised. This means that attempts at typologization of the resources' characteristics are to be made, in line with a set of criteria. The diversified classification of cultural landscape by its types, forms, styles or variations is reflected in the complicated system of valuation or assessment (universal methods of landscape valuation aim to protect chosen spatial units in regard of their appeal, while methods focused on specific undertakings evaluate landscape in regard of its practical value in a certain function /investment project). In practice, this means that we must deal with highly complex landscapes, which combine different types of forms, content and functions. Moreover, on a local scale, one of the most crucial values is diversity, which is a token of human identity and of regional nature of human activity, but it is also one of the most challenging aspects when classifying resources and using universal cultural landscape valuation methods. Perhaps due to this reason, a recent update on the cultural heritage protection system in Poland report (2010) suggests that identification and protection of cultural landscape effort made since 1989 has been scarce.

To develop a universal method – and such undertaking is now undergoing verification (ordinances are being drafted) – is to create a foundation to serve as the basis for a system of classification and valuation of landscape resources, which would adhere to the guidelines set forth in the new landscape act (2015). The act assumes developing research methods that would cater for the needs of a country-wide, voivodeship (landscape audit) and local scale. Formal solutions for landscape policy involving zoning plans also call for verification methods, with particular attention devoted to local zoning plans, whereby the individual characteristics of a cultural landscape (subjective) may get the upper hand over general criteria (biotic - objective) that are important in a wider scale.

An intermediate problem that has some influence on cultural landscape protection in Poland is the long-neglected issue of spatial planning as the most important tool in comprehensive protection of diverse landscape characteristics. The standstill in spatial policing is observed at all levels, which means that even the best sanctioned resource classification methods will not find their way to any actual practice of protection and sustainable shaping of cultural landscape.

Through an analysis involving dozens of landscape papers in Poland and Europe, it may be seen that most of them are based on identifying landscape types by natural environment criteria (considered more objective), while less than 30% used a combination of social, economic and technical criteria, and only few resorted to culture and aesthetic criteria (considered the most subjective of all). The large proportion of anthropogenic criteria renders automated valuation impossible, hence the more accurate evaluation system, the lesser share of objective criteria compared to the subjective ones.

Yet another obstacle which may emerge in the future stems from the shift in competence that appears in the new landscape act (2015): protection of a landscape's visual qualities is now an issue regulated by the act on protection of nature, and as such becomes disassociated from its aesthetic qualities, which are one of the considerations of spatial planning. This unprofessional approach is also apparent in the use of incorrect definitions of the statutory terminology used in the act, which suggests that any further protection effort dedicated to this set of landscape qualities may be insufficiently competent.

Cultural landscape valorisation involves assessment of its market and social value increasingly often. It is presented as a tangible resource (based on economic criteria), which may be bought or be subject to compensation claims, should it be damaged. This method surely makes it easier for the consumer society to understand that the "public property" that a landscape is, is not "nobody's property", as the previous political system implied. These methods do not, however, prove effective in studies which aim to create a broad protection-oriented classification of landscape, which is a necessary thing in landscape policy-making in all levels.

Another important aspect is the management and protection or resources, which is now a matter addressed only incidentally by administrative or scientific bodies. It is assumed that cultural landscape, understood as historical landscape, is an issue within the scope of conservation authorities' interest, whereas contemporary landscape is the matter addressed by urban and spatial planners. All the remaining cultural landscapes, mostly characterised by natural features (e.g. arable fields, systems of green areas), are protected and managed by specialist groups dealing with environment or nature protection. The discordance between landscape policing by different parties is further convoluted by administrative divisions, which delineate otherwise functionally and spatially uniform units of landscape. For instance, in Warsaw, the administrative division of the city into 18 quarters and the creation of multiple central bodies with overlapping landscape responsibilities is the source of tremendous competence havoc.

The fact that new guidelines, instructions and methodological studies are being issued, that training courses and conferences on cultural landscape in Poland are being held, is evidence of the emerging need to shape the right ways of valuation, protection and management of cultural landscape, which is an essential factor in the work of architects, geographers, planners and conservation specialists.

Hence, interdisciplinary cooperation between the parties with landscape within their interest –people involved in the theoretical studies, those with practical experience, politicians as well as local communities – should bring about an improvement in the identification and valorisation of cultural landscape. Development of a coherent model for protection and shaping of landscape, one that would combine natural and cultural, tangible and intangible, physiognomic and aesthetic properties, seems the only appropriate solution to preserve the most precious cultural landscapes of Poland. A coherent policy for comprehensive protection of natural, historical and landscape resources as recommended by the European Landscape Convention is the best model for protecting "flexible" cultural landscape resources. This, however, requires that certain institutions are created, and in particular, that legal tools are provided, which work in concert with each other and not in separation, as has been the practice over the last years.

SQUELCH VS. SNAP, CRACKLE AND POP:
A CASE STUDY OF HOW DIFFERENT SURROUNDINGS SHAPED
THE WORK OF TWO NEW ZEALAND BORN ARTISTS

Julian Rennie

Department of Landscape Architecture, Unitec, Auckland, New Zealand

ABSTRACT

Rosalie Gascoigne (1917-1999) and Colin McCahon (1919-1987) were both New Zealand born artists. Gascoigne moved to Canberra, Australia in 1943. There she gathered the flotsam and jetsam of her adopted landscape and used it to shape her artistic response to that countryside. Meanwhile McCahon stayed within the New Zealand landscape, and transcribed his landscape visions via paint and painted text as a record of his experiences. Many of his resulting images seem to express for many Kiwi's 'a real sense of place.' My intent in this paper is to unpack the contrasting milieu of these two New Zealand artists and explore how each has shaped their co-inhabitants' responses. Referencing each artist's own words along with the writings of other visual artists and landscape architects from around the world, I will attempt to tease out some of the contrasting ways in which landscape can shape an artist's perceptions. The resultant argument is that such contrasting haptic and visual responses may add some layers of meaning for landscape architects as they go about their design business of intervening and engaging with landscape.

Keywords
Haptic Landscape, Rosalie Gascoigne, Colin McCahon

1. INTRODUCTION

Rosalie Gascoigne (1917-1999) and Colin McCahon (1919-1987) were both artists and both born in New Zealand. Gascoigne moved to Canberra, Australia in 1943, where she gathered the cast-offs and abandoned waste of her adopted landscape and used it to shape her response to that countryside. McCahon stayed in his country of birth where, according to his children, whilst out walking he was sometimes 'stopped in his tracks' by a particular landscape; which he then later transcribed largely via dabs of paint and painted text onto canvas as a record of his cathartic experiences. My intent is to unpack the contrasting milieu of these two New Zealand artists and explore how each has shaped their inhabitant's responses. I argue that Gascoigne engaged in a frugal and tactile approach, often recycling elements directly from her arid surroundings in a fashion similar to John Dewey's 'art as experience' approach. McCahon, on the other hand, donned his gumboots and wandered off into the damp and rugged New Zealand countryside seeking 'images afresh' with his eyes but all the while literary words followed him like a loyal sheepdog. His resulting painterly images, including various texts (often from the Bible) hovering over or monumentally set within the painted landscape, seem to express for many New Zealanders some real 'nuances of place'. Drawing upon both artist's own words, the writings of other artists such as Agnes Martin and James Turrell, along with authors such as Gaston Bachelard, James Corner and something unique that has come directly from this milieu – something other than brand-name petrol station type environs that seemingly breed across our landscapes.

Gascoigne described being brought from New Zealand to Canberra as a young bride as "…in the country but not of it" (MacDonald 1998: 14). Did this give her the angle of being an outsider and perhaps better able to perceive elements of a foreign land with a sharper eye than the local inhabitants? Rather like the landscape architect gets called in to help a client, who perhaps has an objective view of their piece of real estate, whereas the landscape architect can view it afresh, listening to the client while listening, hearing and smelling the site; searching out its recent and distant temporalities; mapping phenomena both on the site and beyond (via marks on paper perhaps); absorbing it ALL through a type of 'mental osmosis'; dreaming of the site's possibilities – and then only later, taking up a scale rule to measure and delineate 'something that fits' this site.

James Corner prescribes that we as humans want to 'measure our scapes', whether they be seascapes, 'night-scapes' or landscapes, we seem to think by overlaying some human-made measuring device such as 'fathoms', 'light-years' or 'metre grids' and so forth, we are laying claim over them. When in fact often our measuring "of land…[often] reveal[s] itself, for what we actually find is only an illusion of human order, a screen behind which lies the unceasing cry of the wild" (Corner & MacLean 1996: 41).

Within New Zealand's own colonial history, Wystan Curnow talks about the conquering English nineteenth-century land grabbing tactics over the indigenous Māori, "who took the absence of written maps as an endorsement of the 'emptiness' of the land…unmapped land was unoccupied, and to that extent unpossessed" (Curnow 1998: 254). Yet the Māori had an oral culture, and thus their 'maps' were oral. This paper contends that Gascoigne's wall constructions are not maps (in the 'way-finding' manner), rather they seem like 'sensory jigsaws'. A jigsaw is normally thought of as an 'image' cut up into pieces, with the resultant puzzle task being to complete the original image. For Gascoigne it would seem, the reverse was true; found objects were cut into shapes that pleased an inner rhythm and her mind's eye, and then constructed into a rectangular 'image' that in turn seemingly evoked the milieu from whence they came. They became evocations of landscapes, with a touch of the weathered and untamed about them. Rosalie stated her aim "…to capture the 'nothingness' of the countryside, those wide open spaces…the great Unsaid…the silence that often only visual beauty transcends" (Edwards 1998: 16).

To attempt to capture the nuances of the landscape, Gascoigne worked in an active way, as John Dewey ascertained: "In order to understand the [a]esthetic in its ultimate and approved forms, one must begin with it in the raw" (Dewey 1934: 3). The artist's scouring the landscape, turning up all manner of small things, was a way of 'experiencing that landscape' – not only building up her visual library, but getting to know the landscape first-hand with her gatherings, pausing to take in macro vistas of it, and their contrast with her micro-discovered gleanings; these adding up to a more nuanced sense of place. Her visual memories stored in her mind, along with the tactile bits and pieces that accompanied Gascoigne back to her studio, to slowly build an aesthetic related to this milieu.

I would like to propose that Rosalie's Gascoigne's husband, Ben, with his astronomical work related to the night sky, his expertise in photometry (study in measurement of light effects on the eye), was also trying "to sound out the void" (Corner & MacLean 1996: 149). It could be said that this married couple were both seeking to describe the land/nightscapes associated with their chosen fields of endeavour: "Measures of faith belong to a form of awaiting, admitting and opening that presumes neither closure nor certainty… Such measures are found in gardens, cemeteries, monuments and observatories" (Corner & MacLean, 1996: 149). "The measure of mappings is not restricted to the mathematical, it may equally be spiritual, political or moral" (Cosgrove 1999: 2). This paper asks: are our cemeteries and battleground sites our only sacred sites?

Rosalie Gascoigne also made the point: "Nature selects, makes, abandons, is big. We need to be reminded of this because suburbia is boxed in; we need confirmation of an expanding universe" (Mollison & Heath 1998: 8). Rather obvious perhaps to remind the reader that Gascoigne's wall constructions could hang in those same suburban houses and evoke another place, giving a sense of 'the beyond' – allowing reflection and possibly 'ethereal migration' from within the house's four walled rooms – perceiving that 'otherness' through suggestion, rather than a limiting 'moment in time type' image which constitutes every photograph.

***

Colin McCahon was born in 1919, (just two years after Rosalie Gascoigne) in Timaru, New Zealand. As with Rosalie, Colin also seems to have been largely self-taught in visual art appreciation, although between 1937–39 he "attended King Edward Technical College Art School in Dunedin, but not as a full-time student" (Brown 1984: 212). He grew up surrounded by his Grandfather's landscape watercolour paintings which hung on the house walls (C. McCahon 1966: 363). Colin got exposed to the current art movement via overseas journals, and "…we were a gallery-going family and went to all the [Dunedin] exhibitions" (C. McCahon 1966: 362).

William McCahon, Colin McCahon's son, contends "my father – sought to engage his public with a visual dialogue about himself and his relationship with God…his entire oeuvre is the narrative of his life of spiritual and emotional discovery" (W. McCahon 2002: 29). It appears that Colin McCahon had an epiphany within the landscape, as William explains: "[In 1931] …my father, now in his teens, had a vision, triggering for him a spiritual crisis. Colin wrote much later – in 1966 – and with embellishments, about this event:

> "Driving one day with the family over the hills from Brighton, [New Zealand]…I first became aware of my own particular God…Big hills stood in front of little hills, which rose up distantly across the plain from the flat land: there was a landscape of splendour, order and peace…I saw something logical, orderly and beautiful belonging to the land and not yet to its people. Not yet understood or communicated, not even really yet invented." (C. McCahon 1966: 363-64)

That a landscape could spiritually uplift and enlighten human thoughts is not exceptional; a couple of precedents might be Giotto or J.M.W Turner. However within the modern era it seems rather unique, and especially so within the New Zealand context. McCahon's paintings, not surprisingly, were not understood by the Kiwi public and often ridiculed within the public press. And often his paintings were "judged solely on an aesthetic or art-historical basis by those who, not spiritually participant in the same way as [Colin] was" (W. McCahon 2002: 29). Colin became disenchanted with the critical response to his work: "On those occasions when McCahon did comment specifically on his paintings…his elegant and very quotable statements on his own work often themselves contributed to a process of disinformation and mythologising of aspects of his art practice. Many of these writings, while being in one part truth, often obscured his core meaning – and occasionally even introduced red herrings" (W. McCahon 2002: 36).

As Murray Bail says:
> "There was, too, of course the landscape. It is distinctly [Colin's]… a pair of islands at the bottom of the world. Islands already possess an undiluted separateness: sharp, compact, singular. And McCahon looked around and loved his land more. Soon afterwards he wrote the love, literally, onto his paintings. Generally, McCahon's landscapes have a direct serenity, sense of place being easier to render than the thornier religious feelings. The wonderful undulations of the New Zealand landscape are never far away, often forming a horizon or rearing up as the pictorial coalface in his late big written paintings." (Bail 2002: 43)

McCahon's sense of the immensity of landscape (in comparison to us as humans) manifested itself in large landscape works made up of a number of 'panels' (so much so, that the total length of some individual works can range from 4 to 12 metres). One such example is Fig.3. This requires the viewer to walk past the entire work; to experience it 'side-on' as one does on a bush track, taking in the surroundings whilst in motion, as opposed to a 'lookout' where one stops walking, and pauses, and looks out (of the bush) to the panorama. These dimensions often challenge the space of a gallery (such that there is not room to stand far enough away from the work to view it from a single location). This is a kinaesthetic way of appreciating the artwork, similar to how one experiences a stroll through an *allée* of trees for example. Shadow…light…shadow…light. This too would seem essential for a landscape architect; to experience any site kinaesthetically, not just via *Google Earth* from the isolation of the design office.

Figure 3, is also inspired by New Zealand's unique landscape (that all Kiwis know). As William McCahon suggests: "The series of paintings known as *Waterfalls*…Colin saw a waterfall as the earth bleeding – a sacrament of light issuing from the land recalling the blood shed by Christ in his Passion; Christ becoming the earth" (McCahon, W. 2002: 32).

Fig.3. *The Fourteen Stations of the Cross*, 1966 (750 x 7770 mm), by Colin McCahon.
Image is in the public domain.

Another of McCahon's preoccupations was what might be beyond the 'Gateway' at the juncture of death. Being mortal, most of us don't tend to dwell on this (at least not until the end of our days). And again various bluffs and headlands provided a visual answer to evoke Colin's musings. Especially the two up-thrusting, pillar like, rock formations just off the mainland between Māori Bay and Muriwai Beach (which are long established Gannet nesting colonies), west of Auckland city. For an example, refer to Fig. 4.

McCahon responded to his New Zealand landscapes, although seemingly using them as a tool: "…one feels that there is *something else* to be expressed, besides what is offered for objective expression. What [is] expressed is hidden grandeur [and] depth" (Bachelard 1964: 186).

Fig.4. *Muriwai. A Necessary Protection Landscape*, 1972
(610 x 920 mm), by Colin McCahon.
Image is in the public domain.

As an aside (but still on the topic of how landscape can indeed shape the human journey), a couple, with whom we are friends, lost their daughter to suicide. Following this tragedy they decided to spread their daughter's ashes at this same Muriwai Beach, which according to Māori legend is the place where the soul of the departed begins its journey north up the west coast to Cape Reinga (the tip of the North Island), then onwards to the 'Other World' known as *Hawaiki*. As the Mother herself says, "I started coming out to Muriwai for walks soon after Leah died – and before I knew the legend about souls leaving here on their journey north. It was hard to be at home because Leah was gone from there. Muriwai was the place I felt most alright – the big beach and the big sky and the westerly aspect with the sun going down – so it is the landscape and the rhythm of life going on that drew me here – eventually to live" (Morice, 2016). Is this an example of how landscape can draw humanity in, metaphorically hugging them, providing solace even? As Macfarlane ponders: "What does this place know of me that I cannot know of myself?" (2013: 27).

McCahon could raise strong emotions in people: "[A] student once came in through a window at home at 2.00am, as McCahon slept, and tried to strangle him. Another student hit him on the head with a lump of wood" (Bail 2002: 44). He seemed solely focused on his spiritual journey, often to the detriment of his family: "His widow, [Anne McCahon], looking back, had this to say: 'Colin McCahon? He was the man who was not there…not there when he was needed'" (Bail 2002: 44).

Figure 5, highlights some of the mysteriousness of the spiritual and how that might be manifest in a painting. If the reader looks carefully, on the left hand side are the words 'AM I' to counter the 'I AM' on the right side. As a landscape parallel, it is somewhat akin to submerged objects in a stream where an object 'peers up' from the depths in a mysterious manner.

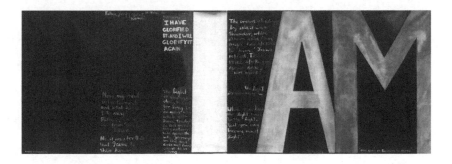

Fig.5. *Victory Over Death 2,* 1970 (2310 x 6710 mm), by Colin McCahon. Image is in the public domain.

Mystery is something that intrigues – the unknown – compelling to those able to perceive these wonders. I contend that the power and awe inspiring nature of New Zealand's landscapes was perfect as a 'vehicle' for Colin to question the mystery of death, that which we will never know about whilst still alive (if there is anything at all beyond?). Flashes of the afterlife, (if there is one), can be evoked by bird visitations. One such example is when Australian artist Brent Whiteley died: "…people had all these birdly experiences when Brent died…[a]s the coffin was lowered in the ground, I saw lots of crows flock. The cemetery was the northern [Sydney] suburbs one – you never see a flock of crows there" (Dickens 2002: 98). I myself, had a similar experience when my mother died. After the funeral, a native New Zealand Pigeon, *Kererū*, was seen perched on the overhead power lines right in front of our house, whilst we had her wake on the front lawn below, and remained there for over an hour. You never see *Kererū* on power lines, (they prefer the cover of trees), and you never see one linger for that long in one spot. Who knows if it was something spiritual, or a mere coincidence, but to this day I hold on to that fond memory. A touchstone perhaps?

"Above all, the characteristic that most distinguishes my father's art from that of his contemporaries is its ambiguity. He believed that this was the key element that made art in the 20th Century 'modern.' Artists were wasting their time, he said, if there were not two or more intertwining visual and thematic meanings in their work. Colin implies and infers, leaving his audience to decide at what level they will engage with his imagery. These multiple meanings allowed him to develop audiences who saw his relevance in different ways – as a spiritual Christian; as a landscape painter; or purely as an abstract modernist. This last view was most often promulgated by those who wrote about him." (McCahon, W. 2002: 33)

Colin McCahon was unusual in the New Zealand context in that throughout his life he remained firmly rooted in his own country, feeling little need to work in, or experience, the wider world. (McCahon, W. 2002: 29). He did travel briefly to Fiji and Australia (Brown, 1984: 212-16). Most Kiwis do an 'OE' ('overseas experience') due to the country's isolation at the bottom of the world, with the next stop being Antarctica. Most people return to what is known colloquially as 'God's Own' after looking around at the rest of the world and surmising that what New Zealand has to offer is special; not perfect, but indeed special.

Quoting Henry Plummer:
"The contemporary artist James Turrell has said: 'Light is not so much something that reveals, as it is itself the revelation'. Attention to light itself, and not to the object it illuminates, is the point…[light itself is a]…'phenomena'… as never before, [can] evoke moods and feelings we feel inside ourselves – helping modern man escape the loneliness of his social system, and fill the void left by a 'disappearance' of God'". (Plummer 2003: 28)

With this different take on the 'world of light' in the twenty-first century, can McCahon's paintings still be valid? Most of his paintings are about light and shadow, for example: the spatial effects drawn from how light seeps from behind natural headland formations forming silhouettes. The sublime nature of such magical light effects within the landscape can still stop people in their tracks.

3. CONCLUSIONS

According to the visual artist Agnes Martin in her essay, *I want to talk to you about the Work…*
"The process of art work is:
The original inspirations
The development of sensibility
The directed inspiration
The function of sensibilities
The finished work.

No thought or notions. Nothing to be discussed or criticised
Just; if your sensibilities respond. THAT'S IT." (Martin 2012: 16)

The above words could equally apply to landscape architects and their work related to design: inspirations; responding to one's sensibilities; the finished work. Full Stop.

These two artists Colin McCahon and Rosalie Gascoigne were of a similar era and both New Zealanders. But because of life's twists and turns, they settled in a different country, in different milieus, and those landscapes shaped their aesthetics to produce work that related to each locale. Each artist looked, saw and perceived the nuances, undertones and overtones of their locale, engaging and responding in different ways, which then shaped a unique response and humble perception of something much bigger than themselves. Robert Macfarlane argues that a "landscape projects into us not like a jetty or peninsula, finite and bounded in its volume and reach, but instead as a kind of sunlight, flickering unmappable in its plays yet often quickening and illuminating" (2013: 27).

This paper contends that visual artists may have the skills to 'more closely read' our landscapes. And thus it may be prudent for landscape architects who need to respond to programmatic and pragmatic briefs set by their clients, to look to such artists (and poets) in order to see how a landscape might be perceived and responded to as a site. To be able to step beyond a pragmatic brief with a design response that has the capacity for reverence and awe in relation to a given landscape is one of the cornerstones of a landscape designer's skill. As Corner says, "Landscape is less a quantifiable object than it is an *idea,* a cultural way of seeing, and as such it remains open to interpretation, design and transformation" (Corner, 1999: x).

In order to engage with a site experientially and even spiritually, as highlighted by these two New Zealand artists, perhaps landscape architects can build their own unique aesthetic and encourage a more humble and caring perception of the world in which we all live.

BIBLIOGRAPHY

Bachelard, G. (1964). *The Poetics of Space,* Boston: Beacon Press.

Bail, M. (2002). I Am. In: Bloem, M. & Browne, M. eds. *Colin McCahon: A Question of Faith.* Amsterdam: Graig Potton / Stedelijk Museum.

Brown, G. H. (1984). *Colin McCahon: Artist.* Wellington, New Zealand: A.H. and A.W Reed Ltd.

Corner, J. (ed.) (1999). *Recovering Landscape.* New York, NY: Princeton Architectural Press.

Corner, J, and MacLean, S. A. (1996). *Taking Measures across the American Landscape.* New Haven: Yale University Press.

Cosgrove, D. (ed.) (1999). *Mappings.* London, UK: Reaktion Books.

Curnow, W. (1999). Mapping and the Expanded Field of Contemporary Art. In D. Cosgrove, ed. *Mappings.* London, UK: Reaktion Books.

Dewey, J. (1934). *Art as Experience.* London: Penguin Books.

Dickens, B. (2002). *Black and White: Barry Dickens in search of Brett.* South Yarra, Victoria, Australia: Hardie Grant Books.

Edwards, D. (ed.) (1998). *Material as Landscape.* New South Wales: The Pot Still Press.

MacDonald, V. (1998). *Rosalie Gascoigne,* Paddington, New South Wales: Regaro Pty., Ltd.

Macfarlane, R. (2013). *The Old Ways: A Journey on Foot.* London: Penguin Books Ltd.

McCahon, C. (1966). Beginnings. New Zealand. *Landfall,* 20(4), 360-364.

McCahon, W. (2002). A Letter Home. In: Bloem, M. & Browne, M. eds. *Colin McCahon: A Question of Faith.* Amsterdam: Graig Potton / Stedelijk Museum.

Morice, L. (2016). *Re: Muriwai Beach.* Type to Rennie, J. J., on 5 March 2016.

Martin, A. (1956-67). I want to talk to you about the Work. In A. Glimcher, 2012. ed. *Paintings, Writings, Remembrances.* London, UK: Phaidon Press Ltd.

Mollison, J. and Heath, S. (1998). Rosalie Gascoigne: In her own Words. In *Rosalie Gascoigne: Material as Landscape.* New South Wales: The Pot Still Press.

O'Brien, G. (2004). Plain Air / Plain Song. In *Plain Air.* Wellington, New Zealand City Art Gallery Wellington and Victoria University Press.

Plummer, H. (2003). *Masters of Light: Twentieth-Century Pioneers.* Bankyo-ku: a+u Publishing Co. Ltd.

THE IMPACT OF THE COUNTRY ESTATE LANDSCAPE ON THE MODERN COTTAGE COMPLEX IN RUSSIA

Tatiana Isachenko

Saint-Petersburg University, Dept. of Regional Geography & International Tourism

ABSTRACT

The role of the noble country estates in the formation and development of modern cottage nature-cultural complexes in European Russia has been identified through the analysis of literature, archival data, old and modern maps, space images, photographic pictures, toponyms and field studies. Modern cottage settlements inherited the idea of an "ideal landscape" embodied in the Russian country estate. On the one hand, their location, planning, architecture reflect the tastes, requirements and possibilities of the modern people, but on the other hand, we can discover both cultural and space memory here. There are the modern country estates - the sort of replicas, which follow to idea of the ancient country estate. They simulate or copy them exactly. Space memory is expressed in inheriting of the old estates places, remained fragments, names, toponyms by modern cottage complexes. Cultural associative memory allows to use names of old country estates for new cottage settlements, though they allocate far from former estate location. The modern cultural landscapes of cottage settlements have imprint of cultural heritage, which determines its perception, development and image.

Keywords
country estate, cottage complex, landscape image, space memory, cultural landscape, nature-cultural complex.

1. INTRODUCTION

Historical-geographic and historical-cultural scientific researches help to reveal a causation of the modern cultural, social, ethnic and economic processes in different regions of the world. The landscape affects the life of the community and at the same time, it changes under the impact of human economic and household activities. Many researchers today wonder, what role space memory plays in forming of the modern nature-cultural complexes, what is the connection of the past and the present. In the beginning of XX century Russian poet Anna Akhmatova wrote in her "Poem Without a Hero": "...As the future ripens in the past, so the past smolders in the future...". These words could be an epigraph to the study of contemporary cultural landscapes.

By cultural landscape (nature-cultural complex) we will mean a territory with certain natural features, for a long time developed by humans who changed it as a result of his economic, social and intellectual-spiritual activities (Sauer 1925; Vedenin 1990). Every historical period has its own idea about the "ideal" cultural landscape. Man's dwelling and the place where he rests and spends his free time is the most important source of landscape preferences analysis. As a rule, for shelter and rest a man selects a territory, that complies with his idea of the perfect space, or tries to create this ideal by himself. Residential-recreational complexes in Russia have passed a long way from elite country estates of the XVIII-XIX centuries to mass summer cottages and gardening associations of the XIX-XX centuries and, finally, to the elite cottage complexes that appeared at the late XX and early XXI centuries.

Country estate in Russia became a materialized view of a perfect world and this explains its ambivalence. On the one hand, it is a reality that combines economic, residential and recreational functions. On the other hand, it is a myth, a dream of an earthly Paradise. In regard to landscape the Russian country estate is a reflection of human genetic memory. It reproduces the traditional Central Russian landscape, which is a combination of ploughed fields and woodlands. For the Russian people an ideal space could be neither too closed nor too open: the forest with Nightingale the Robber (Solovei the Brigand) is dangerous, but the steppe with nomads is very dangerous as well. The country estate creates a model of the traditional landscape by alternating open and closed spaces: house and household building (residential complex), parks and woodland fragments, cropland and hay meadows.

The country estate construction in XVIII –XIX centuries was one of the most important factors in the cultural landscapes formation of European Russia. The country estates gently changed and complemented landscapes by fitting in it, making a significant dash in the shape and image of the region (Anholt 2002; Zamiatin 2013). Russian noble country estate ceased to exist in 1917 and nowadays the cottage complexes replace them in the cultural landscape of European Russia. On the one hand, their location, structure, architecture of buildings, approaches to the territory arrangement reflect the tastes, needs and opportunities of the modern man. On the other hand, we can discover both geographical and historical-cultural memory in the cottage complexes; here the idea of creating an "ideal" landscape develops forward. The modern cottage complex has inherited the two country estate functions: residential and recreational, but only in rare cases - economic. Correspondingly, it has a smaller area compared to the old country estate. However, due to the join of the separate cottage complexes to the large settlements, their role in the landscape is comparable with the role of the country estates 150 years ago. By comparison, in the middle of the XIX century there were about 500 country estates on the territory of present Leningrad region. Today there are about 420 cottage settlements here, and its number is growing rapidly. For example, there were 55 cottage settlements on the same territory in 2006, there were 250 in 2011. For the last three years the number of cottage settlements has increased more than by 1.5 times.

1.1. Research methods

The object of research are nature-cultural complexes of country estates and cottage complexes, which are defined as interrelated combinations of natural landscape and cultural elements emerging during the estate and cottage development.

The role of the noble country estates in the formation and development of modern cottage nature-cultural complexes has been identified through the analysis of literature and archival data, old and modern maps, space images, toponyms and field studies. Figure 1 shows the key vectors of cultural- historic and historical-geographic continuity of the estate and cottage nature-cultural complexes.

North-West European Russia (Leningrad, Pskov and Novgorod regions) were selected as a key area for the study. In XVIII-XIX centuries the country estates were one of the most important factors in the shaping of this "near capital" cultural landscapes. More than 1000 estates existed here in the late XIX century.

2. CONTENTS

The country estate image enters our consciousness in two ways. On the one hand, we can still see actual country estate buildings and parks, survey the surviving realities of estate life, and reconstruct a material image of the noble estate from these fragments. On the other hand, a real image of the Russian country estate is complicated by its artistic image, passing throughout Russian culture. When we read works of the XIX century Russian literature, listen to the music of Tchaikovsky, view the paintings of "The World of

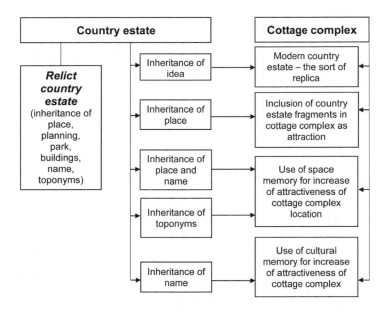

Fig.1. An inheritance from the noble country estates in the modern cottage nature-cultural complexes.

Art" artists, we are introduced to an extraordinarily rich country estate mythology. The border between the reality and the artistic image is erased and the created Russian country estate image is in many respects equal to the image of Russia. For a modern Russian man the country estate is a symbol of an organized life, stability, and adherence to cultural traditions and perfectly arranged space.

1. **The relict country estate complexes (the inheritance of the old country estates: of places, structure, park, buildings, names, country estate toponyms).** Today, a large part of the country estate is lost forever. At best, only small fragments of the parks and bases of the historic buildings are left. Surviving and restored country estates are the relict nature-cultural complexes. Only 14 such complexes remained from 500 country estates on the territory of Leningrad region. Five of them have ruins on a place of constructions, and their parks need significant maintenance and reconstruction work. Today only those country estates that have received the status of memorial estates make an essential contribution to the cultural landscape (Fig.2).

Among these country estates are: Monrepos, Rozhdestveno, Izvara, Priyutino, Suida in Leningrad region; Mikhailovskoye, Trigorskoye, Petrovskoye, Naumovo, Lubensk, Vechasa in Pskov region; Konchanskoye in Novgorod region.

For the last decade investors have restored some of the country estate complexes (country estate houses, farm buildings, country parks). Now they are used either as private residences (Busani, Elizavetino in Leningrad region), or as the public recreation complexes (Marieno, Zapolie in Leningrad region). In the second case their interiors are re-created in the style of the XVIII-XIX and farmstead lifestyle is imitated: masked balls, fancy-dress holidays, horseback riding, historic games, etc. Essentially, this is the material embodiment of the modern idea of how the nobles lived in the old days. This idea lives in the Russian mass consciousness of XXI century, and the recreational complex organizers make use of it to attract tourists.

2. **Modern country estate – the sort of replica (the inheritance of the estate idea).** Modern country estate – the sort of replica is the modern cottage complex which styled after the country estate complexes of XVIII-XIX centuries. They are exact correlated with the old country estate structure. Construction and service of such estate demand huge expenses. The estate-replica does not produce any profit and only

serves for the satisfaction of the owner's ambitions. It is not so much his conception of a beautiful life in a perfect space as a sign of his life success. The estate-replica in Vyritsa village (Gatchina district, Leningrad region) is an architectural model of the XVIII century country estate. Modern house in magnificent Baroque style could compete with an imperial residence buildings in it's architectural decoration and interior design (Fig.3).

However old country estate was focused on the surrounding landscape, it served as a center for the development of the region and stimulated the road network development. Modern estate-replica is closed, surrounded by a huge fence, it is actually removed from the landscape and does not contribute to the road construction: its owners use a helicopter.

The architectural retro styles are often used for the design of individual cottages and area planning in modern cottage settlements. The settlement names also reflect the differentiation of architectural

Fig.2. The memorial estates "Priyutino" (Viborsky district, Leningrad region). Photograph by author.

Fig.3. Modern country estate – the sort of replica (Vyritsa village, Gatchina district, Leningrad region). Photograph by author.

preferences: "Petrovskoe Baroque", "North Versailles". Sometimes multiple styles are used within a cottage settlement, so the potential buyer could choose what corresponds to his idea of the perfect house. For example, in "Harmony" cottage complex (Leningrad region, Vyborg district) they offer 5 types of house style and landscape design. Sometimes the houses are built in different price ranges within one settlement dividing the space into the "manor" and "servant" parts (Leningrad region, Vyborg district, Gazprom settlement). Modern cottage complexes, as well as estate-replica, are surrounded by high fences leading to fragmentation of the territory and opposition the cottage settlement to the surrounding landscape (Fig.4).

But the country estate idea cannot be encapsulated in a space enclosed by a fence: cottage owners eventually start developing and transforming the surrounding area. Moreover, this development follows the landscape arrangement in noble country estates, the ideas of openness, emphasis of natural features and compatibility of architectural details with the environment (Fig.5).

Fig.4. The cottage complex (settlement Leninskoye, Leningrad region). Photograph by author.

Fig.5. The landscape arrangement around the cottage complex (Karelian isthmus, Leningrad region).
Photograph by author.

3. **Cottage complexes of the XX-XXI centuries (the inheritance of the material space memory).** Country estates used to be situated in picturesque, often frontier sites: shores of lakes and rivers, ancient valleys, Glint (the Baltic-Ladoga Cliff), morainic hills and ridges. The cottage complexes of today inherit these locations. In case the fragments of country estate complex are still present, they are included in the cottage villages. The fragments of Mutalahti estate included in "Harmony" cottage settlement, are aimed at declaring a continuity of a tranquil suburban world of the elite. Material and mental symbolic elements form "associative" image of the country estate and increase attractiveness of cottage complexes.

4. **Cottage complexes of the XX-XXI centuries (the inheritance of the mental space memory).** Where the cottage complex is located in place of former noble country estate and with the absence of financial resources, toponymic associations are applied. The estate name and the owner's name join in the title of the cottage complex. For example, the names of the cottage complexes on the territory of Leningrad region are: "Volcovici Estate", "Lopukhinsky Grange", "Ropsha Estate", "Stroganov Estate". The estate toponyms are widely used as names for individual landscape elements in and around cottage settlements: Grafskaya Gorka (Count Hill), Barskii Forest, Gospodskii (Domonical) Meadow.

5. **The use of cultural memory to enhance the attractiveness of cottage complexes.** Cultural associative memory allows to use the names of noble country estates as brands for the names of those cottage settlements located far away from the estate place. Such cottage settlements as "Yasnaya Polyana" (the name of Lev Tolstoy's country estate in Tula region), "Mikhailovskoe" (the name of Aleksandr Pushkin's estate in Pskov region) have appeared in Leningrad region. The names of ten cottage settlements of Leningrad region contain the word estate in various combinations, four of them contain the word "manor" and one contains the word "grange". In the XVIII-XIX centuries the concepts of estate, grange and manor were used to denote a country house with services, a park and agricultural lands.

3. CONCLUSIONS

In conclusion, it is important to compare the role of landscape conditions in the placement of country estate and cottage nature-cultural complexes. The analysis of the country estate complexes revealed a significant role of the natural conditions in its location. This applies both to the choice of the landscape region, and to the choice of landscape location within this region. As an example, the vast number of country estates on the territory of St. Petersburg province were located within the area of Izhorskoye plateau, the place with the most fertile soil in the region. Preference in placement of country estates was given to the river and lake banks, the sites difference of a relief, etc. (Isachenko 2004). The analysis of cottage complexes location revealed that the most important factors were proximity to major cities (St. Petersburg) and transport availability. Unlike country estate complexes, natural factors are of less importance for location of cottage settlements. The fertile soil of Izhorskoye plateau and the picturesque landscapes of the Lugskiy landscape region do not predetermine cottages construction in the extent to which they determined the placement of country estates. However, the landscape factor plays a key role in the selection of a cottage building promotion vector. Northerly direction became a vector of this kind in Leningrad region, and the landscape of the Karelian isthmus is the top leader by the number of cottage settlements, with the distance to the city increasing significantly. A total of 260 cottage settlements were settled on the Karelian isthmus in 2014. This represents a half of all the Leningrad region cottage complexes.

Study of cottage nature-cultural complexes as part of the cultural landscape in the North-West of European Russia, and assessment of the cottage construction scope require further historical-geographic and historical-cultural research, allowing to trace the continuity and trajectory of the further North-West cultural landscape development.

BIBLIOGRAPHY

Anholt, S. (2002). Nation brends: the value of "provenance" in branding. In: Destination Branding: Creating the Unique Destination Proposition, Morgan, N., Pritchard, A. and Pridee E., eds., Oxford: Butterworth Heinemann, pp. 42-57.

Isachenko T. (2004). Old estates near St.Petersburg and their role in forming cultural landscape. In: Cultural landscape as a heritage site, Vedenin Yu., Kuleshova M., eds., Moscow-St.Petersburg, pp.186-196.

Sauer, K. (1925). Morphology of Landscape. University of California Publications in Geography, V. II (2). pp. 19–53.

Vedenin, Yu.A. (1990). Problems of a cultural landscape formation and its studying, Izvestia Akademii Nauk. Series geographic. no. 1, pp. 5-18.

Zamyatin, D.N. (2003). Humanitarian geography: Space and language of geographical images. Saint Petersburg.

HOW TO DEAL WITH UNESCO WORLD HERITAGE ZONES. ANALYSIS OF RESULTS OF THE COMPETITION FOR BAMIYAN CULTURAL CENTRE IN AFGHANISTAN

Damian Poklewski-Koziełł
Mado Architekci

ABSTRACT

At the end of 2014 international architectural competition has been launched for the design of the Bamiyan Cultural Centre in Afghanistan. The town of Bamiyan is located on the western edge of the Hindu Kush mountains, about 120 km northwest of the capital city Kabul. Region comprises of eight elements that in 2003 has been inscribed on the UNESCO world heritage list. Author - participant of the competition, analysis awarded projects for theirs ability to blend into the extremely demanding landscape and cultural context. Article tries to answers the question to what extent the landscape conditions has determined the form of the building and how the modern architecture and landscape can be defined in respect for the outstanding context.

Keywords
Afghanistan, Bamiyan Valley, Buddha Cliff, Bamiyan Culture Center competition, UNESCO World Heritage List

1. INTRODUCTION

1.1. About the competition

At the end of 2014[1] an international architectural competition for the design of a building of a Culture Centre in Bamiyan, Afghanistan (BCC) was announced on the most popular websites devoted to architecture. This one-stage competition was addressed to a broad group of recipients: professionals, as well as architecture students all over the world. The only condition for participation in it was that the team of designers taking part in it should have one person holding relevant licenses in the country of their origin. There were no participation fees in the competition. This extraordinary event was possible thanks to a harmonious cooperation of many actors, including UNESCO, municipal authorities of Bamiyan, the government of Afghanistan, with a generous support from South Korea, which had decided to support the project of the Culture Centre.

Thanks to good promotion, transparency of the rules, an open formula and the lack of any fees, the competition attracted crowds of competitors. Eventually, as of the date of its closure, on 23 January 2015, ca. 1070 works from 113 countries were submitted to the server of the organizer of the competition, making the competition the fifth in terms of popularity in history[2]. The leader in this ranking is a competition for a design of Guggenheim Museum in Helsinki held a bit earlier, where the total of 1715 designs had been submitted from all over the world[3].

An international jury of the competition, consisting of 7 professionals representing different disciplines and countries of origin, selected a design by an Argentinian team consisting of the leader, Carlos Nahuel Recabarren, and other members Manuel Alberto Martines Catalan and Franco Morero. Additionally, 4 distinctions were granted, to designs from Turkey, Cyprus, France, and Holland[4].

1.2. Objective of the article

The objective of this article is not only to analyze the awarded designs in terms of their ability to inscribe in a very demanding cultural and landscape context, but also to bring closer the beauty of the unique place that Bamiyan is.

2. HISTORICAL BACKGROUND

The documented history of Afghanistan reaches back to ca. 500 B.C, when these territories were under the rule of the Achaemenid Empire. There is, however, evidence that confirms the existence of a culture capable of building cities, which dates back to the period between 3000 and 2000 B.C. Afghanistan was one of the provinces of the Persian empire ruled by Achaemenids, known under the name of Bactria. In 330 B.C. Alexander the Great after a victorious battle of Gaugamela, where he beat Persians, arrived at this land together with his army. Before the today Afghanistan found itself in the hands of the tribe of Kushans in ca. 2 century B.C., the ruling dynasty changed twice[5]. It was Kushans who were responsible for the introduction of the Buddhist art, inspired by the Hellenic and Sassanid art. Due to fact that the territory of Afghanistan was intersected by the Silk Route in ca. 1 century A.D. the influences of the Indian Buddhism started to be visible. By around the 6th century A.D., when the Western Turks took over the rule, the ruling dynasties changed several times[6]. Since that moment the culture of Islam had a decisive effect on the further development of the region, which resulted in the decline of the other cultures, including the Buddhist one. Subsequent Turkish dynasties contributed to the further development and growth of importance of this area, until the time when it was dubbed Afghanistan. In 1747 the Pashtu tribes got united and an empire of the Durrani dynasty was established, which is recognized as the beginnings of the modern Afghanistan. At the end of the 19th century Afghanistan was a buffer zone separating two empires: the British one and the Russian one. After the third Anglo-Afghan war, on 19 August 1919 the country recovered its full independence from the British Empire. After a short period of democracy, which was terminated with a coup in 1973, until the Bonn conference in 2001[7], the country suffered devastating armed conflicts[8].

3. LOCATION

3.1. Characteristics of Bamiyan

Bamiyan is located ca. 120 km to the west from Kabul, in the western part of the massif of the Hindu Kush. Due to its special location, it was a centre of trade between the east and the west for ages, but also a place of cultural and religious exchange[9]. Between the 2nd and 3rd centuries A.D., under the rule of the Kushans, it became a place of burial of important saints. About this period the Buddhist culture reached its climax in the territories of Central Asia, from where it had its impact to the east to the territory of China, as well as to the west, marking its effect also on the Christian iconography.

The legacy of Bamiyan stands not only for the remains of the Buddhist culture, but also a rich heritage of the culture of Islam. Bamiyan owes its urban layout, modelled on the Iranian land of Khorasan, to sultan Mahmud of Ghazni. Fortified settlements of Shahir-i-Bamiyan, Shahr-i-Zuhak, and Shahr-i-Sarkhoshak date back to the times of the rule of the Ghurid dynasty[10].

Unfortunately, in the early 13th century Bamiyan was ruined by Genghis Khan, and the Buddhist monasteries were plundered. The 18th century saw the rule of a fanatic Islam believer, Aurangzeb, who ordered its army to shoot off a leg of the Great Statue of Buddha. Since that time, the valley was abandoned for many years. There are, however, traces of settlements from the end of the 19th century, encountered in the mountain caves.

3.2. Cultural landscape

Bamiyan has preserved its agrarian character, also due to the fact that people are strongly bound to the ground. Farming generates ca. 80% of the revenues of the city. Nevertheless, due to its geographical location, the development of agriculture is strongly limited[11]. The mountain ranges that surround the city from all its sides concentrate the city in one point.

The urban layout of Bamiyan resembles a patterned check[12], where arable fields intermingle with residential houses, build most of all of pressed mud[13]. The contour of an irregular check in the landscape is created by a grid of paths between the fields and by low fencing walls. External walls of households are inscribed in this pattern. A characteristic element of the architecture of Afghanistan is a garden and an internal courtyard. The wall separates from the external world. Along its perimeter individual parts of buildings are located – facing the internal patio they secure an optimal level of sunlight. Opening of the rooms to the courtyard blurs the border between the interiors and the external area. Afghans like spending time in the garden, so it constitutes an extension of the living space of the residents.

The city has preserved its historical layout and the identity of a small-scale settlement. The level of the infrastructural development is very low. People get around mainly on foot. Recently, the roads have been hardened, which facilitates the supplies of the missing products[14].

3.3. UNESCO protected areas

In 2003, two years after the destructions of the statues of Buddha by the Taliban, 8 elements were entered in the UNESCO World Heritage List, which can be classified in three main categories: protection of the cultural landscape, protection of the complex of archaeological ruins located in three valleys, and protection of structures referring to the local traditions. These areas represent the artistic and religious development from the 1st to the 13th century and refer to the Buddhist as well as the Islamic culture, but also – as it is believed – they bear the traces of the existence of the Zoroastrian culture[15].

The area of the highest degree of impact on the designed area which is the point of reference for the architecture of Bamiyan is a characteristic cliff located on the northern side of the valley. It spreads over the distance of 2 kilometres and its maximum height is 160 metres over the adjacent area. There are two niches in the perpendicular wall of the cliff, which used to be the place where the statues of Buddha had been, before they were destroyed by the Taliban. On the western side, there used to be a larger statue, 55 metres tall, on the western side – a statue smaller by 38 metres. There are over 1000 caves in the surrounding area, where murals and decorations carved in the rock can be found. The origins of these archaeological remains are still a subject of scientific investigations,. It is believed that the statue of the Great Buddha came into being between mid-6th century and the early 7th century,

3 kilometres to the south-east, in the Kakrak valley, there is another protected place. Among over a hundred caves dating back to the period before the 6th and the 13th century, we will find a 10 metres tall niche with a statue of Buddha and a sanctuary near the rear wall behind the statue. It dates back to the times when the Sasanian dynasty ruled the area[16]. The third place where archaeological remains and other numerous caves can be found is the Foladi Valley, located ca. 2 kilometres to the south west[17]. In the caves situated in two areas: Qoul-i-Akram and Qoul-i-Ghamay, murals and carved decorations have been preserved[18].

Other four places are connected already with the rule of Islam. The furthest to the east, ca. 15 km from Bamiyan, there is the so-caller Red City. The fortress occupies the peak of a hill that divides two rivers: the Bamiyan and the Kalu. Although the beginnings of the settlements date back to the 6th – 7th century, the fortifications are already connected with the period of Islam. Qal'a-i-Kafari A and B are located in the distance of 12 km to the east. The complex consists of ruins of defence walls and of towers, which constitute one of the elements of the defensive system. Below the walls there are caves. The material used

Fig.1. UNESCO World Heritage Protection Zon - Map of eight protected elements.
Photo source: Cassar, B., Mojadidi, K., Noshadi, S. (2014).

for the purposes of building of the complex was unburnt brick, dried in the sun. The last of the elements entered in the UNESCO World Heritage List discussed here, and the one which is located the closest to the Cliff with the statues of Buddha, is Shahr-i-Ghulghulah – a fortified citadel that occupies the surface area of ca. 16 ha. It is situated in the place where the Bamiyan Valley meats the Kakrak Valley. Remnants of city walls and of a graveyard have been preserved here. There are numerous caves to the west and south-west from here.

3.4. Characteristics of the site

The plot of land in question is located on a plateau of Chawni mountain. Its characteristic element is the fact that it has two levels, with the height difference of over 10 metres. The lower part of a prolonged shape is located more to the north, whereas the higher one is of a more regular shape, closer to a square. The passage between the levels is steep. The flat part of the area occupies the surface of ca. 2.6 ha. The western part is dominated by a steep precipice, which forms the southern edge of the Bamiyan Valley. From the east, the plot borders on territories that belong to public institutions: the police, the television, and institutes of culture, and it is directly adjacent to the road, which gradually becomes a path leading to the main commercial street located at the foot of the plateau. Currently, the plot of land is developed, and buildings located on it are planned to be demolished.

The most important, however, is the view towards the north-west of the Great Cliff with the empty niches after the statues of Buddha, surrounded with numerous niches hollowed in the rock. According to the rules of the competition, this view was to be integrated with the design so that it would become a coherent whole with the protected cultural landscape[19].

To the unique location of the plot intended for the culture institution with such a great range of impact, several limitations were imposed in the competition rules. Firstly, the height of buildings on the upper level was limited to a one-storey building with the maximum height of 8 m above the ordinate of 2555.5 m ASL. At the lower level it was allowed to design 2-storey buildings, but their maximum upper height could not be higher than the one specified for the upper level. Along the border of the plot around its perimeter it was necessary to design a 3m tall wall for safety-related reasons, and the buildings had to be at least 15m away from the wall on the eastern and southern side.

Fig.2. The site. Photo source: Cassar, B., Mojadidi, K., Noshadi, S. (2014).
Photo source: Cassar, B., Mojadidi, K., Noshadi, S. (2014).

Fig.3. View from the site toward the Buddha Cliff. Photo source: Cassar, B., Mojadidi, K., Noshadi, S. (2014).

The main advantage of the plot, at the same time the main challenge, is the breath-taking view of the Bamiyan Valley, the Hindu Kush mountains, and most of all the Great Cliff. In a more distant perspective the other places entered in the UNESCO World Heritage List, Shahr-i-Ghulghulah or the Foladi Valley, are visible.

4. ANALYSIS OF THE WINNING PROJECT

The winning design entitled 'Descriptive Memory. The Eternal Presence of Absence' by an Argentinian team managed by Carlos Manuel Recabarren was based on two compositional axes. The first axis leads from the corner created by the intersection of two main roads and is directed towards the niches of the Great Buddha. This axis marks the main entrance, which further behind the gate transforms into a ramp leading to a square – a place of contemplation, and an open theatre. The second axis leads from the square in the direction of the smaller niche.

The authors of the design approached the task from a very theatrical point of view. The external walls imposed by the rules of the competition which surround the entire project make the Culture Centre as if the owner of the view[20]. In order to see the Great Cliff with the entire panorama, we need to enter, to cross the magic wall of BCC. The cultural landscape becomes an integral element of the exposition, constituting still vivid tangible evidence of the richness and greatness of culture. Architects could create a building as a detached structure protruding above the area, which would constitute another visual barrier. The beauty of the landscape would present itself to visitors only after they entered. Nevertheless, they decided to choose a different solution. The building was hidden under the ground, and what visitors who enter the premises see is the extraordinary panorama. As they emphasised themselves, their intentions was not to create a building as such, but rather a place of get-togethers, where the landscape would intermingle with the rich cultural life, which is not limited to the internal spaces only. The entire complex was closed in ruled geometrical outlines. A system of light tunnels, courtyards, resembles the system of architecture with a wall, an internal building, and a patio, dominating in the local landscape and enrooted in the Arabic culture.

The rooms creating the rich programme of the Culture Centre were grouped according to their themes and they were given separate structures. Three buildings can be distinguished in the complex. The first one holds exhibition halls and a warehouse, a multifunctional hall, and auxiliary functions, such as toilets, a shop, and a coffee shop. The exhibition halls face the cliff with the Great Buddha, therefore, their endwalls are glazed in the form of an Arabic arch, or even more a cave hollowed in the rock. The glazing in the multifunctional hall, similar in form, is oriented towards the niche of the Little Buddha. The second building was allocated to research and education. The third one holds administration offices. All of them are linked together with an internal courtyard, equipped with permanent stands for outdoor performances.

The buildings are designed in the form of a negative, and as the authors emphasise, this means that the creation stands not so much for the process of building, as uncovering, digging out, or even carving in the rock. Thanks to this measure, the building blends with the surrounding area even more. The local brick applied reiterates the colours of the surrounding natural and cultural landscape. The windows, although different in shapes and sizes and arranged rather freely, seem to refer to caves hollowed in rocks, thanks to which they create a very logical and coherent system in terms of composition. The whole structure blends with the landscape even better.

Fig.4. Winning proposal. Photo source: Stott, R. (2014).

5. ANALYSIS OF THE AWARDED PROJECTS

From amongst the four works that won distinctions, two are characterised by considerable realism, and two are extremely interesting, but more conceptual rather than implementation works. A pair of Turkish architects, Ahmet Balkan and Emre Bozatli, proposed a structure that protrudes above the adjacent area[21]. The view of the landscape presents itself to visitors only when they enter the complex. The programme has been arranged around an internal closed courtyard. It is a bow towards a characteristic feature of the Afghan architecture, where residential spaces are organised around an internal patio called here 'hawli'. The project consists of one closed patio and a complex of other ones, which are open to the surrounding landscape, including most of all the places subjected to the protection of UNESCO. The building constructs strong spatial relations with the landscape, it does not limit itself to the view of the Bamiyan only. Each of the squares is of a different nature. The authors were more committed to the creation of a place fostering gatherings than to sophisticated architecture, hence the designed building is simple, it consists of limited quantities of materials, mainly obtained locally. This makes BBC have a positive effect not only on culture, but also on the local economy[22].

The work of the French team managed by Noel Dominguez exhibits most of all strong relations with the direct urban context. The designed building corresponds to the sizes of the neighbouring facilities which hold the police and the television, and the main entrance constitutes an extension of a stone road leading from east to west. A characteristic architecture element is a flat roof, which maintains the level of the designed fencing. The concept makes use of the difference in the level of the ground in designing premises which require to be taller. Individual premises in the form of detached buildings are arranged along an internal street. Spaces between them crop attractive views on the surrounding landscape.

A concept of a Cypriot architect, Costas Nicolaou, is inspired by elements which can be found in the landscape of Bamiyan. The first element are walls which separate individual households. The second element – geometrical arable fields which form forefields for vast views. The third element are paths that intersect at acute angles, and the fourth one – steep slopes of the mountains. The building has been designed as an archipelago of these elements[23]. An external wall separates the gardens, which have been treated differently. The external, regular one corresponds to the layout of the fields, the internal, more natural one is to be a safe oasis. The entire project opens to the cliff.

The last awarded proposal belongs to a Dutch team managed by Graham Baldwin. Extremely conceptual in character, it consists of a complex of parallel walls made of pressed earth. Inside, as if in niches in rock massifs, individual rooms have been hollowed, but only those which fulfil utilitarian functions for the very building. The main concept is withdrawn architecture. The main role is played by spaces between the walls, constituting individual functions which build the identity of the designed Culture Centre. These premises have been glazed to a maximum degree, so as to open the interiors to the surrounding landscape. The walls have been designed in a perpendicular system towards the cliff, thanks to which they constitute a minor disturbing element in the orthogonal view. When perceived from the side, they form a massif compact body, like an ancient ziggurat, blending into the landscape.

6. SUMMARY

Each of the proposals described above is characterised by a completely different approach to the context. Nevertheless, it seems that the winning work provided the best solution to the task. Hidden architecture in such a wonderful place is probably the only right way. It is so difficult to compete with such an astounding landscape.

NOTES

[1] 15th of November 2014

[2] u.a. *Ahmet Balkan's proposal for the UNESCO Bamiyan Cultural Center.* Designboom. http://www.designboom.com/architecture/bamiyan-cultural-center-unesco-ahmet-balkan-architects-04-01-2015/. (accessed 13 March 2016)

[3] Stott, R. (2014) *See All 1,715 Entries to the Guggenheim Helsinki Competition Online.* ArchDaily. . http://www.archdaily.com/560207/see-all-1-715-entries-to-the-guggenheim-helsinki-competition-online/. (accessed 17 February 2016)

[4] Architects and urban planners - Zahra Breshna, Ajmal Maiwandi and Young Joon Kim, and Robert Knox former custodian of the art collection of Asia in the British Museum, Elisabeth O'Donell, dean at the Copper Union, Cameron Sinclair, founder of a non-profit organization Architecture for Humanity, the purpose of which is to search for solutions in

the field of architecture focused on providing humanitarian aid in parts of the world affected with global crises, and Jukka Jokilehto, engaged in the cultural heritage, author of a book on management of areas protected by UNESCO.

[5] After the Seleucid Empire there was the time of rule of the Maurya dynasty coming from the north of India.

[6] Sassanids controlled Afghanistan from mid-3rd century and in the 5th century nomadic tribes of Central Asia.

[7] When the foundations for the political reconstruction of the country has been created.

[8] Cassar, B., Mojadidi, K., Noshadi, S. (2014). *Bamiyan Cultural Centre Competition Brief.* UNESCO. http://bamiyanculturalcentre.org/. p.24. (accessed 01 December 2014)

[9] It was a passage to the Hindu Kush mountains and important branch of the Silk Road

[10] See. Frazik, J.T. (1999). *Architektura muzułmańska na terenie Iranu, Afganistanu i Azji Centralnej.* Cracow: Politechnika Krakowska

[11] Bamiyan is one of the poorest regions in Afghanistan. In comparison with the other parts of the country, agriculturally is the least productive area. The amount of valuable land that could be used for cultivation is limited due to its mountainous nature, which results in a large migration to other cities of Afghanistan but also to Iran and Pakistan, where they work as unskilled labor.

[12] Mainly grown wheat and potatoes.

[13] Construction of pressed mud, also known as pakhsa are very popular. The material is widely available, and the method is easy to learn. Physical properties of the material are decisive factor for its popularity. The thick walls of pressed mud parameter are characterized by high thermal insulation - in the summer they prevent overheating, in the winter they effectively store generated heat.

[14] Cassar B., Mojadidi K., Noshadi S. (2014). p.52

[15] At the cemetery, located on the eastern side of the Great Cliff the pot-burial containing the complete human skeletons were found. This way of burial indicates the presence of Zoroastrianism.

[16] UNESCO official website. http://whc.unesco.org/en/list/208. (access 08 March 2016)

[17] It is believed that the caves were interconnected by a tunnels, that were leading to situated on a top of the hill watchtowers, and used to defend the Bamiyan Valley from the south side.

[18. Currently, unfortunately in a very bad condition.

[19] Cassar B., Mojadidi K., Noshadi S. (2014). p.56

[20] Direct function of the the the wall is to ensure the safety of a users, indirectly wall functions as an effective barrier that keeps the magnificent view within its borders

[21] Unlike the authors of the winning design

[22] Foster J.T. *UNESCO Reveals Winning Scheme For The Bamiyan Cultural Centre In Afghanistan.* ArchDaily. http://www.archdaily.com/600403/unesco-reveals-winning-scheme-for-the-bamiyan-cultural-centre-in-afghanistan/. (accessed 13 March 2016)

[23] As author describes it.

BIBLIOGRAPHY

Baker, P. H. B., Allchin, F. R. (1991). *Shahr-i Zohak and the History of the Bamiyan Valley, Afghanistan.* British Archaeological Reports.

Blair, S. S., Bloom, J. M. (1996). *The Art and Architecture of Islam, 1250–1800.* Yale University Press

Cassar, B., Mojadidi, K., Noshadi, S. (2014). *Bamiyan Cultural Centre Competition Brief.* UNESCO. http://bamiyanculturalcentre.org/ (access 01 December 2014).

Foster J.T. *UNESCO Reveals Winning Scheme For The Bamiyan Cultural Centre In Afghanistan.* ArchDaily. http://www.archdaily.com/600403/unesco-reveals-winning-scheme-for-the-bamiyan-cultural-centre-in-afghanistan/ (access 13 March 2016).

Frazik, J.T. (1999). Architektura muzułmańska na terenie Iranu, Afganistanu i Azji Centralnej. Cracow: Politechnika Krakowska.

Knobloch, E. (2004). *Archaeology & Architecture of Afghanistan*. Tempus Pub Ltd.

Stott, R. (2014). *See All 1, 715 Entries to the Guggenheim Helsinki Competition Online*. ArchDaily. http://www.archdaily.com/560207/see-all-1-715-entries-to-the-guggenheim-helsinki-competition-online/ (access 17 February 2016).

u.a. *Ahmet Balkan's proposal for the UNESCO Bamiyan Cultural Center*. Designboom. http://www.designboom.com/architecture/bamiyan-cultural-center-unesco-ahmet-balkan-architects-04-01-2015/ (access 13 March 2016).

UNESCO official website. http://whc.unesco.org/en/list/208 (access 08 March 2016).

CASTLES OR CULTURAL AND NATURAL LANDSCAPES?
A NEW APPROACH TO THE MANAGEMENT OF FORTIFICATIONS
IN THE SOUTH OF THE VALENCIAN COMMUNITY (SPAIN).
EXAMPLES OF CASTALLA AND SAX (ALICANTE)

Juan Antonio Mira Rico
ICOMOS-ICOFORT; Castalla Municipal Service for Cultural Heritage

ABSTRACT

The current management of cultural heritage requires a joint administration of their tangible and intangible assets, as well as the natural heritage in their environment. However, it is an approach that is not always carried out. In the case of those castles located in the south of the Valencian Community (Spain), this management is in themselves. From the work developed in Castalla since 2005, and the doctoral thesis carried out between 2013 and 2016, it has been possible to meet their real – cultural and natural – heritage diversity: in many cases and to date it was practically invisible. Thus, with reference to Castalla Castle and Sax Castle, the concept of heritage site will be defined, cultural and natural assets that make them up will be listed, their similarities and differences will be showed and it will be reflected on the need to understand them as heritage sites that are cultural and natural landscapes, larger or smaller, to be integrally managed as the only way to achieve a proper administration.

Keywords
Castalla, Sax, heritage, sites, management, landscapes

1. ALICANTE, A LAND OF CASTLES

The province of Alicante is an administrative unit belonging to the Valencian Community, one of the 17 autonomous communities that make up Spain, which is located in the southeast of the Iberian peninsula (Figs. 1 and 2). Its historical vicissitudes – as a part of al-Andalus and the crowns of Aragon and Castile – have encouraged the existence of a large number of castles. All of them mark the province from north to south and east to west. In many cases, they are configured as real landmarks of reference in their landscape. Some working documents, as the *National Plan for Defensive Architecture* (1), highlight the importance of the landscape in managing defensive architecture (Cultural Heritage Institute of Spain 2010: 14 and 17). So, without a deep knowledge of the landscape, it will be impossible to understand completely this kind of architecture.

Thus, the province of Alicante is configured as a privileged place for the analysis of castles and landscapes (2) in any of its forms and at different scales. Its study as a part of the defense system in the southeastern border of the Crown of Aragon with the Crown of Castile highlights on a large scale (Guinot 1995) (Fig. 3); while the analysis of the fortifications must be mentioned on a middle scale, whether in general works (Azuar 1981; Ferrer and Català 1996; Segura and Simón 2001) or specific works (Azuar 1994; Menéndez *et al.* 2010; Mira *et al.* 2015: 381-388).

However, there is an absence of studies at micro level, such as that developed in this project, which allows to better understand the reality of castles. This is a fundamental and necessary issue because the

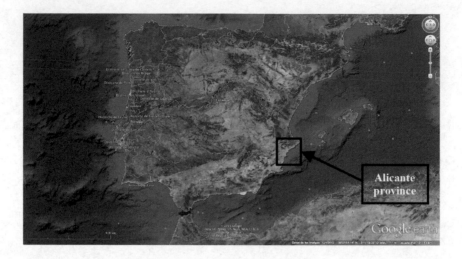

Fig. 1. Alicante province with the location of the heritage sites. Source: prepared by the author.

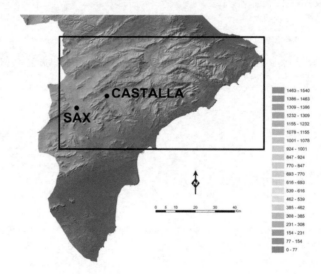

Fig.2. Alicante province with the location of the heritage sites. Source: Juan José Mataix Albiñana.

current management of cultural heritage requires a joint administration of their tangible and intangible assets, as well as the natural heritage in their environment. But this approach is not always carried out. Consequently, it is not surprising to see how the management of certain cultural and natural assets comes first, depending on those specific interests at the expense of others. If the subject is focused on castles in the province of Alicante, it can be seen that the management is in themselves. In this sense, many fortifications are presented as single heritage landmarks that grab all the performances carried out in their sites to the detriment of others. Taking as reference Castalla Castle and Sax Castle, this project will make known their heritage. It also will serve as a starting point for a new approach of the total management regarding to cultural and natural heritage on the sites of these fortifications to achieve an adequate

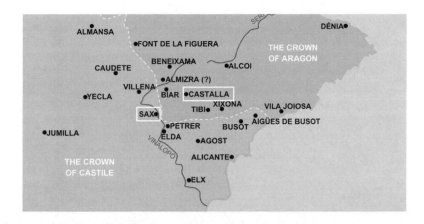

Fig.3. South border of the crowns of Aragon and Castile in 1244. Heritage sites are pointed out.
Source: https://es.wikipedia.org/wiki/Tratado_de_Almizra#/media/File:Tratado_de_Almizra.png.

management. This approach embraces castles, not as isolated elements in the landscape, but as heritage sites that are complexes and interesting, cultural and natural landscapes with a rich heritage going beyond the fortification.

According to the definitions given in previous work (Mira *et al.* 2015: 381), heritage site means the grouping of cultural – tangible and intangible – and natural assets, with common historical, environmental and heritage values, located and/or held on the hill of Castalla Castle and the rock of Sax Castle.

This denomination is the result of a process of work and reflection whose origin lies in the research on cultural heritage management in Castalla, developed within the University of Alicante between 2003 and 2005 (Mira 2005). It was an approach to the castle where an architectural intervention (2003-2006) was performed under the direction of Màrius Bevià i Garcia, and it also served to become aware of the heritage reality on the hill of the fortification. A reality that was closely related to, going beyond the castle and its management, but that also was paradoxically unknown because the castle had attracted the attention of society –something logical because, apart from its historical and heritage significance, it is the emblem of the municipality – On this basis, the work developed within the Castalla Municipal Service for Cultural Heritage, since 2009, allowed to deepen and improve the knowledge of the Castalla Castle Heritage Site.

On the other hand, the doctoral thesis project developed within the Department of Prehistory at the University of Alicante between 2013 and 2016 – to know how municipalities of the province of Alicante manage their castles– has served to better understand, among other things, its real heritage diversity – cultural, tangible and intangible, and natural – that in many cases, such as Castalla, was invisible. Particularly, it has allowed to recognize other heritage sites as Sax Castle, whose characterisation has been carried out by those professionals dealing with the *Master Plan of Sax Castle Cultural Park* (3) (Ponce *et al.* 2011).

2. FROM CASTLES TO HERITAGE SITES: A REQUIRED CHANGE?

The overcoming of a cultural heritage tandem regarding to monuments, whether isolated or including environment and/or nature, and works of art from the second half of the 20th century has allowed to value as cultural heritage those assets not regarded as such to date. Thus, as the UNESCO sets up at the World Conference on Cultural Heritage (Mexico 1982):

"The cultural heritage of a people includes the works of its artists, architects, musicians, writers and scientists and also the work of anonymous artists, expressions of the people's spirituality, and the body of values which give meaning to life. It includes both tangible and intangible works through which the creativity of that people finds expression: languages, rites, beliefs, historic places and monuments, literature, works of art, archives and libraries" (http://portal.unesco.org

Therefore, we are faced with an heritage diversity that, in the case of Spain and specifically in the area of study, has been recognized by different Valencian laws on cultural heritage, such as the Act 5/2007, February 9, of the Valencian government, amending the Act 4/1998, June 11, on Valencian Cultural Heritage, which considers as cultural heritage: those tangible and intangible assets of historical, artistic, architectural, archaeological, paleontological, ethnographic, documentary, bibliographic, scientific and technical value, and any other kind; those creations, skills, practices and the most representative and valuable uses of life styles and traditional Valencian culture, as well as knowledge; and those musical, artistic, gastronomic and entertainment expressions – especially those transmitted orally supporting and improving the use of Valencian.

In the words of Juan Agudo Torrico (1999: 40), it is a change of mind, as well as terminological, that is not still complete, from an old model made up by the historical and artistic heritage – restricted and elitist, it is focused on tangible culture – to other new composed of cultural heritage – open-minded and not elitist, it is focused on tangible and intangible culture and natural anthropized assets (cultural landscapes) – This new model requires the full management of all cultural and natural anthropized assets, without regard to their monumentality, value or interest. Without a comprehensive management, there will always be abandoned assets, and even outcasted in favour of others that could disappear. In order to answer the question arisen in the title of this subsection, this terminological change from castles to heritage sites is required to understand the true heritage, cultural and natural reality. It is the only way to manage it properly, as well as to know, preserve, disseminate and learn from it. Without this change, it will be impossible to carry out an integral management of our heritage and these fortifications will be regarded as single heritage landmarks from a social, and even legal, point of view.

3. CHARACTERISATION OF HERITAGE SITES (SUBJECT OF STUDY)

3.2. The Castalla Castle Heritage Site (Fig. 4)

It is located in the municipality of Castalla, in the north of the province (see fig. 2) (4). As was pointed out in other studies (Mira *et al.* 2015: 382), it has an extension of 11 ha and consists of the following cultural and natural assets: Castalla Castle (nº 1) (Menéndez *et al.* 2010), ancient medieval village (nº 2) (Ortega and Esquembre 2010: 61-106; Torró 1988-1989: 53-82), likely site of the lower ward (nº 3) (Ortega and Esquembre 2010: 91 and 92), likely site of the Fossar Vell necropolis (nº 4) (Ortega and Esquembre 2010: 90), traditional cultivated strips and terraces (nº 5), Dipòsit Vell archaeological site (nº 6) (Cerdà 1994: 99 and 100), stations of the Cross (nº 7) (http://www.cult.gva.es/dgpa/etnologia/Detalles_etnologia.asp?IdFicha=2792 and http://www.cult.gva.es/dgpa/etnologia/Detalles_etnologia.asp?IdFicha=2793), likely site of the battles of Castalla (nº 8) (González 2010: 255-265), water tank (1928) (nº 9), water tank (1960) (nº 10), Holy Week (Ariño *et al.* 1999: 59-87), Moors and Christians Festival (Ariño 1988: ///), hand-ringring of the María bell, and 224 elements belonging to 59 different families of plants and 37 species of vertebrates (Mira and Liñana 2014)

This site has a rich cultural heritage that embraces from Prehistory – the Dipòsit Vell archaeological site is dated from the 2nd millennium B.C. – to nowadays, a period where the role of this heritage site can be highlighted – specifically the castle and the ancient medieval village – as a border enclave between the crowns of Aragon and Castile. It also notes its importance as a scene of many celebrations in Castalla,

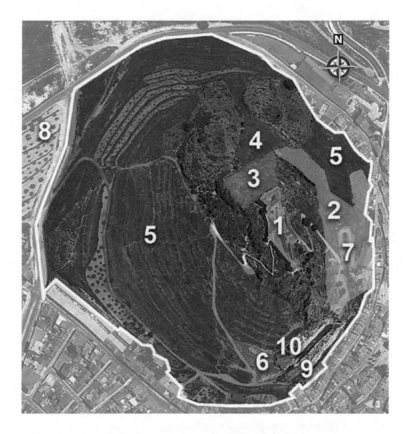

Fig.4. The Castalla Castle Heritage Site. Source: Juan Antonio Mira Rico and Daniel Liñana Torres (2014: 1).

such as Moors and Christians Festival and Holy Week; or its role as a strategic place during the War of Independence against French invaders (12 July 1812 and 13 April 1813). Its natural values cannot be forgotten: this site is closely linked to the Protected Landscape of Serra del Maigmó and Serra del Sit (5). Both have common geological features because the rock mass is part of Serra del Maigmó (Marco 1987: 17, fig. 1), as well as plants and animals: 31 animal species found in this site are also present in the protected landscape. And the same happens with 8 plant species documented. In terms of animals, it is noted the house martin (*Delichon urbicum*), while in terms of plants it is highlighted the man orchid (*Aceras anthropophorum*): a protected orchid in the *Valencian Catalogue of Threatened Plant Species*.

In light of the above, it can be seen that the enormous wealth of the Castalla Castle Heritage Site goes beyond the potential of the castle. In addition, this heritage site has a defined environment of protection with its own rules in order to preserve heritage values (6). All its cultural and tangible assets are included in the *General Inventory of Valencian Cultural Heritage* (7). The castle and its walls have the highest degree of protection according to the Spanish legislation on cultural heritage: asset of cultural interest with the category of monument, while other cultural assets are of local relevance. Under Section 2 of the Act 4/1998, June 11, of the Valencian government, on Valencian Cultural Heritage, assets of cultural interest "*are those that, due to their characteristics and relevance for cultural heritage, become the object of special protection, dissemination and promotion measures*". Assets of local relevance are those that do not have such values to be declared assets of cultural interest, but they have their own significance in that area.

3.2. The Sax Castle Heritage Site (Fig. 5)

This site is located in the municipality of Sax, also in the north of the province (see Fig. 2) (8). It has an extension of 9.47 ha and consists of the following cultural and natural assets: Sax Castle (nº 1) (Simón and Segura 2005: 295-334), well to store snow (nº 2) (http://www.cult.gva.es/dgpa/brl/detalles_brl. asp?IdInmueble=7173), Peña de Sax archaeological site (nº 3) (http://www.sax.es/ruta-del-castillo/en-el-frio-horno-metalurgico), cross (nº 4), triangulation station (nº 5), Municipal Natural Landscape (nº 6), and 226 elements belonging to 56 different families of plants and 21 species of vertebrates (Maestre and Pascual 2001: /173-294).

This site presents some features in common with Castalla. It has a cultural heritage dated from the 2nd millennium B.C. – Peña de Sax archaeological site – to nowadays, with the fortification as a border enclave between the crowns of Aragon and Castile. In terms of natural features, it also presents a wealth in plants with 25 endemic species (Maestre and Pascual 2001: 182 and 183). Most of them are common in the Iberian peninsula – such as *Carduus bourgeanus* –, but there are single species of the Valencian Community – such as *Rhamnus lycioides* subsp. *borgiae* –. In terms of animals, it can be highlighted the house martin (*Delichon urbicum*).

On the other hand, both heritage sites coincide with their animal species: house sparrow (*Passer domesticus*), Iberian wall lizard (*Podarcis hispanica*) and west European hedgehog (*Erinaceus europaeus*); as well as with their plant species: *Hypericum ericoides* subsp. *ericoides*, *Rhamnus lycioides* subsp. *borgiae*, *Silene mellifera* and *Teucrium thymifolium*.

As in the previous example, the Sax Castle Heritage Site has an enormous potential that goes beyond the fortification. Some of its cultural and tangible assets are included in the *General Inventory of Valencian Cultural Heritage*. The castle is protected as an asset of cultural interest, while the well to store snow and the archaeological site (Peña de Sax) are assets of local relevance. Nevertheless, the cross and the triangulation station do not appear in that inventory. Besides the protection focused on cultural heritage, part of the rock is protected as a municipal natural landscape.

Fig.5. The Sax Castle Heritage Site. Source: edited by the author.

3.3. The current management of Castalla and Sax heritage sites

The analysis carried out as part of the doctoral thesis has served to find out the management of both heritage sites between 2003 and 2013. As can be seen, the Castalla Castle Heritage Site has been managed integrally, continuously and in a coordinated way (Mira *et al.*, 2015: 381-388). That is, it has covered the entire cultural heritage, whether or not monumental or historical-artistic, as well as the natural heritage located on the hill, with some performances carried out continuously, not only punctually. Since 2009, the need of a joint management for these heritages has been developed (Querol 1995: 301-306). It is a common practice in the Anglo-Saxon world, like in Castle Campbell (Scotland) (http://data.historic-scotland.gov.uk/pls/htmldb/f?p=2400:15:0::::GARDEN:GDL00089), Castle Hill National Historic Site (Canada) (http://www.pc.gc.ca/eng/lhn-nhs/nl/castlehill/index.aspx) and Dover Castle (England) (http://www.english-heritage.org.uk/visit/places/dover-castle/), but not in the Spanish context. In fact, it rather separates the management of both heritage sites without taking into account their respective rules (Querol 2010: 24 and 25, 28**).**

All actions carried out have been performed, until the corresponding master plan in drafting stage is approved, under *The Castalla Castle Heritage Site Social Regeneration Project* (10). This is a management plan (Mira *et al.* 2015: 384):

> *"(...) started and promoted by the City Council of Castalla in 2009, and managed directly by the Castalla Council Department for Cultural Heritage and its Municipal Service for Cultural Heritage. It is based on research, preservation, restoration, didactics and dissemination. The municipal service staff coordinates and co-leads an interdisciplinary team – whose origin lies in the team that began the recovery of Castalla Castle in 1984 – made up of 20 researchers and professionals of cultural and natural heritage. This team is in charge of designing and performing many actions – research, preservation, restoration, didactics and dissemination – according to the needs. In addition, the municipal service has close collaboration with other departments of the city council – Culture, Environment, Urban Maintenance and Tourism – as well as local and scientific educational institutions, like the University of Alicante and the University of Valencia.*
>
> *The financial resources to carry out these performances come mainly from the city council. Nevertheless, it has been vital the financial support of the Valencian government, throughout its Conselleria d'Educació, Cultura i Esport (a regional department of education, tourism and sports)".*

On the other hand, although the economic situation in which Spain is involved is not the best,
> *"(...) the heritage site management has a good projection at the moment that allows to reach the purposes progressively. In general, it consists of this heritage site social recovery implementing a professional management model based on research, preservation, restoration, didactics and dissemination. Specifically, trying to:*
> - *Increase and improve the knowledge of those cultural and natural assets making up the Castalla Castle Heritage Site.*
> - *Ensure its good condition.*
> - *Create a cultural and tourist product of quality contributing to the economic and social development of Castalla.*
> - *Promote both access and enjoyment of the Castalla cultural heritage by society in general, and the Castalla Castle Heritage Site in particular."*

Nevertheless, a full management has also been carried out in the Sax Castle Heritage Site between 2003 and 2013 although it differs from that of Castalla. It has been performed integrally and continuously but in an uncoordinated way. That is, it has been carried out regarding to cultural and natural heritage on the hill where the fortification is located, following the parameters explained above. This also has been uncoordinated because there is not a team to work together in its heritage management. Therefore, each professional of the city council who participates in its management – archivist and librarian, architect, cultural assistant and technical of environment – acts independently on the area. Moreover, it has been managed continuously because many interventions have been made over time.

However, the Sax Castle Heritage Site has a master plan drafted but it has not yet been approved by the local government and therefore it has not come into force. This planning document is designed, according to its authors *"(...) as a scientific document suitable for planning, coordinating and managing its future interventions, and harmonizing those pre-existing performances with the true environment of (...) Sax Castle"* (Ponce *et al.* 2011: 4).

Its purposes are to (Ponce *et al.* 2011: 1):

- *"Ensure the protection of this asset of cultural interest (Sax Castle) in its entirety: on the heritage aspect (movable and immovable assets) and on the environmental and landscape appearance.*
- *Define its perimeter and areas in accordance with current state, community and local legislation.*
- *Combine the management of this asset with that of the municipal natural landscape where it is located.*
- *Value this asset and the municipal landscape in order to set up a space for cultural and environmental knowledge.*
- *Promote scientific studies on both of them, in order to improve their knowledge and disseminate their values.*
- *Ensure their use and enjoyment for both local and foreign citizens, under sustainable assumptions.*
- *Establish an annexed inventory of assets of local relevance and define their management rules".*

Those differences in management do not mean that there is a better heritage site, although the achievement of a master plan for Castalla and the entry into force of that in Sax, as well as the creation of a team, will enhance and improve their management.

4. RECOGNITION OF THE HERITAGE REALITY: FROM MONUMENTS TO CULTURAL PARKS

The Castalla Castle Heritage Site and the Sax Castle Heritage Site are not recognized as such under the Spanish and Valencian laws on cultural heritage at the moment. However, as noted in paragraphs 3.1 and 3.2, part of those cultural and natural assets are protected in terms of cultural and/or natural heritage, while other assets have no protection.

It is a priority to solve this situation in order to recognize that reality and manage them properly. To this end, and following the Valencian framework on cultural heritage, Section 26.1.A.h of the Act 5/2007, February 9, of the Valencian government, amending the Act 4/1998, June 11, on Valencian Cultural Heritage (11), these heritage sites are protected as assets of cultural interest with the category of cultural park: *"An space that contains significant elements of cultural heritage in a relevant physical environment for its scenic and ecological values"*.

As seen in its definition, the figure of cultural park protects all tangible and intangible cultural heritage located on both sites. Therefore, the teams in charge of drafting their master plans have chosen this legal concept. Furthermore, in spite of being a concept from the laws on cultural heritage, it also serves to protect the natural heritage as it has a previous declaration. In the case of Sax, this heritage site is already protected as a municipal natural park, while Castalla could be protected with this category or that of natural monument – which includes unique, rare or beautiful natural elements deserving special protection, as the hill that supports the heritage site, a singular landscape –. However, as Fernando Tomás Maestre Gil and Vicente José Pascual Abellán (Maestre and Pascual 2001: 189 and 190) point out, perhaps the category of municipal natural landscape is the most suitable because, unlike the natural monument and in spite of being similar figures, the first one requires less bureaucracy.

On the other hand, it is curious that, despite the advantages offered by the category of cultural park since 1998 (12), this has hardly been developed in the Valencian Community. In fact, there is only one: Valltorta-Gasulla Cultural Park, whose protection is recently started on 25 February 2015 (13). It is located in the municipalities of Ares del Maestrat, Morella, Catí, Tirig, Les Coves de Vinromà, Albocàsser, Vilar de Canes and Benasal (Castellón). Its dimensions exceed those of Castalla and Sax heritage sites because it includes many municipalities completely and/or partially. However, it is interesting to note that, as the examples discussed, this space is a unique combination of cultural and natural heritage, but on a larger scale, in which "(...) *the nature and the human work come together to give us a single landscape and a historical territory already disappeared in other places of our country*" (Valencian government, 2015). It consists of the following cultural and natural heritage: caves, shelters and rocks with cave art, military buildings, industrial buildings, boundary crosses, monuments of local interest, ethnological areas of local interest, areas of archaeological protection, areas of archaeological surveillance, inventoried ethnological assets, cattle track, sites of community interest, municipal natural landscapes, plant micro-reserves and catalogued caves.

In order to identify the true reality of these heritage sites, improve their management, and consider them cultural parks and not only monuments, a master plan must be drafted, adopted and entered into force.

5. CONCLUSIONS

The work developed in the municipality of Castalla since 2003 has served to recognize, characterise, deepen and improve the knowledge of the Castalla Castle Heritage Site (Mira *et al.* 2015). Subsequently, the doctoral thesis *Analysis of the Municipal Management of Castles in the Province of Alicante* (Mira 2016: ///) has allowed to identify some fortifications that in fact are heritage sites in the province of Alicante – an administrative unit of the Valencian Community, located in the southeast of the Iberian peninsula –. Both are located in places with a cultural and natural heritage wealth that goes beyond the castles. Actually, they are small cultural and natural landscapes that stand as landmarks of reference in their respective administrative and geographical contexts.

On the other hand, both heritages have similarities and differences based on their heritage wealth or management. After shelling them, these must be recognised and not seen as monuments. Making use of the existing laws and focusing on the current approaches of cultural and natural heritage management, they must be declared as cultural parks. This would enable an better management of both heritage sites. Furthermore, their characteristics

"(...) *make them perfect laboratories in order to put into practice the integral management of cultural and natural heritage and take advantage of them, developing the concept of heritage site as a superior entity that embraces a diverse number of cultural and natural assets. On the other hand, their common features make them very attractive to establish synergies of management and become heritage sites of interest at provincial and community level*" (Mira 2016: 576).

Some laboratories represent a new and interesting line of study focused on fortifications and cultural and natural heritage management in the province of Alicante. In this case, although without castles, there are other heritage sites that, as good cultural and natural landscapes, are the result of human activity on the environment. For example, Tabarca, a small island in the south coast of the province of Alicante (14), protected as an asset of cultural interest with the category of historical-artistic site (15), also treasures an important natural heritage (http://www.alicante.es/es/contenidos/reserva-marina-tabarca) with a full management (Pérez 2014: 78).

NOTES

[1] More information at http://ipce.mcu.es/conservacion/planesnacionales/defensiva.html.

[2] Landscape *"(…) means an area, as perceived by people, whose character is the result of the action and interaction of natural and/or human factors (…)"* (European Landscape Convention, Section 1 a). Other definitions to take into account are those included in the *Charter of Cracow*, that considers a landscape as *"(…) result from and reflect a prolonged interaction in different societies between man, nature, and the physical environment. In addition, they are testimony to the evolving relationship of communities, individuals and their environment (…)"* (*Charter of Cracow*, Section 9); and the *National Plan of Cultural Landscapes* where *"(…) a cultural landscape is the result of people interacting over time with the natural medium, whose expression is a territory perceived and valued for its cultural qualities, the result of a process and the bedrock of a community's identity"* (http://www.mecd.gob.es/planes-nacionales/dms/microsites/cultura/patrimonio/planes-nacionales/textos-planes-nacionales/05-paisajecultural-eng.pdf).

[3] More information at http://www.agricultura.gva.es/web/parajes-naturales-municipales/pnm-ladera-del-castillo-de-sax-sax.

[4] DATUM ETRS 89. 1-UTM X: 702.560.65 and UTM Y: 4.274.938.16; 2-UTM X: 702.753.03 and UTM Y: 4.274.726.07; [3-UTM X: 705.582.61 and UTM Y: 4.274.506.71; and 4-UTM X: 702.375.77 and 4.274.743.51.

[5] Protected landscapes are specific locations of the natural environment that deserve special protection due to their aesthetic and cultural values. More information at http://www.citma.gva.es/web/espacios-protegidos/paisajes-protegidos.

[6] The environment of protection came into force in March 2014. More information at https://www.boe.es/diario_boe/txt.php?id=BOE-A-2014-3218.

[7] The *General Inventory of Valencian Cultural Heritage* is a protection tool of moveable, immovable and intangible assets of the Valencian cultural heritage. More information at http://www.cult.gva.es/dgpa/inventario_c.html.

[8] DATUM ETRS 89. 1-UTM X: 690.073.08 and UTM Y: 4.268.128.60; 2-UTM X: 690.073.08 and UTM Y: 4.267.888.40; 3-UTM X: 689.747.22 and UTM Y: 4.267.680.79; and 4-UTM X: 689.987.14 and 4.267.980.95.

[9] Municipal natural landscapes are areas embracing one or more municipalities with special values of local interest. More information about the Sax Castle Municipal Natural Landscape at http://www.cma.gva.es/web/indice.aspx?nodo=55853&idioma=C.

[10] More information at http://www.gestioncultural.org/buenas_practicas.php?id_proyectos=299223.

[11] More information at http://www.cult.gva.es/dgpa/Ley/DOGV_13-02-07_LEY%205_2007%20de%20modificación%20del%20Patrimonio%20Cultural%20Valenciano_2%20Modoficación%20de%20la%20Ley.pdf.

[12] Act 4/1998, June 11, of the Valencian government, on Valencian Cultural Heritage. Section 26.1.A.a.g.

[13] More information at http://www.docv.gva.es/datos/2015/03/16/pdf/2015_2184.pdf.

[14] ATUM ETRS 89. UTM X: 721.170.37 and UTM Y: 4.227.406.15.

[15] More information at http://www.cult.gva.es/dgpa/bics/detalles_bics.asp?IdInmueble=1492.

BIBLIOGRAPHY

Agricultura.gva.es, (2007). *Paisaje Protegido de la Serra del Maigmó i de la Serra del Sit.* [online] Avalaible at: http://www.citma.gva.es/web/espacios-protegidos/presentacion-55853. [Access 6 Feb. 2016].

Agricultura.gva.es (2008). *Paraje Natural Municipal Ladera del Castillo de Sax.* [online] Avalaible at: http://www.agricultura.gva.es/web/parajes-naturales-municipales/pnm-ladera-del-castillo-de-sax-sax. [Access 6 Feb. 2016].

Agudo, J. (1999). Cultura, patrimonio e identidad. *PH: Boletín del Instituto Andaluz del Patrimonio Histórico*, [online] Volume 29, pp. 36-45. Available at: http://www.iaph.es/revistaph/index.php/revistaph/article/view/904/904#.VrcYizYU5bw. [Access 29 Dec. 2015].

Ariño, A. (1988). *Festes, Rituals i Creences. Temes d'Etnografia Valenciana*, IV. València: Institució Alfons el Magnànim.

Ariño, A., Martí, G.M. and Melis, A. (1999): El Ciclo Pascual. In: A. Villarroya and V. L. Salavert, dirs., *Calendario de Fiestas de Primavera de la Comunidad Valenciana*. Valencia: Fundación Bancaja, pp. 59-87.

Azuar, R. (1981). *Castellología medieval alicantina: área meridional*. Alicante: Institución de Estudios Alicantinos.

Azuar, R. (coord.) (1994). *El castillo del Río (Aspe, Alicante). Arqueología de un asentamiento andalusí y la transición al feudalismo (siglos XII-XIII)*. Alicante: Diputación Provincial de Alicante.

Cerdà, F.J. (1994). El II mil·lenni a la Foia de Castalla (Alacant): excavacions arqueològiques a la Foia de la Perera (Castalla). *Recerques del Museu d'Alcoi*, [online] Volume 3, pp. 95-110. Available at: http://www.raco.cat/index.php/RecerquesMuseuAlcoi/article/view/184406/237482. [Access 29 Dec. 2015].

Council of Europe (2000). *European Landscape Convention*. [pdf] Florence: Council of Europe. Avalaible at http://www.convenzioneeuropeapaesaggio.beniculturali.it/uploads/Council%20of%20Europe%20-%20European%20Landscape%20Convention.pdf. [Access 1 Dec. 2015].

Cult.gva.es/dgpa/direccion_c.html (n.d.). Direcció General de Cultura i Patrimoni. Website. (///) [online] Avalaible at: http://www.cult.gva.es/dgpa/direccion_c.html/ [Access 3 Jan. 2016].

English-heritage.org.uk/visit/places/dover-castle/ (n.d.). Dover Castle Website. (///) [online] Avalaible at: http://www.english-heritage.org.uk/visit/places/dover-castle/. [Access 3 Jan. 2016].

Ferrer, P. and Català, E. (1996): *El Comtat: una terra de castells*. Cocentaina: Centre d'Estudis Contestans.

Generalitat Valenciana (1998). *Ley 4/1998, de 11 de junio, de la Generalitat Valenciana, del Patrimonio Cultural Valenciano*. [pdf] Valencia: Generalitat Valenciana. Presidencia de la Generalitat. Avalaible at: http://www.cult.gva.es/dgpa/Ley/DOGV_18-06-98%20-%20LEY%204_1998%20del%20Patrimonio%20Cultural%20Valenciano.pdf. [Access 14 Jan. 2016].

Generalitat Valenciana (2007). *Ley 5/2007, de 9 de febrero, de la Generalitat, de modificación de la Ley 4/1998, de 11 de junio, del Patrimonio Cultural Valenciano*. [pdf] Valencia: Generalitat Valenciana. Presidencia de la Generalitat. Avalaible at: http://www.cult.gva.es/dgpa/Ley/DOGV_13-02-07_LEY%205_2007%20de%20modificaci%C3%B3n%20del%20Patrimonio%20Cultural%20Valenciano_2%20Modoficaci%C3%B3n%20de%20la%20Ley.pdf. [Access 14 Jan. 2016].

Generalitat Valenciana (2014). *Decreto 36/2014, de 7 de marzo, del Consell, por el que se complementa la declaración de bien de interés cultural del Castillo y Murallas de Castalla, sitos en el término municipal de Castalla, mediante la delimitación de su entorno de protección y establecimiento de su normativa de protección*. [pdf] Madrid: Generalitat Valenciana. Avalaible at https://www.boe.es/diario_boe/txt.php?id=BOE-A-2014-3218. [Access 14 Jan. 2016].

Gestioncultural.es (n.d.). Portal Iberoamericano de Gestión Cultural. Website. (///). [online] Avalaible at: http://www.gestioncultural.org/. [Access 3 Jan. 2016].

González, M.Á. (2010). De castillos y guerrilleros. Las milicias de voluntarios honrados de la Foia de Castalla en la Guerra de Independencia (1812-1813). In: J.L. Menéndez, M.Bevià, J.A. Mira and J.R. Ortega, eds., *El Castell de Castalla. Arqueología, arquitectura e historia de una fortificación medieval de frontera*. Alicante: MARQ, pp. 255-265.

Guinot, E. (1995). *Els límits del Regne. El procés de formació territorial del País Valencià medieval (1238-1500)*. València: Institució Alfons el Magnànim, 1995.

Instituto del Patrimonio Cultural de España (2010). *Plan Nacional de Arquitectura Defensiva*. [pdf] Madrid: Instituto del Patrimonio Cultural de España. Avalaible at http://ipce.mcu.es/conservacion/planesnacionales/defensiva.html. [Access 1 Feb. 2016].

Instituto del Patrimonio Cultural de España (2010). *Plan Nacional de Paisaje Cultural.* [pdf] Madrid: Instituto del Patrimonio Cultural de España. Avalaible at http://ipce.mcu.es/conservacion/planesnacionales/ paisajes.html. [Access 1 Feb. 2016].

Maestre, F.T. and Pascual, V.J. (2001). Estudio sectorial para un proyecto de paraje natural municipal en el Castillo de Sax (Alicante). *Investigaciones geográficas*, [online] Volume 25, pp. 173-194. Available at: http://rua.ua.es/dspace/handle/10045/372. [Access 18 Dec. 2015].

Menéndez, J.L., Bevià, M., Mira, J.A. and Ortega, J.R. (eds.) (2010). *El Castell de Castalla. Arqueología, arquitectura e historia de una fortificación medieval de frontera.* Alicante: MARQ.

Mira, J.A. (2005): *La gestión sostenible del patrimonio: propuestas de revalorización del patrimonio arqueológico del municipio de Castalla (Alicante).* University Degree / Master of Advanced Studies in Antiquity. Universidad de Alicante.

Mira, J.A. (2016): *Análisis de la gestión de los castillos municipales en la provincia de Alicante.* PhD. Universidad de Alicante.

Mira, J.A. and Liñana, D. (2014). *The Castalla Castle Heritage Site. An introduction to our natural heritage. Field Guide of the Fauna and Flora*, [online]. Available at: https://arepaccastalla.files.wordpress. com/2014/10/ingles.pdf. [Access 14 Dec. 2015].

Mira, J.A. and Ortega, J.R. (2015). Castalla Castle. Architecture and restoration in the 21st century in Alicante. In: R. Amoêda, S. Lira y C. Pinheiro, eds., [cd-rom]. *REHAB 2015. Proceedings of the 2nd International Conference on Preservation, Maintenance and Rehabilitation of Historical Buildings and Structures.* Barcelos: Greenlines Institute. [Access 10 Dec. 2015].

Mira, J.A., Bevià, M. and Ortega, J.R. (2015). Del Castell de Castalla al Conjunt Patrimonial del Castell de Castalla: un nuevo enfoque en la gestión del patrimonio cultural valenciano. In: P. Rodríguez-Navarro, ed. *Proceedings of the International Conference on Modern Age Fortifications of the Western Mediterranean Coast Defensive Architecture of the Mediterranean XV to XVIII Centuries (Universitat Politècnica de València October 15th-17th 2015).* [online] València: Universitat Politèncina de València, pp. 381-388. Avalaible at: http://ocs.editorial.upv.es/index.php/FORTMED/FORTMED2015/paper/viewFile/1748/1069.

Ortega, J.R. and Esquembre, M.A. (2010). Intervención arqueológica en el interior del recinto fortificado del Castell de Castalla. In: J. L. Menéndez, M. Bevià, J.A. Mira and J.R. Ortega, eds., *El Castell de Castalla. Arqueología, arquitectura e historia de una fortificación medieval de frontera.* Alicante: MARQ, pp. 61-106.

Pérez, J.M. (2014). Nueva Tabarca: un testimonio de un devenir singular. Cultura y Naturaleza. In: G. Canales, J.M. Pérez and F. Lozano, coords., *Nueva Tabarca, un desafío multidisciplinar.* Alicante: Instituto Alicantino de Cultura Juan Gil-Albert, pp. 69-80.

Ponce, G. (coord.) (2011). *Identificación y delimitación Parque Cultural Castillo de Sax y Laderas de la Peña y de los BIC's escudos heráldicos y cruz de término.* Master plan. Universidad de Alicante.

Portal.historic-scotland.gov.uk (n.d.). Castle Campbell Website. (///). [online] Avalaible at: http://portal. historic-scotland.gov.uk/hes/web/f?p=PORTAL:DESIGNATION:::::DES:GDL00089. [Access 3 Jan. 2016].

Querol, Mª. Á. (1995). Patrimonio cultural y natural ¿Una pareja imposible? *Extremadura Arqueológica*, Volume 5: pp. 301-306.

Segura, G. and Simón, J.L. (coords.) (2001): *Castillos y torres en el Vinalopó.* Petrer: Centre d'Estudis Locals del Vinalopó.

Simón, J.L. and Segura, G. (2005). El Castillo de Sax. In: *Historia de Sax*, III. Sax: Comparsa de Moros de Sax, pp. 295-334.

Torró, J. (1988-1989). El problema del hábitat fortificado en el sur del Reino de Valencia después de la segunda revuelta mudéjar (1276-1304). *Anales de la Universidad de Alicante. Historia Medieval*, [online] Volume 7, pp. 53-82. Available at: http://rua.ua.es/dspace/handle/10045/7002. [Accessed 29 Jan. 2016].

Various authors (2000). Charter of Cracow. *Trieste Contemporanea*, (///). [online] Volume 6/7. Avalaible at: http://www.triestecontemporanea.it/pag5-e.htm. [Access 10 Jan. 2016].

UNESCO (1982). Mexico City Declaration on Cultural Policies. Website. (///). [online] Avalaible at: http://portal.unesco.org/culture/en/ev.phpURL_ID=12762&URL_DO=DO_TOPIC&URL_SECTION=201.html/. [Accessed 10 Dec. 2015].

Wikipedia.org (2015). Tratado de Almizra. Website. [online] Avalaible at: https://es.wikipedia.org/wiki/Tratado_de_Almizra/. [Access 10 Jan. 2016].

CONSERVATION PROBLEMS OF GÖKÇEADA (IMBROS)'S CULTURAL LANDSCAPE VALUES

Ayşe Ceren Bilge
Istanbul Technical University, Faculty of Architecture

ABSTRACT

Cultural landscapes are the reflections of the interaction between the natural and cultural forces in the environment. This interaction attracts more attention where the relationship of nature and culture become intense under the limited circumstances, such as islands.

Gökçeada, which is the biggest island of Turkey, has a special natural environment. This environment is an inseparable whole with the cultural structure that is changing and developing over the years along with the social diversity. The island has many cultural assets owing to its generous historic and cultural background. After WWI Gökçeada has lost greater part of its inhabitants. Thus, abandonment process has been the beginning of problems. Traditional settlements and structures fell to ruin due to not being maintained. Moreover, there are significant conservation problems today that damage historic, natural and cultural properties of the island.

The aim of this study1 is to investigate the conservation problems that threat the future of Gökçeada and to clarify what can be done for the natural and cultural values. Also this study may lead to other researches about conservation of cultural landscapes.

Keywords
cultural landscape, cultural heritage, conservation problems

1. INTRODUCTION

Gökçeada, which is the biggest island of Turkey, is located at the north Aegean Sea just at the entrance of Gulf of Saros and also at the mouth of Dardanelles (Fig. 1). The island has named since ancient times as "İmbros" that replaced as "İmroz" with the Ottoman rule (Orhonlu 1972: 15). The island has taken the name of "Gökçeada" with decree of Council of Ministers of Turkish Republic in 1970. Because of being on a strategically important location, Gökçeada has been inhabited since the ancient times by various communities (Kahraman 2005: 39). As in the other Aegean islands, Gökçeada has also changed hands in time because of serving as a bridge between Asia and Europe (Çağaptay 2012: 34). According to the recent researches and archaeological excavations settlement on the island dates back to ancient times approximately 6500 BC (Erdoğu 2012: 1). People that engaged in agriculture and came from northwest Anatolia were thought to be the first settlers of the island (Erdoğu 2012: 9). After that according to the literature about Gökçeada, Pelasgians, Persians, Athenians, Romans, Byzantines, Genoese, Venetians and Ottomans gained dominance on the island respectively throughout the history (Herodotos 2004, Oberhummer 1898, Miller 1921, Mellink 1988, Kritovulos 2007, Orhonlu 1972, Aziz 1973). Although Ottomans began to dominate Gökçeada after the conquest of Constantinople, the island continued to change hands between Venetians and Ottomans for a while (Miller 1921: 333-334, Orhonlu 1972: 17). By the 17th century long term Ottoman rule began on the island (Orhonlu 1972: 17). However Ottomans had lost the island's control between the years 1912-1923 because of the Balkan Wars and World War I that took place in this period (Küçük 1998: 37). After the Turkish war of independence Turkish Republic has gained the control of Gökçeada again with the 1923 Treaty of Lausanne (Meray 2002: 56-57).

Although Gökçeada had varied rulers throughout the history, it has been inhabited mostly by ethnic Greeks (Kahraman 2005: 46). The previously Byzantine island Gökçeada, remained largely unchanged of its cultural, religious and ethnic composition while under Ottoman rule (Kahraman 2005: 46). In the Ottoman period only a small group of administrators and their family had settled on the island (Kahraman 2005: 46). The population of 6712 inhabitants was composed of 6555 Greeks and 157 Turks in 1927 (TUIK, 2015). By Turkish Republic rule, this situation has changed with population planning policies of government on the island. In 1946, Turkish Government brought first Turkish citizens to the island and then there were more of them after 1960s in order to increase Turkish population on the island (Kahraman 2005: 47-49). Moreover new settlements were established after 1960s on Gökçeada with the initiative of the Government. Not only this social alteration with these new settlers on the island but also there were political, cultural and economic changes that occurred after 1960s. All these significant changes had been the factors that motivating the migration of especially Greek inhabitants of the islands.

Social, economic, cultural and politic features have always been significant constitutive factors for the natural and physical structure of the island from past to present. Consequently changes of these features have affected mostly the physical environment of the island. Gökçeada's physical environment has been damaged with the loss of social and cultural diversification, which has shaped with over the years, after economic, social, cultural changes and also migration. In the recent years, Gökçeada is on the verge of change again with increasing population due to the return of those who left the island before and also developing tourism. Therefore threats have increased also on the physical and natural environment of the island.

Islands all around the world have unique ecosystems under the limited natural and cultural resources. According to this, most of the islands have valuable cultural landscapes that formed with these natural and cultural effects. Similarly, Gökçeada as an island settlement has significant cultural landscape areas that reflect relationship between the man and nature from past to present. However, pressure on the physical and social environment has increased and significant changes occurred. Due to the lack of resources for being an island Gökçeada is stricter and could not exhibit a flexible structure against change.

This paper[1] concerns conservation problems of cultural heritage and cultural landscape areas on Gökçeada. For the protection of Gökçeada's cultural landscape values and cultural heritage it is crucial to determine the conservation approaches. However in order to achieve this, root of the conservation problems have to be understood in detail primarily. With this study it is aimed to investigate conservation problems that threat the future of the island and at the end to recommend what can be done for the conservation of natural and cultural values.

2. CULTURAL HERITAGE AND CULTURAL LANDSCAPE VALUES OF GÖKÇEADA

Cultural landscapes are the reflections of the interaction between the natural and cultural forces in the environment. This interaction attracts more attention where the relationship of nature and culture become intense under the limited circumstances. Gökçeada has special cultural landscape values with its special physical conditions and natural environment for being an island and culture that has shaped this environment for many years. In spite of the massive variations and problems occurred in the past, Gökçeada still maintains evidences of its rich history and preserve its traditional villages, architectural texture and settlement characteristics, natural sites, archaeological sites, traditional production types, traditional agricultural sites and also culture, traditions and customs which are crucial representatives of its culture.

2.1. Architectural texture and settlement types

Today, historic traditional villages are the most representative elements of cultural landscape values of the island. They are organically developed settlements that occurred according to interventions to island's physical environment of the people over the years. These interventions are not based on decided plans or models. Although they comprise of serious of choices among the other alternatives that reflect knowledge, culture, traditions and customs. From settlement types to construction techniques, materials and craftsmanship, they are all outcomes of many decisions and results of evolving knowledge over the years.

According to the historical development of the island, settlement types and areas also have affected and changed. Settlements that preserved with a castle in Byzantine period expanded outskirts of the castle with the increase of population and than in the period of pirate attacks increased they became lots of small and scattered settlements in the interior and relatively safe parts of the islands (Ousterhout and Held 2000: 128, Kahraman 2006: 28). After the increase of security measures on the island with the Ottoman rule, scattered settlements have come together and formed larger settlements (Emecen, 2002: 57-61). Most of these settlements are the villages on the island that have reached today. The center of the island, which is known by the same name with the island and also is an old settlement, is Gökçeada. There are five historic traditional villages known as Kaleköy, Dereköy, Bademliköy, Tepeköy and Zeytinliköy except the island center. In addition, there are five more settlements called Eşelek, Şirinköy, Uğurlu, Yeni Bademli and Şahinkaya, which have started to be established by the mid-20th century with the government initiative (Kahraman 2006: 35) (Fig.1).

One of the oldest settlements in Gökçeada is Kaleköy (Kastro) that located on the northeast side of the island. It is considered to be the same area where Kaleköy established with the ancient city of "Imbros" that the island took its name from (Ousterhout and Held 2000: 62). For many years Kaleköy named as Kastro because of the castle that constructed in Genoese period and remains of which can still be seen today (Moustoksidis and Bartholomeos 2010: 153). In the 16th century Kaleköy maintained its importance and it was one of the two settlements that Piri Reis who was an important sailor and commander of Ottoman showed on his map with the name "Kal'a-i İmroz" (Piri Reis 1973: 119). Kaleköy was also the center of the island in this period. The other settlement showed on Piri Reis's map was Dereköy with the name "Kal'a-i İskinit" (Piri Reis 1973: 119). Dereköy has preserved its importance since 16th century same as Kaleköy, even it became the biggest village of the island in 20th century. Bademliköy, Tepeköy and Zeytinliköy are the other historic settlements that established in mid-16th century and have maintained their importance until today.

These organically developed settlements still preserve their authentic rural texture that comprise of residential buildings and other monumental or communal buildings. All of these buildings are constructed

Fig.1. Location of Gökçeada (right) and settlements on the island (left).

with traditional materials and techniques due to the requirements of inhabitants and the needs of social and cultural life. Also, they have designed according to be compatible with other structures and their environment.

Most of the traditional villages have settled to the outskirts and high zones of the mountains on the island. It is thought that there are several different reasons for this circumstance. One of these reasons is safety. In order to be protected from pirate attacks, which were crucial threats for the period, higher zones that could not be seen from sea have chosen for the establishment of these traditional settlements. Another reason is not to use already scarce fertile lands for the settlements. Traditional settlements of the island have established outskirts of the mountains around the arable lands and they could benefit thus more from these lands (Fig. 2).

Traditional residential buildings have constructed with natural materials like stone and wood that can be found on the island. Despite rare different samples, residential buildings are generally two-story, stone masonry-structured buildings with courtyards. They have annexes like shelter, oven and stores associated with daily life needs in the courtyards (Fig. 3).

Fig. 2. Historic traditional settlements of Gökçeada, Bademliköy (left) and Dereköy (right). Photographs by author.

Fig. 3. Residential buildings from traditional settlements of Gökçeada. Photographs by author.

Ground floors of the buildings also have designed according to the daily life needs. They were usually used for storage. First floors have designed for sitting, resting, sleeping, eating and drinking functions. Residential buildings in the villages are the examples of traditional construction techniques and craftsmanship. Natural stone material has used for foundations, load-bearing walls and wood material has used for partition walls generally. Also, wood has used for floor covering, doors and windows as the basic material.

As well as residential buildings, monumental and communal buildings in the villages have also constructed with traditional materials and techniques. All traditional historic villages have similarly at least one or more church, school, laundry and fountain. There are also other structures around villages like chapels, monasteries or residential buildings that are used seasonal for agricultural activities. There used to be also wind and water mills in the history of island (Fig. 4).

However, new settlements, which established after 1960s with government initiative, have not planned in connection with island's potential and features. These new settlements consist of mostly two storied, reinforced concrete structured buildings that are constructed according to a prototype plan. Also, these settlements have a poor relation with traditional settlements of the island, which has existed for many years.

Fig. 4. Monumental and communal buildings in the villages of Gökçeada; a church (top left), a laundry (top right), chapel, olive oil atelier, coffeehouse and a fountain (at the bottom from left to right). Photographs by author.

2.2. Natural features

Gökçeada has a special physical and natural environment due to being an island. It has considerably mountainous and rugged structure that is comprised 10% of plains, 1% of lakes and the rest of mountains and hills (Aziz 1973: 89). This mountainous structure constitutes various natural formations especially at the high northern part like "Kaşkaval Reefs" and "Marmaros Waterfall".

Also, the island is the richest one of Turkey and fourth one in the world in terms of water resources (Öztürk 2001: 1). In addition, one of the most important natural formations is Salt Lake, which is located at the southeast of the island (Yücel 1966: 69). Kefalos Cape was used to be an independent island before and than merged to the island from southeast part and has constituted the Salt Lake (Yücel 1966: 68). The lake that is fed from sea was used for salt production until World War I (Yücel 1966: 69). Today, it provides food, water and shelter for migrating birds.

Although, it may seem quite arid with treeless hills when getting close to the island by ferry, Gökçeada is a green island. Throughout the island mostly at the north parts there are protected natural sites since 1985. Endemic plant species are grown also on these protected natural sites. Olive tree is another special plant specie growing on the island. Greek inhabitants of the island produce olive and olive oil for many years with traditional techniques. In fact olive and olive oil production was the main source of livelihood in the past for island. Recent days, organic agriculture, olive and olive oil production trying to be improved by government investments after the migration of the island and than immigration circumstances.

Inhabitants of Gökçeada have formed the physical and natural environment of the island by building structures using natural materials like stone and wood in the surrounding. They used upper parts of the hills for settlements and outskirts for growing fruits and vegetables. Also, plains that have fertile soils are used for agriculture and olive production.

2.3. Archaeological features

Throughout the island, there have been various crucial archaeological findings and remains related to its rich history and culture. With the archaeological excavations and researches in recent years, Gökçeada's rich history has get out day by day. In the beginning, surface surveys have carried out on the island by local and foreign specialists and then systematic archaeological excavations have begun after 1990s. Most of the archaeological findings have removed to the archaeological museum in Çanakkale. Some of them still remain on the island.

Yeni Bademli mound is the first systematic archaeological excavation on the island, which is thought to be located in the boundaries of ancient Imbros city at Kaleköy. Except the excavation, it is also possible to see archaeological remains in Kaleköy and its environment. One of the most important remains is the castle on the top of the hill of Kaleköy. The area that the castle is located on is a protected archaeological site and Kaleköy village is also an urban archaeological site (Fig. 5).

According to the researches castles are thought to be the defense mechanism against attacks of the island especially in the Early Byzantium period. From south to north there were castles on the island periodically for communication. It is still possible to see the remains of these castles on the island and also surface surveys and researches have been done before on this subject. However, most of these areas are not under protection and not protected archaeological sites like in Kaleköy. Moreover, one of these important sites called Pirgos, which is located on the south part of the island and is thought to be an ancient port settlement, have damaged dramatically in the recent years. The settlement is located on the small cape also called Pirgos and there is a castle remaining from the middle Ages. In order to build resorts traditional residential buildings have been demolished around the castle in Pirgos.

Fig.5. Castle of Kaleköy from World War I period (left, www.awm.gov.au) and current situation (right).
Photographs by author.

2.4. Culture, traditions and customs

For many years, ethnic Greeks have inhabited the island. They are mostly Orthodox Christians and they have been faithful to their traditions and customs from past to present. The island remained largely unchanged of its cultural, religious and ethnic composition while under the regime of Ottomans. Even today, people come to the island for their religious holidays after they have migrated to other countries. They continue to celebrate their special name days of chapels together on the island. The most important and famous ceremony is "Panagia Ceremony" that carried out each year on 15 August. From all around the world the Greeks who once upon a time lived on Gökçeada return for a few days to the island and take part in this Panagia ceremony. The most important representative element for island culture is also architectural texture and historic traditional settlements. Monumental and residential buildings on the villages all together reflect this rich culture.

3. CONSERVATION PROBLEMS AND THREATS

In order to develop conservation model for the cultural landscape values and cultural heritage of Gökçeada current circumstances need to be understood and conservation problems required to be analyzed deeply. For this purpose researches, investigations, field studies and observations were performed on Gökçeada in order to reveal factors that threat maintenance of island's cultural values. These factors can be classified as natural reasons, socio-economic reasons, political reasons, reasons arising from current legislation, improper planning decisions, unplanned constructions and unqualified repairs as a whole.

3.1. Natural reasons

Among the factors threatening cultural heritage, natural reasons are the important ones. Cultural properties that are open to the external factors such as rain, snow and wind could be damaged easily and even lost in time. Historic traditional structures are mostly fragile structures because of being constructed by natural materials as wood, stone or earth. They need continues maintenance in order not be damaged rapidly. Abandonment endangered the traditional structures and making them vulnerable to external factors such as rain, snow or wind. Therefore abandoned structures that are not maintained continuously can easily be damaged and even demolished after a while.

In addition to these natural disasters such as erosions, floods and earthquakes are also among the threats for cultural heritage. Moreover, Gökçeada's climate, soil and geological features tend to natural disasters structurally. Because of being in the first-degree earthquake zone Gökçeada has experienced destructions and damages due to earthquake since it has inhabited. According to the earthquakes that occurred on the island in the recent times it can be said that the risk of earthquakes originated on the island and cultural values still continues. Lastly, magnitude 6,5 earthquake has caused serious damage on the island in 2014.

3.2. Socio-economic reasons

Another factor threatening the cultural heritage of the island is socio-economic reasons. Gökçeada has experienced significant social changes from past to present. Among these changes population movements could have been the most effective one on physical, cultural and natural environment of the island throughout the history. After 1960s Greek inhabitants started to abandon the island because of the changing politic, economic and social balances. These balances have changed with World War I, tensions that occurred on the island with the Cyprus dispute and also exchange period arising from the treaty of Lausanne.

Gökçeada excluded from the process of exchange but unfortunately it still has affected as politically and socially. Consequently, island has started to lose its inhabitants rapidly due to the consequences and troubles of these events. Among these consequences and troubles, the closure of schools providing Greek language education, expropriation of the most viable agricultural lands for military purpose, construction of airport or establishment of an agricultural based open prison and also for establishment a governmental agricultural enterprises can be said. Actually, all listed above are factors motivating the abandonment of the island by its inhabitants that live for many centuries on. However, abandonment is the main problem for cultural heritage and cultural landscape conservation.

In 1990s traditional villages of the island, which has existed for centuries, were mostly vacant. Dereköy, which was the biggest village of the island, has become almost empty. Although some inhabitants have stayed in Dereköy until today, a great majority of structures have been abandoned. After abandonment some new settlers came from Anatolia and started to live in empty houses not just in Dereköy also in other villages of the island. But mostly these new settlers have made improper interventions to the buildings in order to rehabilitate them. On the other hand abandoned structures have remained neglected and vacant for many years therefore most of them have become vulnerable to external factors by loosing their protective layers like roofs or external plasters. Finally extant buildings in the village have been damaged considerably even some of them are just ruined today. However Dereköy like the other traditional villages in the island still maintain the cultural significance and cultural landscape values by the cultural heritage it has.

3.3. Reasons arising from current legislation and policies

Although there are other important factors threatening the cultural heritage, most of the threatening factors originate from legislation on preservation and conservation. In such circumstances either legal structure would not appropriate for cultural heritage conservation or there would be problems in practice. In Gökçeada both of them could be problem about conservation. Political approaches to the preservation and conservation are privileged for the problems about cultural heritage conservation. One of the most important steps to be taken to protect cultural heritage is to provide related legal infrastructure properly.

First of all, national conservation laws are not appropriate for conservation of rural areas neither for cultural landscape areas. There is no legal definition for rural conservation areas in "Law on the Conservation of Cultural Properties" numbered 2863 which is the general law in Turkey regarding conservation. Historic traditional villages of Gökçeada are listed as urban conservation sites since 1990s. Rural conservation areas of the island as in Turkey, are trying to be preserved with current laws for urban sites. However, these circumstances certainly pose problems about conservation.

Furthermore, there is no definition of cultural landscape areas in national law. As a result of this, apart from understanding the importance of these areas also these areas could not protected integrally with tangible and intangible heritage. Historic villages in Gökçeada reflect traditional lifestyle, traditions, culture, traditional building materials and construction technology, traditional handcrafts of Greek inhabitants who live on these settlements for many years. With these features, they all could define as cultural landscape areas. Registering as protected areas could not maintain all tangible and intangible features of sites. In addition to protect cultural monuments individually and bringing regulations for other structures, it is crucial to preserve settlements integrally with their historic features, settlement patterns, agriculture culture, daily life culture and traditions.

According to national law Kaleköy, Dereköy, Bademliköy, Tepeköy, Zeytinliköy and Gökçeada City Center, which are traditional villages of Gökçeada, have been declared as conservation areas since 1990s. They all should have conservation development plan but only two of them could have completed until today. In other villages even registration and determination studies have not been finalized yet.

Before 1993, people had to have special permission from Çanakkale Governorship to visit Gökçeada. After that, this requirement has been removed and more people have started to visit the island. People, who had once left their village and home, began to come to the island for holidays after political circumstances have normalized. Consequently, rehabilitation and restoration works have increased because of people trying to repair their old, abandoned and damaged houses. Çanakkale Conservation Board, which is a department of Ministry of Culture and Tourism, is in charge of registration and determination process of cultural monuments and sites in Çanakkale and also in Gökçeada. However, this conservation board is located on Çanakkale. People need to go there for taking permission. Also, it takes sometimes quite long time because people are unaccustomed to legal procedures. Finally, some of them may choose the illegal way. Most of the repairs could have done out of permission from Municipality and Conservation Board.

With the increasing of government investments and plans in the field of tourism numbers of people that returns back and settled on the island are growing day by day. Also, there is a group of people who have come from big cities of Turkey and have settled to the island. In addition to this, there is a new upper scale plan for Çanakkale region that has approved by Ministry of Environment and Urban Planning. According to this plan a bridge is going to be constructed to the Dardanelles. In this case a further increase of population is foreseen for the region and also for Gökçeada. All of these circumstances bring more pressure on cultural, natural and archaeological conservation sites and cultural heritage of the island. But there seems to be no vision for these developments and no conservation development plan for the island.

4. CONCLUSION

Island's physical and natural environment that has been continuously inhabited since ancient times has changed, modified and reached today with the human factor. Today it has valuable cultural landscape areas that reflect interaction between the nature and culture for centuries. However, in the recent years, changing physical, economic and social conditions cause damages on these areas and destroy the values that give meaning and identity to the island. One of the most important reasons for this is lack of integrated conservation development plan for the whole island.

Furthermore, there are still crucial problems about current legislation and politics. There are archaeological, natural and urban conservation sites that are under protection on the island. According to the Decree number 648 dated 2011, some arrangements were made in the content of the Law on the Conservation of Cultural and Natural Properties numbered 2863 (Decree number 648, 2011). In this context, the term "natural" was omitted from the name of the law and it was changed to "Law on the Conservation of Cultural Properties" (Decree number 648 2011). By doing this, duties and authorizations regarding natural properties and natural sites, which are under the authorization of the Law numbered 2863, were transferred from Ministry of Culture and Tourism to the Ministry of Environment and Urban Planning (Decree number 648 2011). In spite of development on the integrated conservation approaches in the world this would be the reversed with international norms. A study should be made as soon as possible that deal with the whole cultural heritage and cultural landscape values of the island. While developing conservation method for cultural heritage of Gökçeada it would be appropriate to the island's identity to approach with cultural landscape concept.

In addition to these, there are no legal definitions neither for rural conservation areas nor cultural landscape areas in Turkey's current conservation law. By taking into consideration international standards and definitions of international organizations about cultural and natural heritage like UNESCO or IUCN, a legal definition should add to the conservation law of Turkey about cultural landscapes and rural conservation areas immediately.

Moreover the Conservation Board that is in charge of registration and determination process of cultural monuments and sites is located on Çanakkale. Because of being quite a large area with its districts, towns and villages Çanakkale needs more attention with its wide range of cultural heritage values. It could be better for the island establishing an office (KUDEB) that will be in charge of implementation and supervision in the sites according to the law 2863.

At the end, it is crucial that people should notice the importance of cultural heritage values of the island. It is just because that a majority of problems arise from lack of awareness in this regard. Educational activities and seminars should be provided about the significance of this cultural heritage and importance of preservation especially for the people who live on the island. Also, international cooperation and researches should take in consider about problems.

NOTES

[1]   This paper is derived from the ongoing doctoral thesis of Ayşe Ceren Bilge at Istanbul Technical University, Graduate School of Science Engineering and Technology, under the supervision of Prof. Dr. Yegan Kahya. The title of the doctoral thesis is "Gökçeada'nın Kültürel Peyzaj Değerlerinin Korunmasına Yönelik Bir Model Önerisi (A Proposal Model for the Conservation of Cultural Landscape Values of Gökçeada)".

BIBLIOGRAPHY

Aziz, A. (1973). *Gökçeada Üzerine Toplumsal Bir İnceleme.* Volume 1/28. Ankara: Ankara University Faculty of Political Sciences, pp. 85-119.

Çağaptay, S. (2012). *Bir Adanın Arada Kalmışlığının Öyküsü, İmroz'un Osmanlı Öncesine Bakış, İmroz Rumları Gökçeada Üzerine.* İstanbul: Heyamola, pp. 34-49

Decree number 648. (2011). Statutory Decree Regarding Changing the Statutory Decree in Relation to the Organization and Duties of the Ministry of Environment and Urban Planning and Some Additional Laws and Statutory Decrees. 28028, 17.08.2011.

Emecen, F.M. (2002). *İmbros'tan İmroz ve Gökçeada'ya Bir Adanın Tarihi Geçmişi.* Gökçeada: Gökçeada Municipality, pp. 53-68.

Erdoğu, B. (2012). *Uğurlu-Zeytinlik:Gökçeada'da Tarih Öncesi Dönemlere Ait Yeni Bir Yerleşme.* Volume 2/4. Edirne: Trakya University Journal of the Faculty of Letters, pp.1-16.

Herodotos. (2004). *Herodot Tarihi.* Müntekim Ökmen. İstanbul: İş Bankası, pp. 300-366.

Kahraman, S.Ö. (2005). *Gökçeada'da Göçlerin Nüfus Gelişimi ve Değişimi Üzerine Etkileri.* Volume 3 (2). Ankara: Journal of Geography Sciences, pp. 39-53.

Kahraman, S.Ö. (2006). *Geçmişten Günümüze Gökçeada'da Yerleşmelerin Dağılışında Etkili Olan Faktörler.* Volume 14. İstanbul: İstanbul University Faculty of Literature Department of Geography, Journal of Geography, pp. 25-42.

Kritovulos, M. (2007). *İstanbul'un Fethi,* İstanbul: Kaknüs Press, p. 23.

Küçük, C. (1998). Temel Sorun Egemenliği Tartışmalı Adalar. *Ege Adalarında Türk Egemenliği Dönemi,* Volume VII/182. Ankara: Turkish Historical Society Publications, pp. 33-80.

Mellink, M. (1988). *Anatolia. The Cambridge Ancient History.* Volume IV, Chapter 3, Eds. Boardman, J., Hammond, N. G. L., Lewis, D.M. Ostwald, M., *Cambridge Histories Online* Cambridge University Press, pp. 211-219.

Meray, S.L. (2002). *Lozan Barış Konferansı: Tutanaklar-Belgeler.* İstanbul: Yapı Kredi Publications, pp. 56-95.

Miller, W. (1921). *The Gattilusj of Lesbos 1355-1462. Essays on the Latin Orient.* Cambridge University Press. Available at https://archive.org/stream/essaysonlatinori00milluoft.

Moustoksidis A. and Bartholomeos, K. (2010). *A Historical Memorandum Concerning the Island of Imbros.* Gökçeada: Protection, Solidarity, Improvement and Development Association of Imbros.

Oberhummer, E. (1898). *Imbros*. Beitrage zur Alten Geschichte und Geographie, Festschrift für Heinrich Kiepert, Berlin, pp. 277-304.

Orhonlu, C. (1972). *Gökçeada (İmroz)*. Volume X/112. Ankara: Journal of Turkish Culture Studies, pp.15-21.

Ousterhout, R. and Held, W. (2000). Imbros/Gökçeada 1998. *XVII. Araştırma Sonuçları Toplantısı*, Volume 1. Ankara: Ministry of Culture National Library Publications, pp. 123-136.

Öztürk, H. (2001). Gökçeada'nın Jeomorfolojik ve Hidrojeolojik Yapısı-Yerleşim Planlaması için Önemi, *Ulusal Ege Adaları Toplantısı 2001 Bildiriler Kitabı*. Volume 7. İstanbul: Turkish Marine Research Foundation, pp. 1-8.

Piri R. (1973). *Kitab-ı Bahriye*. İstanbul: Tercüman 1001 Temel Eser, pp. 119-120.

TUIK. (2015). *Turkish Statistical Institute*. Available at www.tuik.gov.tr.

Yücel, T. (1966). *İmroz'da Coğrafya Gözlemleri*. Volume 1. Ankara: Journal of Geography Researches pp. 65-109.

LEGISLATIVE PROBLEMS OF LANDSCAPE PROTECTION

Barbara Wycichowska

Technical University of Lodz, The Institute of Architecture and Urban Planning

ABSTRACT

After the transformation of the political system in Poland the process of natural and cultural landscape degradation advanced due to the lack of radical pro-landscape changes and insufficient enforcement of the existing laws.

The responsibility for the definitely bad visual state of the landscape lies first of all with the imperfect legal system. Landscape protection in Poland has been limited to the protection of special areas, as well as to the protection of particularly valuable natural features. The present regulations are not enforced effectively enough.

Currently, we deal with the regression of landscape protection, compared to the previous legal system, which included other regulations concerning landscape protection apart from the established forms, i.e. the common nature and landscape protection.

In order to achieve the desired effects of landscape protection, it is necessary to make specific moves, which will ensure smooth functioning of the landscape protection system and forming the landscape from rational landscape planning, through shaping it to caring for it. The range of the activity will require precise definition in the country's jurisdiction.

Keywords

protection, landscape, law, act, legislation, legislative problems

1. INTRODUCTION

The scientists' appreciation of landscape (accepting the fact that it is an important element of the natural environment, responsible for the quality of life) was not followed by state jurisdiction, which means that so far effective laws concerning its protection have not been established. In contrast to the degradation of other environment resources (water, air, fauna and flora), destroying and polluting landscape is not penalized. What is more, sometimes landscape degradation is generated by legal regulations. The liberal character of the law concerning landscape protection and management, as well as its ineffective execution lead to an increasing depreciation of the landscape of Polish cities, villages and open spaces.

The activity of the Polish legislative bodies (the president, government, parliament and territorial authorities) does not result in effective protection of high quality cultural and natural landscape, which is a very important factor as regards satisfying human needs. The progressing inflation of national jurisdiction justifies starting a discussion about the problems of Polish post-war legislation concerning landscape protection.

1.1. Methods

Polish post-war legislation can be divided into two periods: before and after the transformation. They are separated by the year 1989, which introduced qualitative changes into the political, social and economic system of the county, opening the way to Poland's membership in the European Union (2004). After the war, Poland moved from central management subordinated to the ideological and economic targets of the state, to democratic governance and market economy, leaving a permanent record of the changes taking place in landscape.

Based on an analysis of the post-war legal acts concerning landscape protection, we may divide them into positive, neutral and negative ones, the last of them limiting the scope of earlier pro-landscape regulations. We may also define the main problems resulting from the activity of different ministries as regards landscape protection.

2. LANDSCAPE PROTECTION IN POST-WAR POLAND

After the war, until 2015, despite the lack of the legal definition of landscape, landscape protection in Poland had functioned due to the provisions of subsequent laws regarding the protection of nature, historical monuments and environment, as well as spatial planning acts. The legal definition of landscape had not appeared in Polish jurisdiction until 2015 and was included in the amended Spatial Planning and Management Act (Journal of Laws of 2015, No. 0, item 199). According to this definition, landscape should be understood as "space perceived by people, containing elements of nature or civilization products, created as a result of natural factors or human activity" (Article 2 point 16e).

The amendment was forced by the Landscape Act of 24th April 2015, changing some regulations with regard to strengthening the tools of landscape protection, which came into force on 11th September 2015 (Journal of Laws of 2015, No. 0, item 774). The same act changed the interpretation of the already functioning terms, i.e. "cultural landscape" and "landscape assets", introduced legal definitions of "priority landscape", "planning", "landscape protection and management", and – which is particularly important – it introduced new legal instruments of landscape protection: landscape audit and the Advertising Act. As it will not be possible to assess the legal regulations established by the Landscape Act sooner than in a few years' time, they will not be analyzed here. A similar decision regards the Revitalization Act of 9th October 2015 (Journal of Laws of 2015, No.0, item 1777), which became effective on 18th November 2015. Owing to the introduction of new revitalization tools (revitalization committees, commune territorial revitalization programs, local revitalization plans and special revitalization zones), it creates an opportunity to implement effective protection of the degraded cultural and natural landscape of Polish cities.

Particularly significant forms of landscape protection have been those which regard the preservation of landscape assets, and were established by consecutive post-war Acts on the Protection of Nature (Acts from 1949, 1001, 2000 and 2004) and Historical Monuments (1962, 1990, 2003).

It must be stressed that by the early 1990s, landscape protection had been focused on the natural-geographical environment and was implemented through strictly landscape-related forms of nature protection: landscape parks (they started to be created in 1976, despite the fact that as a legal form of nature protection they came into existence only in 1991, in the Nature Conservation Act), protected landscape areas (the first ones were established in 1971, on the strength of the local law, while as a legal form of protection they appeared in the Act of 1991), as well as natural landscape complexes (established on the strength of the Act of 1991). Landscape protection is also provided through forms with pre-war tradition, i.e. national parks, nature reserves and monuments of nature (Wolski 2011: 22-24).

Cultural landscape as an object of legal protection appeared only in 1990, in the act on the change of the Act on the Protection of Cultural Property and Museums (Journal of Laws of 1990, No. 56, item 322). The legislator not only extended the definition of "cultural goods" by including the concepts of cultural landscape, historical space and intangible cultural goods, but also introduced new forms of protecting cultural environment: a culture reserve, a culture park and a conservator's protection zone. In this way, the structure of cultural environment protection was constructed, complementary to the forms of protecting natural environment assets (Myga-Piątek 2001). The subsequent Act on the Protection and Care of Monuments from 2003 (Journal of Laws of 2003, No. 162, item 1568) excluded culture reserves from the list of the established protection forms.

Considering their significance for landscape, we should distinguish here the Nature Conservation Act from 1991 and the act on the change of the Act on the Protection of Cultural Goods and Museums from 1990.

In post-war Poland, the shape of landscape, except the areas protected by legal forms of protection, is determined by regulations concerning spatial planning and development, included in the Acts on Spatial Planning (1961 and 1984), on Spatial De velopment (1994) and on Spatial Planning and Development (2003).

Table 1. Existing forms of protection landscape. Edited by B. Wycichowska

Applicable Law	Kind of protected landscape	Forms of protection	Year in w hich this form of protection w as introduced in legal documents	Legal document in w hich this form of protection w as first introduced
Act of 16 April 2004 on Nature Conserv ation (Journal of Law s of 2004, No. 151, item 1220, as amended)	Natural landscape	Natural Monument	1919	Regulation from the Minister of Religion and Public Education of 15 September 1919 on protection of nature and monuments, Official Gazette "Monitor Polski" No.2, item 208.
		National Park	1934	Act of 10 March1934 on Nature Conservation (Journal of Law s of 1934, No. 31, item 274)
		Nature Reserve	1949	Act of 10 March1949 on Nature Conservation (Journal of Law s of 1949, No. 25, trm. 180)
		Natural Landscape Park	1991	
		Natural and Landscape Complex	1991	Act of 16 October 1991 on Nature Conserv ation (Journal of Law s of 1991, No. 114, item 492)
		Protected Landscape Area	1991	
Act of 23 July 2003 on the protection of monuments and the care of monuments. (Journal of Law s of 2003, No. 162, item 1568, as amended)	Cultural landscape	National Register of Historic Monuments	1928	Ordinance of the President of the Republic of Poland of 6 March 1928 on protection od monuments (Journal of Law s of 1928, No. 29, item 265 as amended)
		Historic Monument	1990	
		Cultural Park	1990	Act of 19 July 1990 on the amendment of the Act on Protection of Cultural Property and Museums (Journal of Law s of 1990, No. 56, item 322)
		Establish a protection in Local Spatial Management Plans	1990	

By the end of the 1980s, in accordance with the law, the basic tool of spatial management were local plans, both general and detailed. A general plan referred to the area of the whole commune and was an act of local law (the Act on Spatial Planning of 12th July 1984; Journal of Laws of 1984, No. 35, item 185). The Act additionally introduced a new type of spatial development plans – plans of functional areas, intended for areas distinguished on account of the special cultural or natural-environmental functions they perform. This was a good solution as regarded protecting cultural and natural landscape assets. Functional plans were abolished in 1994, on the strength of the Act on Spatial Development (Journal of Laws of 1984, No. 89, item 414).

After 1989 – the year of the transformation, it turned out that it was necessary to adjust the law to the conditions of market economy, which meant introducing changes in spatial planning. The new system of spatial planning involved the decentralization of spatial planning tasks and their communalization. On the strength of the Act on Spatial Development from 1994 (Journal of Laws of 1994, No. 89, item 414), establishing area development was considered to be a responsibility of the commune. The legislator created two planning tools from the former local plan: (1) an obligatory Study of the Conditions and Directions of the Spatial Management of a Commune, corresponding to the former general plan but not having the status of the local law, and (2) facultative Local Spatial Management Plans having the status of the local law and given spatial freedom (they could be made even for individual plots of land).

In the case when there is no plan, the Act imposes defining the ways of developing and the terms of building up the area, based on the land development decision, which, contrary to plans, is not subordinated to the study ("administrative decision concerning terms of construction and land management" is a common name of two types of decisions: the decision concerning the location of a public purpose investment and the decision concerning land development). It should be added that the land development decisions lack indications against interference into culturally or naturally valuable space.

The facultative and fragmentary character of plans accepted by the legislator, as well as the wide implementation of land development decisions as a planning instrument made the plan an ineffective tool of landscape protection and the obligatory study also lost its significance.

A positive novelty was the obligation to prepare a forecast concerning the influence of the local spatial development plan on the environment (the resolution of the Minister of Environmental Protection, Natural Resources and Forestry of 9th March 1995, Journal of Laws of 1995, No. 29, item 150), as a tool supporting the spatial planning process: to revise urban planning solutions and/or provisions of the plan from the point of view of securing protection for natural assets and resources, the quality of landscape and the inhabitants' living standard (Szulczewska 2010: 65).

In 2003, all local plans devised before 31st December 1994 lost legal validity. Moreover, issuing a land development decision was based on the good neighborhood principle (the Act on Spatial Planning and Development of 27th March 2003; Journal of Laws of 2003, No. 80, item 717, Art. 61, paragraph 1, point 1)., which states the necessity to adjust new buildings to the existing ones (urban and architectonic features and parameters).

Replacing local plans with land development decisions due to the fact that old plans have expired and new ones are scarce stands in opposition to the sustainable development principle declared in the Polish Constitution. It shows the imperfection of law as regards spatial economy and care for spatial order. In accordance with the law, spatial planning which involves designating areas to particular purposes as well as establishing the rules of their development is based on spatial order and sustainable development (the Act on Spatial Planning and Development of 27th March 2003).

To make matters worse, the problems of the legal system started to be resolved by the legislator by passing special purpose acts according to which investments are located on the basis of administrative decisions issued irrespective of spatial planning and development regulations, threatening the quality of landscape. The first special purpose Road Act from 2003 was followed by other ones, due to which nearly all strategic infrastructural investments in Poland are realized (special purpose acts: Rail, Shipyard, LNG Terminal, EURO 2012, Airport, Flood, Anti-Flood, Nuclear, Energy Transfer).

The Act from 2003 and the subsequent special purpose acts certainly largely contributed to the degradation of landscape.

An important aspect of landscape assets protection is the registered level of competency connected with the landscape protection forms. As a rule, the changes targeted at lowering the previously established level (moving from governmental to self-governmental) are unfavorable. This situation was caused by the Act of 23rd January 2009 on Voivode and government administration in the Voivodeship (Journal of Laws of 2009, No. 31, item 190), which changed the provisions of the Nature Conservation Act from

2004: from then on it has not been the province governor but the regional councils (provincial assemblies) that are responsible for creating, enlarging, liquidating or decreasing the areas of parks and protected landscape, while creating and abolishing the forms important for the protection of the local landscape assets (monuments of nature and natural landscape complexes) takes place exclusively on the strength of the resolution passed by the commune council. By August 2009, they had also been established by the province governor. The bodies responsible for establishing the abovementioned forms of nature protection are free to act; it has not been defined yet what competency they have and what responsibilities rest upon them and their subordinates (Kistowski 2012: 33-37).

Changes concerning landscape parks, introduced upon the request of the President, were even discussed by the Constitutional Tribunal, but the Act remained unchanged. Beyond any doubt, however, delegating the competency to approve protection forms to the self-governmental level due to the small interest of self-governments in creating new protected areas does not benefit landscape protection (Wolańska-Kamińska, Ratajczyk 2014: 139-140).

2.1. The case of universal landscape protection in post-war legislation

Despite the fact that landscape protection in Polish jurisdiction was limited to special areas (the established forms of protection), for a short time some legal provisions went beyond that and they were bearing the hallmarks of universal landscape protection. Art. 47 of the Nature Conservation Act of 16th October 1991 (Journal of Laws 1991, No. 114, item 492) contains the legislator's provision that: "Landscape assets are to be protected no matter if they are included in special forms of nature protection" (Art. 47a, point 1). Seventeen years earlier, Article 4 of the Construction Law of 24th October 1974 (Journal of Laws 1974, No. 38, item 229) stated that "The architectural form of buildings should be harmonized with the surroundings, take landscape assets into account and have an influence on the aesthetics of the surroundings."

2.2. Law inflation

Even the Landscape Act was not free from flaws. First of all, one may have reservations about the very definition of landscape, which does not correspond to the original interpretation of this term included in the European Landscape Convention, as it has been clearly narrowed down.

Serious doubts are raised by the fact that the same act introduces two definitions of landscape at the same time: one of "landscape" and the other one of "cultural landscape". The element that differs them is the expression "historically developed space", which the legislator referred exclusively to the cultural landscape, while every landscape usually has its own historical dimension.

We should also notice that in the current legal system, newly amended by means of the Landscape Act (amended in 2015), the terms "environment" and "natural environment" are defined differently and as a consequence "landscape" has been ascribed a different rank in the context of "environment" and "natural environment" (a double interpretation of landscape). According to the definition included in the amended act of 27th April 2001 (Environmental Protection Act), "environment" is "the whole of natural elements, including those transformed as a result of human activity, particularly the land surface, minerals, waters, air, landscape, climate, and the remaining elements of biological diversity, as well as the mutual influence of these elements" (Art. 3, point 39, section II: Definitions and general rules). Within the meaning of the amended Nature Conservation Act of 16th April 2004, "natural environment" is "landscape together with the items of inanimate nature and natural and transformed natural habitats of all the plants, animals and fungi" (Art. 5 point 20).

A sign of good legislature is first of all stability, which guarantees firm legal regulations. In Poland, the necessary legislative changes forced by the changing political, social and economic situation are constantly accompanied by objectively unjustified legislative battle – too much poor quality law is being created (an increasing number of low standard MPs' bills). Acts, most often the new ones, are amended several to several dozen times, which points not only to their faulty preparation but also to the poor quality of the amendments (lack of legal and specialist expertise combined with legislative haste) (Wycichowska 2013: 532). The Nature Conservation Act from 2004 has been amended 25 times, its predecessor from 1991 – 18 times, while the first post-war Act on Nature Conservation from 1949 which was standing law for 42 years – only 5 times. The record number of amendments were introduced to the Environmental Protection Law from 2001 – it has been amended about 70 times (Szymkowiak 2011: 6; Kotowski 2014: 121).

What is more, the number of collective amendments is growing (one act forces amendments in several other acts). They have problems maintaining internal and external coherence, e.g. the Landscape Act from 2015 forced amendments to 10 other acts.

The problems of landscape legislation result mainly from the fact that law is created for the use of economic policy, frequently for the benefit of specific groups of interests influencing the decision-making process (political and economic lobbing). Such behavior affected even the Landscape Act. While proceeding with the government act, support for the wind energy led to the exclusion of the provision about the spatial dominant from the Act.

Landscape regulations are usually treated instrumentally, mainly for achieving immediate aims by means of orders, bans, permits and obligations. Regulations concerning landscape protection are not clear (lack of precision leads to multiple interpretations), basic terminology is often unreliable (several definitions of the same term). Moreover, landscape legislation lacks definitions of the basic terms connected with landscape protection, which makes it difficult to apply the established law. "Landscape" gained its legal definition only in 2015, in the Landscape Act, while the term "landscape development" still does not have a legal definition despite the fact that it is particularly important as regards landscape protection and is used in current legislature (e.g. in Article 20.4 of the Act on the Protection and Care of Monuments from 2003; many times in the Landscape Act).

2.3. The biggest legal paradoxes regarding landscape protection

Firstly, despite the fact that local spatial development plans are the acts of local law and as such are generally applicable, preparing them is not mandatory.

Secondly, the obligatory Studies of the Conditions and Directions of the Spatial Management of a Communes are not mandatory for making administrative decisions, which very often replace local plans (land development decisions, special purpose acts).

Additionally, the risk of introducing sanctions for interfering with the landscape is small, which can be seen in the lack of disciplinary measures taken against entities operating on the brink of the law or even crossing this line (the case of introducing abolition for land use violation intensifies the phenomenon of "going round" the law (abolition for land use violation / buildings erected without permission after 1st January 1995 but before 11th July 1998, as well as those against which Construction Supervision did not conduct proceedings before 11th July 2003, in accordance with the act of 10th May 2007 on the change of the Building Law and some other laws, Journal of Laws of 2007, No. 99, item 665).

3. CONCLUSIONS

Polish legal system has not created conditions favoring the protection and development of landscape. First of all, the problem of general protection has not been solved (individual attempts). Landscape is protected by the law with varying degrees of success, only in special areas, within the boundaries of the established forms of protection. Although the legislator has increased the number of forms of protection over the years, deciding to transfer competency to a lower level of administration (from governmental to self-governmental), their range is not growing fast enough. Territorial authorities, who took over planning, value economic development more than landscape assets. In a situation where there is a deficit of local plans created facultatively, managing local space defined in commune studies is replaced with land development decisions. The real problem of legislation is allowing a situation in which shaping the space of communes and cities is based first of all on the land development decisions, which leads to random parceling of space and, consequently, to the degradation of landscape.

Polish landscape loses a lot due to creating and applying poor quality law and its ineffective execution. The multitude of passed legal acts and their slackness clearly prove that Polish parliament does not care about securing the comfort of quality and stability of law. The authors of the law are usually not specialists but politicians, who abuse legislative initiative in the name of building their own political prestige, and do not solve real problems, including those connected with landscape protection. There are definitely too many low quality legal acts which contain a range of editorial, factual and legal mistakes. The legislative chaos combined with the progressing liberalization of regulations responsible for the state of landscape, leads to a dangerous degradation of resources instead of protecting them. Poor quality law generates conflicts related to interpretation. Frequent changes of the acts lead to the deregulation of the legal system, and consequently make it difficult to implement and execute law.

In order to obtain the desired effects of landscape protection, it is necessary to initiate specific activities which will ensure smooth functioning of the landscape protection and development system, based on legislation. These activities, from rational landscape planning (based on thorough recognition, valorization and monitoring), through shaping it, to caring about it, will require precise definition at different levels of state jurisdiction (these two terms have not been defined so far).

BIBLIOGRAPHY

Kistowski, M. (2012). The prospects for landscape conservation in Poland with special attention to landscape parks, *Przegląd Przyrodniczy* XXIII, 3, pp. 33–37.

Kotowski, W. (2014). Ochrona środowiska w ustawodawstwie pozakodeksowym, *Prokuratura i Prawo 5,* Wydawnictwo IES, pp.. 121.

Ratajczyk, N., Wolańska-Kamińska A. (2014). Establishing local forms of nature protection by rural district governments, *Woda-Środowisko-Obszary Wiejskie* (I–III). T. 14. Z. 1 (45), Instytut Technologiczno-Przyrodniczy w Falentach, pp. 139-140.

Myga-Piątek, U. (2001), Refleksja nad ochroną krajobrazów Górnego Śląska. *Gazeta Uniwersytecka UŚ,* [online], No. 10 (89). Available at: http://gazeta.us.edu.pl/node/209851 [Access 17 Jan. 2016].

Szulczewska, B. (2010). Environmental impact prediction as an important tool in physical planning process. In: Radziejowski, J. ed., Physical Planning in Poland. Status and problems. *Zeszyty Naukowe No. 2,* The Higher School, of the Universal Education Society in Warsaw, Warszawa, p. 65-73.

Szymkowiak, T. (2011). Dwie dekady ekologii, *Przegląd Komunalny* 3, p. 6.

Wolski, P. (2011). Szkic do polityki kształtowania krajobrazu, In: Dziekoński, O. ed., *Ochrona krajobrazu przyrodniczego i kulturowego a rozwój cywilizacyjny,* Polskiej Biuletyn Forum Debaty Publicznej, Nr 3, Kancelaria Prezydenta Rzeczypospolitej Polskiej. Biuro Polityki Społecznej, Warszawa 2011, pp. 22-24.

Wycichowska, B. (2013). Directing the development of a medium-sized city - the holistic approach. In: Juzwa, N., Sulimowska-Ociepka, A. ed., 7ULAR. *Urban Landscape Renew. Middle-sized cities.* Vol.2, Wydział Architektury Politechniki Śląskiej; Gliwice, Łódź, pp. 515-522.

Legal references

Regulation from the Minister of Religion and Public Education of 15 September 1919 on protection of nature and monuments, Official Gazette "Monitor Polski", No.2, item 208.

Ordinance of the President of the Republic of Poland of 6 March 1928 on protection od monuments (Journal of Laws of 1928 No. 29, item 265 as amended).

Act of 10 March 1934 on Nature Conservation (Journal of Laws of 1934, No. 31, item 274)

Act of 7 April 1949 on Nature Conservation (Journal of Laws of 1959, No. 25, item 180).

Act of 15 February1949 on Protection of Cultural Property and museums (Journal of Laws of 1999 No. 98, item 1150).

Act of 24 October 1974 – Building Law (Journal of Laws of 1975, No. 38, item 229).

Act of 31 January 1980 on environmental protection and forming of the environment (Journal of Laws of 1994 No. 49, item 196 with amendments).

Act of 12 July 1984 on spatial planning (Journal of Laws of 1984, No. 35, item 187)

Act of 19 July 1990 on the amendment of the Act on Protection of Cultural Property and Museums (Journal of Laws of 1990, No. 56, item 322).

Act of 16 October 1991 on Nature Conservation (Journal of Laws of 1991 No. 114, item 492).

Act of 7 July 1994 Building Law (Journal of Laws of 1994 No. 89, item 414).

Act of 7 July 1994 on the Spatial Management (Journal of Laws of 1999, No. 89, item 415).

Regulation of the Minister of Environmental Protection, Natural Resources and Forestry on 9 March 1995. on determining the requirements to be met forecasts of the impact of Local Spatial Development Plan on natural environment (Journal of Laws of 1995, No. 29, item 150).

Act of 27 April 2001 – Environmental Protection Law (Journal of Laws of 2006, No. 129, Item 902, with later amendments).

Act of 27 March 2003 on Spatial Planning and Management (Journal of Laws of 2003, No. 80, item 717, with amendments).

Act of 23 July 2003 on the protection of monuments and the care of monuments. (Journal of Laws of 2003 No. 162, item 1568, as amended).

Act of 16 April 2004 on Nature Conservation (Journal of Laws of 2004, No. 151, item 1220, as amended).

Ac t of 23 January 2009, on Voivode and government administration in the Voivodeship (Journal of Laws of 2009, No. 31, item 190).

Act of 24 April 2015 on changing some regulations with regard to strengthening the tools of landscape protection (Journal of Laws of 2015, No. 0, item 190).

Act of 9 October 2015 on revitalization (Journal of Laws of 2015, No. 0, item 1777).

THE IMPACT OF WORLDS' EXHIBITIONS ON LANDSCAPE AND DEVELOPMENT OF CITIES. URBAN, ARCHITECTURAL, PARK AND SYMBOLIC LEGACY OF EXPOS

Izabela Sykta

Institute of Landscape Architecture Faculty of Architecture Cracow University of Technology

ABSTRACT

The Worlds' Exhibitions have been creating the special circumstances favoring an implementation of extremely original architectural forms and objects. In time they have become significant dominants or landmarks in the urban landscape of hosting cities. Exhibition sites became a kind of testing grounds where the latest technical inventions, new constructions and forms were presented and tested, unhindered by views of the traditionalists, commonly shared tastes and aesthetic habits or determinants of urban context. Sometimes, despite the presumed temporariness of exhibition structures, they have remained at the exhibition areas, often radically changing cityscape. Very often – as Eiffel Tower or others – they have become icons or symbols of a much broader sense. Expo-cities were built in the areas within existing city field reserves as parks, commons or river waterfronts or on neglected and abandoned terrains, degraded by industry. After the Exhibition they were restored to the city with new infrastructure and multi-purpose buildings, contributing to development of the city. This article is an analysis of urban, landscape, architectural and symbolic legacy of Worlds' Exhibitions, based on selected case studies.

Keywords

Worlds' Exhibitions, Expo, city landscape, urban development

1. INTRODUCTION

Amazing buildings original in both their form and scale, great plazas, promenades, alleys, expansive and modern parks – these are the physical traces left in cities by world exhibitions. Their role in shaping the landscape and development of host cities is invaluable. Cities in which such exhibitions took place changed, became more beautiful, developed, increased their potential in many fields (culture, exhibitions, trade, tourism, economy, transport, ecology etc.) – in every case their urban status and image improved. This influenced their position with regard to world leaders – those cities whose development is most dynamic and multi-directional. Sometimes the boost toward development and urban and landscape changes generated by the world exhibitions exceeded the local scale of the host city. This was the case of the Chicago's World Exposition of 1893 where the incredible urban-architectonic arrangement of the Expo city – the White City – inspired changes in the spatial environment of American cities, which led to the establishment of a social movement aimed at improving their image – the City Beautiful Movement – and the latter implementation of the City Beautiful plans which positively changed the image of many cities. In this way the spatial and landscape heritage of world exhibitions achieved a supra-local and far-reaching dimension.

A major role, also exceeding the scale of the city host, was played by the buildings and structures remaining after the exhibitions, distinct and often controversial and widely discussed among professionals, many of which constitute milestones in the history of architecture. To show their significance, one need only point to such post-exhibition structures as the Eiffel Tower (Paris 1889), the German Pavilion by M. van der Rohe (Barcelona 1929), the Space Needle (Seattle 1962), the Geodesic Dome or Habitat (Montreal 1967). Many of these objects became unique logos of the host cities, their main tourist attractions, but some achieved an even higher rank. One must not neglect to mention those structures which, although dismantled after the exhibition, played a key role in the history and development of the theory of modern architecture. These avant-garde objects predicted new trends and lay down new paths in architecture for decades to come. The Crystal Palace, raised for the Great London Exhibition in 1851, deserves a special mention. It was followed by many equally innovative structures. Usually they were preserved in photographs of the exhibitions, inspiring future generations of architects. Although not preserved physically, such structures also constitute an important heritage of world exhibitions.

Although on a smaller scale, the various symbolical spatial structures – installations and sculpture compositions – which served as the exhibitions' logo often strongly influenced the host city's landscape. Most notable are the statue of Christopher Columbus (Barcelona 1888), Atomium (Brussels 1958) and Unisphere (New York 1964). Similarly to architectonic objects, many symbolical structures of the exhibitions were dismantled or relocated. The most expressive structures found a permanent place in the history of art and architecture.

The scale and scope of the changes brought about by world exhibitions in cities was enormous. The construction of the Expo city spanned wide areas, using partly-developed urban locations but also often restoring areas which had been neglected, degraded by industry, belonging to no one, until then presenting no value. After the exhibition they were transformed into attractive public spaces – both plazas and parks, filled with numerous cultural institutions. Many of them remained after the Expo, bringing the exhibition host profits for many years after its conclusion. Such spaces, exhibiting a strong sense of the *genius loci* of the biggest fairs in modern times, which constitute distinguishing landmarks in urban architecture, often connected through a network of synergistic links, can be found nowadays in Paris, Barcelona, Seville, Chicago, New York, Shanghai and many other cities which hosted exhibitions in the past.

Besides the aesthetic benefits, the organization of the exhibition generated numerous practical and economical benefits for the host city. In preparation for the exhibition, the city had to make a great effort to improve the transport network, the tourist base, the gastronomy etc. in order to accommodate millions of visitors. These efforts proved beneficial both during the exhibition, when the city appeared as open and modern, as well as after its conclusion when the city would use the new infrastructure to improve its operation and the quality of life.

1.1. Remarks / Methodology

The purpose of this article is to present the heritage of world exhibitions and their significance in shaping the landscape, image and development of the host cities. Taking into account the exhibitions' impact on urban development, architecture, parks or symbolism, the author illustrates the above notions with cities which hosted great events, such as Paris, Chicago, Barcelona, New York, Brussels, Montreal, Seville, Shanghai or Milan, and in whose spaces there remain numerous traces and remnants of the Expos.

2. CONTENTS

2.1. Urban legacy

World exhibitions, organized since late 19th century, changed, often radically, the landscape of the host cities. These global-scale events often provided a strong boost to local urban development, transforming "lost spaces" (Trancik 1986) – unused, abandoned areas of low value – into high-quality public spaces which continued to function after the exhibition, bringing many benefits, both visual and economical, to the host city. These processes often occurred in synergy, binding the post-Expo structures to the city with a network of belts or public spaces surrounding distinguishing cultural landmarks (e.g. Paris 1889, Barcelona 1929, Seattle 1962), and through the inclusion of post-Expo areas in the city's green areas system (e.g. Barcelona 1888, Milan 1906, Seville 1929, New York 1939, 1964, Shanghai 2010), contributing to the improvement of the green balance, as well as raising the quality of spaces and the life of the residents. The networks of post-Expo urban and natural areas and structures are superimposed over the city's landscape structure, efficiently and effectively shaping the city's macro-enclosure. The panoramas of host cities gained new minor and major landmarks, accents, eye-catchers etc. which are identified with the world exhibitions and shape the city's identity. They created specific *genius loci* and became significant elements of the mental landscape where, to quote K. Lynch (Lynch 2011: 23) post-Expo areas can be identified as "nodes" or "districts", while the distinguishing post-Expo structures can be viewed as "landmarks".

Paris 1855 1867 1878 1889 1900 1925 1937 Paris hosted a record number of international exhibitions which changed the city's landscape between 1855 and 1937. Subsequent exhibitions left such a distinct mark on the city, both in terms of its urban and architectural development, that the landscape of today's Paris is largely determined by them. The exhibitions reinforced the role of the axis Ecole Militaire – Champ de Mars – Palais de Chaillot as the main exposition area, and also sometimes included additional locations such as: Avenue des Champs-Élysées, Esplanade des Invalides, the wharf of Seine, Bois de Vincennes, connecting them into a kind of constellation with a network of alleys and passageways, which crossed each other in subsequent points of interest marked in Expo guides. Relations between the exhibition areas and objects were formed according to E. Haussman's mid-19th century principle of great interrelated and crossed axes, accentuating the crossing of axes with plazas which highlight distinguished public buildings. The axis Champ de Mars – Trocaderó, further accentuated by the vertical landmark of the Eiffel Tower, has such a strong formal influence (Żórawski 1973: 101-115) on the city's urban structure that its position can be compared even to the great Parisian axis Louvre – Place de l'Étoile. Before the exhibitions, the Champ de Mars was an open field used for purposes requiring wide space, such a military drills, open-air meetings, shows and spectacles, national ceremonies, parades, horse racing etc. (Sykta 2007: 80) Thus, the exhibitions were staged in locations which were central, undeveloped and well suited for the construction of temporary exhibition structures. The first exhibitions of 1855 and 1867 were based on the model of one common exhibition structure. The 1855 exhibition took place in the Palais de'l Industrie on Champs-Élysées with a glass gallery running along the Seine. For the first exhibition on Champ de Mars in 1867 the city constructed a large round gallery (by J.B. Krontz), surrounded by freely designed gardens. The landscape of subsequent exhibitions on Champ de Mars was shaped by quadrangle-based complexes which were constructed since 1878 and included various types of halls and pavilions surrounded by public spaces and gardens. Since that time, the Champs de Mars was connected by a common axis with areas on the other side of the Seine where the Palais du Trocaderó (by G. Davioud) was erected, serving as an art gallery. For the 1937 exhibition this "moorish-byzantine" building was replaced by the monumental classic-modernistic Palais de Chaillot (by L.H. Boileau, J. Carlu, L. Azéma), and the Champ de Mars axis was crowned by terraced gardens (by J.C. Alphand) with cascade fountains. This layout became the basic spatial organization principle of all latter Parisian exhibitions. In 1889, on the Champ de Mars – Trocaderó axis, the Eiffel tower appeared, serving as a new gate to exhibition areas. It was this tower which most radically changed the Parisian landscape, becoming a symbol of a much wider meaning and an attraction without parallel in the world, drawing tourists from the whole world (Sykta 2007: 92). Since then, the 300-meter tower has presided over the Expo areas and the whole city. At the beginning of the 20th century, the garden and the whole block of the Champ de Mars gained its current appearance. The area on both sides was fenced off and developed with residential buildings. Preserving the post-Expo structures, i.e. the axis and the Eiffel tower, the city used their space to create a garden under the direction of J.C. Formigé.

The central part was composed of blocks of lawns with straight alleys, while the perimeter was filled with foliage shaped *à la francaise* (Champigneulle 1973, Sykta 2007: 80). The compositional-scenic axis of Ecole Militaire – Champ de Mars – Palais de Chaillot, the urban heritage of Parisian exhibitions, today a representative public space, perfectly fits the city's urban structure, drawing upon the tradition of great Parisian axes. Its significance is reinforced by the unfading attractiveness and popularity of Paris's Eiffel tower, an original gateway and a logo of Paris exhibitions.

Barcelona 1888 1929 Significant and permanent marks in the city's landscape and space were left by the world exhibitions in Barcelona, which hosted them twice in 1888 and 1929. Just like in Paris, the city tried to connect the exhibition areas both with themselves and with the city using axes: alleys, nodes, plazas, landmarks, architectonic and sculpture accents.

The 1888 exhibition took place in the Ciutadella Park built over the premises of the former citadel, situated between the organic fabric of the Medieval town and the regular grid of the modern 19th century city, according to designs by I. Cerdà. The entrance to the park is preceded by the Saló de Sant Joan promenade (by P. Falqués) which is framed by sculptures and decorative lamps. The exhibition's entrance was formed by an original brick triumphal arch (by J. Vilaseca i Casanoves) with relief decoration created by Catalan modernist-era sculptors. Today these objects constitute one of the most representative public spaces in the city. Another distinguishing feature of Barcelona's landscape is the statue of Christopher Columbus, erected as the symbol of the 1888 exhibition (Ellingham et alt. 1995: 174-176; Simonis 2008: 110-111, 138; Spencer-Jones 2008: 712; Sykta 2012a: 106-107, 116; Sykta 2012b: 228-231; Sykta 2014c: 8, 11, 18, 22; *The end of the Century, the beginning of the Century. The 1888 exhibition*).

The 1929 exhibition was staged in a particularly exposed location of the city's landscape – the Montjuïc hill, a topographic city dominant. The composition of the main exhibition areas (by J. Puig i Cadafalch) was based on the monumental axis Plaça d'Espanya – Avinguda de la Reina Maria Cristina – Palau Nacional – Olympic Stadium. The whole, situated amphitheatrically on a slope, was very exposed in the cityscape. The axis began at the foot of Montjuïc in the Plaça d'Espanya, accentuated by a centrally situated group of sculptures. Next the axis, crossing the symbolic gate formed by two twin towers, rose toward the hill's peak through the wide promenade of Av. de la Reina Maria Cristina, framed by monumental pavilions, with sculpted stairs, the cascade fountain La Font Màgica, columns, decorative balustrades and lamps. The main alley culminates in the most spectacular building of the exhibition: the Palau Nacional (by J. Puig i Cadafalch), crowned by a dome visible from the distance. The representative Expo axis between the Plaça d'Espanya and the Palau Nacional was complemented by other structures scattered on the side of Montjuïc and surrounded by green areas. These include the Olympic Stadium, constructed for the Olympics coinciding with the exhibition and modernized for the 1992 Olympics, which operates to this day as part of the wider Anella Olimpica Park, and the amphitheatre Teatre Grec, as well as the Spanish Village (Poble Espanyol) (by F. Folgera, R. Reventós), which constitutes a kitsch conglomerate of replicas of old buildings and characteristic forms of Spanish architectural styles and landscapes.

Another location, constituting an important node in the network of links between exhibition structures, was the Plaza Catalunya constructed in 1927 (by F. de Paul Nebot). It included a small temple, a central colonnade and decorative details – a monumental fountain and a series of sculptures by leading artists of the period, of which the most famous is the marble *Deessa* (by J. Clarà, 1909), now beautifully reflected in the surface of the large pond (Bonta 1975; Capó and Catasús 2003: 14; Ellingham et alt. 1995: 177-180; Haduch and Haduch 2012: 190; Simonis 2008: 184-190, 192-194, 200-201; Sykta 2012a: 106, 109; Sykta 2012b: 230-231; Sykta 2014c: 8, 11, 18, 22; Williams 2010: 73-76, 184-190; *The era of the 1929 Internacional Exhibition. The first third of the 20th century; Poble Espanyol*).

The exhibitions of 1888 and 1929 contributed greatly to Barcelona's landscape. They provided the city with significant public structures and representative public spaces: plazas, alleys and passageways, as well as parks and sculptures. Connected in a synergistic network of urban and landscape links, to this day they constitute dominant and rife with symbolism elements and landmarks in the city's structure.

Chicago 1893 1933 Chicago's World Columbian Exposition of 1893 awed the world with its scale and the surprisingly cohesive aesthetic and stylistic concept for the arrangement of the exhibition areas. Created on the shore of Lake Michigan, on the premises of today's Jackson Park, White City was a neoclassical dreamworld defined by the uniform white of the monumental Grand Buildings, the sophisticated sculptures and its landscaped gardens. Designed by architects under the direction of D.H. Burnham and J.W. Root, as well as the landscape architects F.L. Olmsted and H.S. Lodman, it presented the contemporary audience with a stunningly beautiful antithesis of the grim urban environment of the American cities of that era (Bolotin and Laing 2002: 5, 155-156; Greenhalgh 2011: 172; Mattie 1998: 9, 88-89; Sykta 2014a: 355-362, 367-375). The impressive White City was destroyed in a fire. Today only two objects from the Columbian Exposition remain in Chicago: the Palace of Fine Arts, which was reopened as the Museum of Science and Industry for the Century of Progress Exhibition in 1933 and serves this function to this day, and the Statue of the Republic, a 1:3 scale of the original Republic (by D.C. French), once the main sculpture of the Court of Honor (Bolotin and Laing 2002: 155-156; Sykta 2014c: 10, 11, 13; *World's fair*).

The Columbian Exhibition made a great spatial and visual impact, not only on the city, but also on a supralocal and national scale. It exerted a significant but also controversial influence over the trends in American architecture and urban planning in the next half-century (Bolotin and Laing 2002: 8). The neoclassical features it presented – plaster-covered white façades in the neoclassical style, in sheer contrast to the modern trends observed in the most advanced designs and the towering skyscrapers of Chicago – became *de facto* the national style, used in countless government and public buildings throughout the whole United States (Greenhalgh 2011: 172; Mattie 1998: 89, 96; Sykta 2014a: 355-362, 367-375). Enchanted by the exhibition, the poet K. Lee Bates wrote *America the Beautiful*, while walks in the White City inspired L. Frank Baum to write the famous *Emerald City* (Bolotin and Laing 2002: 158). These are only a few examples of the extraordinary influence exerted by the Expo city on the imagination and tastes of its visitors. The White City raised unprecedented public interest in urban aesthetics, which led to the creation of a social movement aimed at making cities more beautiful – the City Beautiful Movement. As a result City Beautiful plans for, among others, Cleveland, Washington D.C., San Francisco and Chicago itself, were developed by D. Burnham in cooperation with F.L. Olmsted and other architects (Bolotin and Laing 2002: 96, 158; Mattie 1998: 9, 89, 96; Greenhalgh 2011: 172; Sykta 2014a: 358, 370-371). The spacious, landscaped areas connected with wide green promenades which break, and at the same time unify the grid layouts of many American cities, constitute a long-lasting legacy of Chicago's Exhibition. The synergistic network of architectonic and urban links, originating in the world exhibition areas, developed to encompass nearly the whole country, becoming the model for shaping a City Beautiful!

Seattle 1909 1962 In 1909 Seattle hosted the Alaska-Yukon-Pacific-Exposition. The exhibition areas were planned according to the City Beautiful principles, originated in the 1893 Chicago Exhibition and were applied in practice to the urban space by the Olmsted Brothers / Brookline Massachusetts Landscape Architecture company, invited in 1903 by the city authorities to elaborate the project of the urban green areas system. It was then that the foundations of the system of parks, green areas and green promenades, which was implemented throughout the next century, were laid down. In the design of the exhibition areas, supervised by J.C. Olmsted and conducted by J.F. Dawson of Olmsted Brothers, the city's dominant feature, Mount Rainier, was used as a landscape termination of the Rainier Vista – the main axis of the whole concept, composed alongside a long pool with fountains and framed by neoclassical buildings. This compositional arrangement became the basis of the layout of the University of Washington campus. Two buildings preserved on the university premises constitute the Expo's architectonic heritage: Architecture Hall (former Fine Arts Palace) and Cunningham Hall (former Women's Building) (Lasiewicz-Sych 2015: 100, 110, 112; Cotter 2010: 7; *Alaska–Yukon–Pacific Exposition*).

Another Expo in Seattle – the Century 21 Exhibition, known also as the 1962 Seattle World's Fair, transformed the modest city into a rapidly developing, state-of-the-art centre of the West Coast. This change was brought about in large part by the futuristic narration of the exhibition, which was rooted in the idioms of science, cosmic space and the creation of the world of the 21th century. To give material form to these ideas, the chief architect P. Thiry created an Expo futuristic city (Cotter 2010: 8). It was not based on the rules of Beaux-Arts or City Beautiful with wide alleys framed by monumental buildings. Rather it was composed of expressive futuristic objects freely dispersed throughout the whole area. The most distinguishing Expo structure was the Space Needle – a high tower, presiding over the exhibition areas and the whole city. Futuristic style also characterized the the Washington Square Coliseum (by P. Thiry) and the US Science Pavilion (by M. Yamasaki) (Mattie 1998: 215). The elevated monorail train brought visitors to the exhibition areas from the city centre, while two rubber-wheeled trains took the passengers for a 90-second tour. To bring this futuristic scenario to life, the city chose a relatively small lot (74 acres) in the Queen Anne neighborhood, neglected and full of derelict buildings. The former "lost space" (Trancik 1986) developed into a modern city of the future for more than just the 6 months of the exhibition. After its conclusion, the space was transformed into the Seattle Centre – a constantly growing collection of museums, theatres and exhibition halls distributed on the premises of the actively utilized park. After the Expo, the most emblematic structures were preserved to serve both their original and new functions: the Space Needle (today an observational tower and restaurant), the Coliseum (currently the multi-purpose Key Arena) and the US Science Pavilion (currently the cultural complex Pacific Science Center, Boeing IMAX) (Cotter 2010: 7, 8, 15, 34-35; Greenhalgh 2011: 42, 189; Lasiewicz-Sych 2015: 100, 111; Mattie 1998: 211, 212, 214, 215; Sykta 2014b: 108-110, 119). The Century 21 Exposition objects are an endless source of inspiration for subsequent contemporary buildings raised in the Seattle Center. The monorail was used by F.O. Gehry (2000) in his design for the EMP Museum. The museum, constituting part of the revitalization of post-Expo'62 areas, was situated on the axis of the monorail – a high-velocity train, moving along tracks raised on poles, drives between the metallic folds of the building's "skin" and disappears in its interior to then speed toward the downtown (Lasiewicz-Sych 2015: 117-118, 124). The monorail continues to be one of the city's main tourist attractions. The urban structures of the city and the 1962 exhibition are integrated in a synergistic manner. The city's space based on a topography-adjusted grid (Lasiewicz-Sych 2015: 110), seems to flow through the post-Expo areas without creating visual or physical boundaries. The functional offer of the Seattle Center areas seems to fully suit both the local needs and the purposes of a cultural centre of a national or international range. The architectonic icons of Expo'62 – especially the Space Needle, whose dominant position in the city's cultural landscape was not mitigated even by the continuously rising downtown skyscrapers – lend this location an original identity, shaping the image of a modern and optimistic city. The heritage of the 1962 Expo can also be observed in the urban "placemaking" strategy applied since the beginning of the 20th century (Lasiewicz-Sych 2015: 97-125). The authorities created a place with a character which Seattle residents identify with and take pride in and which serves as an important testimony to their history. Without doubt the exhibition constituted one of the strongest impulses toward development and played a great role in the improvement of the city's image.

Shanghai 2010 Expo 2010 in Shanghai was located on the opposite banks of the Huangpu River, while 2/3 of it took place in the modern district of Pudong, which has been developing rapidly since the 1990s, the rest – in the post-industrial district of Puxi. Despite a considerable distance from the city center, the location through the axis of the river provided scenic links between Expo Celebration Square and Pudong's skyline with modern skyscrapers, a contemporary showcase of Shanghai. Built from scratch, the area of the Shanghai Expo has become a great contribution to transform the city. In keeping with its industry restructuring strategy, the city used the vast areas, until now occupied by shipyards and steel mills, degraded terrains alongside the Huangpu waterfront were cleaned and transformed to public spaces and parks, restoring them to the city and contributing to its development (Lang and Min 2010; Linden and Creighton 2008: chapt. VI; *Expo 2010*). Before Expo large urban investments were made, such as the development of the subway and railway network, new airport, the construction of new bridges, including Lupu and Nanpu, between which the Expo site was stretched, hotels and an Expo city (de Dios Perez 2008: 152-155; Lang and Min 2010; Linden and Creighton 2008: chapter VI; *Expo 2010*). The largest

Expo to date featured the emblematic objects intended to leave after the end of the exhibition. They were ranked in the area of the main compositional and functional axis of Expo Boulevard, ending at the Expo Celebration Square at the waterfront. The role of the main gate and the characteristic Expo landmark was served by the half-open membrane structure Expo Axis, the metallic saucer of the Expo Performance Center dominated the square at the river bank. This side of the large axis was complemented by complex of the Theme Pavilions, which architecture is a reference to the typical Shanghai street with mansards (*A Preliminary Tour of the Expo Site*). The large axis culminated in the most original Expo building the China Pavilion, distinct from other buildings in terms of its scale, original stepped form and red colors (Expo 2010 Shanghai China 2010: 8-19; *A Preliminary Tour of the Expo Site*; *Expo 2010*).

The functional chart of post-Expo use indicated a later continuation of operation, using the preserved buildings for representative, museum, exhibitions, congresses, fairs purposes, etc. A significant part of the areas in Pudong, organized around the Expo Boulevard, is to serve as a congressional-exhibition-business centre. The areas located further to the north are designated as the Government Building Zone. The areas, in which national pavilions stood during the Expo, are now the Expo Houtan Development Zone, taking advantage of Houtan Park's location, as a stimulator of housing development. Areas located on the other bank of the river, in Puxi, belong to the Culture and Exhibition Zone, where the World Expo Museum (*2010 Shanghai*; *Expo 2010*; *World Expo Museum*) is actually realized and the areas where the "Best Urban Practices" are to be presented (Functional chart of post-Expo use. Urban Planning Museum in Shanghai).

Post-Expo usage of the main axis of the Expo Boulevard is currently limited to the function of the museum in the former China Pavilion, the organization of artistic events and fairs at Expo Center, the Performing Arts Center (now Mercedes Benz Arena). The neighboring areas are mostly surrounded by temporary fences behind which construction work is taking place. One may only hope that, in keeping with the Expo theme, these areas will one day function as vibrant districts of "Better Life" in "Better City", applying high quality urban practices, and that the opportunity and energy shot occasioned by hosting the World Exhibition's will not be lost. The Expo was an opportunity to optimize the spatial structure of the metropolis; to use the latest trends in 21th century urbanization with a view to sustainable development and "green ecology", as announced by the exhibitions slogans (Lang and Min 2010). These grand plans were, to a large degree, realized, mainly thanks to the Huangpu Riverside Revitalization Program which provided answers to many difficult environmental problems of the degraded post-industrial areas (de Dios Perez 2008: 152-159; Enquist 2008: 258-267; Lang and Min 2010: 2, 9, 74; Linden and Creighton 2008: chapter IV; Un Tong 2011: 2-3, 9; *2010 Shanghai*; *Expo 2010*).

2.2. Architectural legacy

The formula of world exhibitions, which are not only international fairs, but a place to present state-of-the-art architectonic solutions in terms of design, construction and technology, transformed them into the cradle of hyperindividual architecture. The temporal nature of the objects made it possible to test experimental forms, structures and materials which were not taught at traditional architecture schools such as the École des Beaux Arts (Mattie 1998: 9). The competition between subsequent exhibitions drove the creation of more and more original and surprising objects, both in terms of form and technical solutions. In order to amaze the visitors with something new and unique, the Expo organizers strove to create architectonic attractions which would attract many visitors. This opened the gate to a series of unprecedented installations (de Jong and Mattic 1994: 143; Sykta 2007: 25). It was the world exhibitions which brought many avant-garde solutions into the vocabulary of modern architecture. The theory, critique and practice of contemporary architecture would not exist in its present form without the technical triumphs of the steel trussed constructions of 19th century exhibition pavilions, such as the Crystal Palace or the Eiffel Tower, artistic provocations by icons of modernism, which abandoned the ornament for the simplicity of geometry, such as the pavilion L'Esprit Nouveau by Le Corbusier (Paris 1925) or the Pavilion by Mies van der Rohe (Barcelona 1929), the paradoxical expression of the parabolic post-war exhibition objects such as the hyperbolic-paraboloidal Philips pavilion by Le Corbusier (Brussels 1959), the futuristic creation symbolized by the Space Needle (Seattle 1962), the beauty of geodesic domes of B. Fuller's or the daring of F. Otto's tent roofs (Montreal 1967). These innovations increased the importance of aesthetics in architecture. The people began to perceive, although not without some hesitance and usually after some time, their extraordinary spatial and visual values, as well as the meaning and propaganda conveyed by them. However, one must not forget another, decisively non-avant-garde side of exhibitions, especially those from the turn of 19th an 20th centuries. At many of these events wonders of new construction technologies were masked behind pseudo-historical decorations, wooden cladding and plaster, which concealed the true construction, creating a false image of the architecture. Sometimes these presentations were further dressed in an obnoxiously nationalistic costume, intensifying the sense of artificiality and distracting from the main ideas of the exhibitions, as the propagation of modernity and progress (Jencks 1989: 28; Mattie 1998: 9; Sykta 2007: 25-30).

Eiffel Tower 1889 The Eiffel Tower is the most famous of post-Expo objects. This controversial structure was a milestone both in the history of architecture and in the history of Paris's landscape, which changed beyond recognition. This 300-meter tower (by E. Nougier and M. Koechlin of G. Eiffel's office) was to serve as a symbolical logo and a gateway to the Paris 1889 exhibition which presented contemporary technical achievements. For many years the source of great emotions and the subject of disputes and controversy, it managed to resist a wave of protests and attacks aimed at dismantling the tower, and with time became a much more enduring and popular symbol – the symbol of Paris, its inherent attribute, competing with other Parisian icons such as the Notre Dame or the Pantheon. In this role, it has never lost its significance (Szolginia 1985: 249-252; Sykta 2007: 90). The Eiffel Tower shocked not only with its dimensions, but also, and with equal strength, the boldness of its design and architectonic details, which were incompatible with contemporary canons of beauty and aesthetic taste. The tower's design, reminiscent of iron bridge structures, was externally exposed in an unprecedented manner. The construction elements, traditionally hidden behind stone façades, were shamelessly displayed on the tower's naked skeleton, provocatively aspiring to artistic pretension. The Eiffel Tower was a pioneering example of high-tech architecture, which creates art by exposing the structure's interior and *de facto* continued to triumph even a century later. Among the tower's avant-garde features, one may highlight the overlapping of its interior and exterior, achieved thanks to the perforated trussed construction, or the externalized vertical passageways. These solutions gave the tower the character of a "non-building", a structure which cannot be defined as a building in the traditional meaning of this term. To ease the shock of a practical engineering structure becoming an architectonic dominant of historical Paris, S. Sauvestre, the Beaux-Arts architect, introduced a series of decorative details – a gesture on the part of the tower's constructors aimed at satisfying the public taste (Giedion 1968: 240; de Jong and Mattic 1994: 144-145; Sykta 2007: 85-86). When discussing the incredible phenomenon of the Parisian tower, one may quote the sociologist Roland Barthes: "Glance, object, symbol, such is the infinite circuit of functions which permits it always to be something other and something much more than the Eiffel Tower" (Szolginia 1985: 250; Sykta 2007: 91).

Pavilion Mies van der Rohe 1929 An icon of modernist architecture, the German Pavilion (by M. van der Rohe) was erected for the 1929 exhibition and exerted a special influence on the circle of professional architects. The pavilion's purist form, a spatial and abstract mosaic of glass sheets, marble, onyx, travertine and water, contrastively reflected off the rich and eclectic background of the exhibition areas. Dismantled after the exhibition, the pavilion was reconstructed in 1986 (Haduch and Haduch 2012: 14; Simonis 2008: 191) and continues to distinguish itself with its minimalistic form from the formally rich landscape of the main axis of 1929 the exhibition. The Van der Rohe Pavilion is the symbolical beginning of the era of modern architecture and a model for latter interpretations of modernism or minimalism, whose role in the history of architecture, despite a decisively smaller scale, can be compared to the Crystal Palace or the

Eiffel Tower. It is an excellent illustration of the expansion and crossing of boundaries in architecture and its social reception, as well as the meaning of world exhibitions on this way (Banham 1979: 387-389; Blake 1977: 31; Bonta 1975; Capó and Catasús 2003: 92-93; Ellingham et alt. 1995: 180; Haduch and Haduch 2012: 14, 190; Miralles and Sierra 2007: 194; Simonis 2008: 191; Sykta 2007: 31; Sykta 2014c: 11; *The era of the 1929 Internacional Exhibition. The first third of the 20th century*).

Space Needdle 1962 The most explicit embodiment of science as the idiom of progress and a spectacular manifestation of the technological jump and the conquest of space was the symbol of the Seattle Century 21 Exposition – Space Needle (by J. Graham). This extremely popular, 600 feet high observation tower with a rotating restaurant, located on a teapot-like observation platform, became the most spectacular landmark of Seattle, representing not only the city, but also growth and prosperity, as the most expressive American monument connected with the tradition of world's expositions, often compared to Eiffel Tower. Today Space Needle – still functioning as a tourist information point with the fashionable restaurant on the top – is a significant logo of Seattle Center, not distanced and unbeaten by rising skyscrapers of downtown (Cotter 2010: 7-8, 15, 34-35; Greenhalgh 2011: 42,189; Lasiewicz-Sych 2015: 100, 111; Mattie 1998: 211-212, 214-215; Sykta 2014b: 106, 109, 117, 119; Sykta 2014c: 11).

Geodesic Dome 1967 A whiff of avant-garde at Montreal Expo was most discernible in the US Pavilion (by B. Fuller) dominating over the site. The pavilion – a huge sphere of geodesic dome with a diameter of 80 meters, the largest and the most celebrated of Fuller's inventions – was an identifying symbol of the Expo. It symbolized technological innovation and scientific understanding of nature. The legendary dome – burnt in 1976 – was reconstructed and now it functions as the museum Biosphere (Jackson 2008: 63, 112; Greenhalgh 2011: 185; Mattie 1998: 231; Sykta 2007: 29-30; Sykta 2014b: 112-113, 115, 121-122; Sykta 2014c: 11, 31).

Habitat 1967 The other most conspicuous building at the Montreal Expo, inhabited till the present time, was the Canadian Pavilion Habitat (by M. Safdie, D. Barrott and Boulva) – a box three-dimensional structure consisting of a set of concrete prefabricated modules representing an ideal habitat unit. A spectacular example of achieving variety through standardization, and at the same time a construction perfectly fitting the humanistic dimension of Expo'67, expressed in a motto 'Man and His World'. (Jackson 2008: 63; Mattie 1998: 230-231; Sykta 2007: 30; Sykta 2014b: 113, 121; Sykta 2014c: 11).

2.3. Park legacy

The post-Expo parks played a major role in shaping the cultural and natural landscape of the Expo host cities. The exhibitions were large fair events and as such needed spacious, undeveloped land, preferably in a good location that would be well-connected to the city centre. These criteria were usually met by new parks, which offered leveled terrains where foliage was still not as dense, or the fields and grounds found on the city premises. This was the case with many exhibitions: in Chicago 1853, in Paris since 1867, in Barcelona 1888, Milan 1906 or Seville 1929. In this way the exhibition organizers received land ready for the placement of temporary objects, while for the parks the exhibition constituted a boost to further development, often also leaving physical traces in the form of permanent structures, elements of landscape architecture or sculptures, creating specific *genius loci*. Many exhibitions were also developed "from scratch". In these cases, the organizers often used abandoned or neglected areas degraded by industry, the so-called "lost spaces", of little value but, as the exhibitions' latter success demonstrated – great potential. The exhibitions restored these areas to the city, transforming barren lands into green spaces equipped with transport and technical infrastructure and modern post-Expo objects. Additionally, many environmental and ecological problems were solved, including that related to flood protection or the reclamation of post-industrial land. This was the case of the exhibition in New York 1939 and 1964, in Seville 1992 or in Shanghai 2010. These processes occurred in synergy, bringing many benefits to all participants involved: exhibition organizers, exhibition areas, parks and the city as the host.

Chicago 1893 1933 Chicago's 1893 world exhibition was organized on the shore of Lake Michigan and made use of the spacious park, designed here 20 years earlier by the Olmsted & Vaux company, which had previously designed the Central Park in Manhattan. However, the park's construction reached a dead end. The Columbian Exhibition, which was organized here, constituted a strong impulse toward the latter construction of a complex of three parks: Jackson Park, Midway Plaisance and Washington Park (Bolotin and Laing 2002: 8-9; *Jackson Park (Chicago)*. It is thanks to the exhibition that the parks were created. The landscaped Expo areas are the fruit of the cooperation between landscape architects F.L. Olmsted and H.S. Lodman (Bolotin and Laing 2002: 5; Mattie 1998: 88; Sykta 2014a: 355, 357-358, 368, 370). Situated between the Jackson and the Washington parks – Midway Plaisance, the Expo Entertainment Zone included the famous Ferris Wheel, the icon of the exhibition, which would be emulated countless times in amusement parks all over the world (Bolotin and Laing 2002: 155-156; Sykta 2014a: 359-360, 372). As the heritage of the 1893 Columbian Exhibition, and also the 1933 Century of Progress Exposition, organized here Chicago received a complex of three parks connecting the Michigan Lake shore with the city centre, shaping the urban system of green areas, serving important eco-systemic functions as well as representative ones with various commemorative objects and gardens that made reference to the exhibitions. In Jackson Park, entered into the National Register of Historic Places in 1972, the Columbian Exhibition left a permanent trace in the Wooded Island with Osaka Garden – a Japanese garden, by Olmsted, with the Phoenix Ho-O Den temple which served as Japan's pavilion during the exhibition. Severely damaged during World War II, but later renovated and restored to former glory, the garden was recognized as one of "150 great places in Illinois" by the American Institute of Architects (AIA). Today it is a favorite recreational destination for the residents of Chicago, invoking the spirit of the world exhibitions (Bolotin and Laing 2002: 11; *Jackson Park (Chicago)*; *Jackson Park*). In 1926, Midway Plaisance became a park axis of the University of Chicago campus, framed by university buildings. In 1999, the landscaping office of OLIN developed a new master plan for Midway Plaisance, constituting a tribute to the original concept by F.L. Olmsted. The plan is currently being implemented (*Midway Plaisance*; *Midway Plaisance Park*). The parks were expanded to serve numerous sports, recreational, cultural, educational and other functions for the benefit of Chicago's residents (Bolotin and Laing 2002: 155-156; Sykta 2014c: 11, 13; *Jackson Park (Chicago)*; *Jackson Park*).

Barcelona 1888 1929 Two world exhibitions in Barcelona also contributed to the creation of parks. The 1888 exhibition took place in the Ciutadella Park, developed since 1871 on the premises of a former fortress, by J. Fontseré. Today the park is famous for one of the first works of A. Gaudi – the *La Cascada*, fountain designed in cooperation with J. Fontseré in 1878. The scenery of the freely shaped park landscape was enriched with the objects of the 1888 exhibition, architecturally supervised by E. Regent, artistically reminiscent of the spirit of *modernisme* – the Catalan Art Nouveau. The following architectural attractions remain today after the exhibitions: the building of the restaurant Castell dels Tres Dragons (by L. Domènech i Montaner), the emblematic work of the *modernisme*, and the garden structures L'Umbracle i L'Hivernacle. The Ciutadella Park, later expanded to include other attractions such as: the ZOO, the Museum of Contemporary Art, the Museum of Zoology and the Catalan Parliament (in the former arsenal of the citadel), is now the largest and most popular green area, much needed in the city centre (Capó and Catasús 2003: 32, 38; Ellingham et alt. 1995: 174-176; Jellicoe 2006: 290; Simonis 2008: 110-111, 118, 133-135, 138; Spencer-Jones 2008: 712; Sykta 2012a: 106-107, 109, 116; Sykta 2012b: 228-231; Sykta 2014c: 22; Williams 2010: 20, 33, 58-60; *Modernismo catalán*; *The end of the Century, the beginning of the Century. The 1888 exhibition*)

The representative axis of the 1929 exhibition, running between Plaça d'Espanya and the Palau Nacional and the Olympic Stadium, was complemented by park areas distributed in the shade of the trees growing on the slope of Montjuïc. Remnants of the exhibition include Jardines de Laribal. This tranquil and picturesque park, made up of a series of terraces, linked by narrow paths and stairways, was designed by J.C.N. Forestier and N.M. Rubió Tudurí. The combination of shady pergolas, fountains and water cascades, characteristic for Forestier's style, is a reminiscent of Alhambra gardens (*Laribal Gardens – Montjuïc*). The exposition pavilions and the buildings of the Poble Español, Teatre Grec and Estadi Olímpic, were "submerged" in park foliage. Today Montjuic holds numerous parks and gardens – from castle gardens to the olympic park Anella Olimpica to the new botanic garden Jardi Botanic (Ellingham et alt. 1995: 177-180; Haduch and Haduch 2012: 190; Simonis 2008: 184-185, 194; Spencer-Jones 2008: 702; Sykta 2012a: 106-107, 109, 116; Sykta 2012b: 228-231; Williams 2010: 73-76, 184-190).

Sewilla 1929 1992 Two world exhibitions took place in Seville: in 1929 in the Maria Luisa Park, in the Plaza España and on the Guadalquivir embankments, and in 1992 on the Isla de la Cartuja. Both of them left behind excellent and multifunctional park areas.

The Ibero-American Exposition of 1929 was organized on the premises of the Maria Luisa Park, situated by Guadalquivir and developed since 1893. In 1911 intensive work was commenced under the direction of J.C.N. Forestier, aimed at redesigning the park for the planned exhibition. Forestier developed an unique take on the style termed as "pseudo Moorish", inspired by traditional Moorish tradition and the art of Mudejar, which were strongly identified with the cultural landscape of Seville. On the park's spacious premises, crossed by long shady plane tree alleys, Forestier created a series of Moorish garden-inspired park enclosures complete with water features – fountains, ponds, channels, with spacious lawns and hedges, framed by pergolas, decorated with ceramic amphoras and sculptures, with Mudejar decorations made of colourful *azulejos*. In fact, the neo-Mudejar style was the predominant aesthetic style represented in the architectonic structures of the exhibition, some of which, such as the Mudejar Palace and the Alfonso XIII Hotel remain until today (Dutkowska et alt. 2007: 760, 763; Hintzen-Bohlen 2008: 82-83; Mattie 1998: 148; Spencer-Jones 2008: 735; Sykta 2014c: 22-23).

Expo 1992 was organized on Isla de la Cartuja, an artificial island on the Guadalquivir. Preparing the exhibition site was a great challenge – the dry and barren land by the river, untended for many years, was, after extensive work in 1975, marked for development. The river Guadalquivir was redirected into an old riverbed. The city dug out a channel, cultivated and greened the land at a scale and scope compared to the cleaning of the Forest Park for the 1904 Saint Louis exhibition or the leveling of Corona Dumps for the 1939 Expo in New York. As a result of these actions, the island was transformed into a blooming complex of parks and gardens. Today the post-Expo areas are used in various ways: the main pavilions, including the Pabellón de España, the Torre Panorámica observation tower and other buildings were connected to form a theme park offering multimedia shows and exhibitions. At the Lago de España one can find exotic islands and the reconstruction of a 16th century Sevillean port. West of the Expo area there is a new Science and Technology Park with the headquarters of international companies. The diverse offer of the post-Expo park is complemented by an entertainment zone complete with a water park (Greenhalgh 2011: 73, 232, 235; Hintzen-Bohlen 2008: 110-111; Mattie 1998: 246).

Milan 1906 The 1906 exhibition was organized in the very heart of the city, on the premises of the Sempione Park established by the Sforzesco Castle in 1890-93. Under the artistic supervision of S. Locati, exposition pavilions were built in the park and its surrounding, of which today only the Art Nouveau building of Acquario Civico remains. The greatest heritage of the 1906 exhibition in Milan is the Parco Sempione, a masterpiece of landscape architecture and garden art with a spacious central plain framed by freely traced paths and groves, which curtain the main compositional axis, which perceptively connects the Castello Sforzesco and the triumphal arch l'Arco della Pace located at the edges of the establishment. One can find a large picturesque artificial lake and numerous sculptures and statues. After the exhibition many significant architectural and outdoor works of arts appeared in the park and its surroundings. Among them was the Palazzo dell'Arte (1933), currently the headquarters of the Triennale Design Museum with the famous *Fontana dei Bagni Misteriosi* (by G. de Chirico) in its gardens or the observation tower Torre Branca (1933). The park is connected to the l'Arena – Stadio Civic (1806) or the Biblioteca del Parco (1954). Since the 1906 exhibition, Park Sempione and its surroundings were home to many exhibition and fair structures, which became Milan's specialty (Sykta 2014c: 11; Szyma et alt.

2007: 272-273; Villa 2015: 18, 22, 29, 31, 79, 145-150, 153, 156-157; *Milan World's Fair 2015*. 2014: 58-60; *Park Sempione*).

New York 1853 1939 1964 The first New York exhibition in 1853 left behind two blocks in Manhattan – the Bryant Park – a small but extremely precious green area in a landscape heavily dominated by cultural material (Mattie 1998: 195). However, the next two exhibitions, organized in the 20th century, gave New York a park of a much greater scale and meaning for the city's structure. The 1939 exhibition took place on the marshy lands of Corona Dumps in Queens, formerly the location of the city's landfill. This risky decision on the part of the organizers, which required them to clean up the degraded, flooded land, which involved changing the course of a river, create 62 miles of new roads, technical infrastructure and 200 buildings, as well as plant thousands of trees and millions of bushes, ended with a great success. As a result, the second largest Expo area in the world was created, where two large exhibitions were hosted in 1939 and 1964. The 1939 exhibition left behind a large land complete with utilities where further events could be staged. Most objects were dismantled. In practice, the only architectonic trace of the exhibition was the classicist New York City Pavilion (by A. Embury II), which houses the Queens Museum of Art since 1972. The Expo 1964 left behind the New York Pavilion (by P. Johnson, R. Foster) with futuristic observation towers presiding over the park, and the symbolic Unisphere structure, today an expressive architectonic accent situated in the centre of the park (Cotter 2009: 9-10; Koolhaas 2013: 310, 332; Mattie 1998: 199, 222; Olszewski 2012: s. 15, 20). Thanks to the boost provided by the world exhibitions in New York, the once degraded, valueless land became the multifunctional Flushing Meadows park, the second largest park in New York. It constitutes an important part of the city's greenery system, with a few distinguished architectonic artefacts, which date back to the two exhibitions organized here.

Shanghai 2010 In order to fulfil the Expo's slogan "Better City. Better Life", great effort was put into the improvement of the environment – this is yet another benefit brought about by Shanghai's transformation. Focus was placed on green infrastructure, wide greenbelts, parks, cultivated green areas, increased walking and bicycling infrastructure, multifunctional spaces (combining the residential and commercial sectors, the services industry and art), highly intensive residential complexes, limitation of car traffic in the city centre and the development of public transport (Un Tong 2011: 76). The special zone of Huangpu River Central Area, encompassing also the Expo areas, was part of the large-scale green space development and waterfront regeneration project taking into account environmental problems of the waterfront, including pollution of land, air and water and flood protection (Environmental Transformation 2008: 218-255). The aim was to lay down the foundation of a sustainable green space system, which would efficiently integrate the post-Expo areas with the urban space. In the long-term perspective, this was expected to increase the balance of green areas and improve the environment, thus improving the quality of life in the city. The Expo's green space system took the form of an ecological network spreading from the Huangpu waterfront to the urbanized areas, encompassing "the green core, the green axis, the greenbelts and the green wedges", described "as a combination of water and plants, an interaction within the green network, a space rich in green wedges and green chains" (Lang an Min 2010). The most important elements of this structure were river parks. The "green core" – Expo Park (by Zhu Sheng X.) was the main scene of Expo activities. The concept of the park is based on the motifs of 'bund' (1), associated with the historical district of Shanghai Bund, and 'fan', and also on eastern philosophy of nature 'Shanshui' (2), which strongly accentuate the *genius loci*. Fan-like shapes and terraces, based on natural topography of riverside, created an effective link between the city and the river. A rich plant environment was created using natural ecosystems, fitting the planted species to the waterside environment and simulating a riverside landscape. The park – still operating after the Expo conclusion – incorporates the innovative solutions in landscape architecture and ideas of urban ecology. The project includes ecological approach, the biological purification and recycling of water, the development of a balanced natural environment and alternative solutions in the field of technical infrastructure, especially with regard to flood protection (Jun and Nannan 2010; *A Preliminary Tour of the Expo Site*). Another important element of the post-Expo eco-network – Houtan park, shaping with Bailianjing park, the "green belts", was designed in keeping with the Turenscape concepts. The aim of the project was restoring the degraded environment to life and transformation of post-industrial areas into a permanent public riverside park. The area was transformed into a living system offering comprehensive ecological services: food production, urban farming, flood protection, water treatment and the creation of habitats, combined with educational aspects and contemporary architectural aesthetics. The axis of the park is a self-cleaning marsh, a natural habitat to numerous species of plants, live organisms and birds. The narrow, degraded area between the dirty river and the noisy express road has been transformed into an eco-safe, friendly and esthetic public space (*Shanghai Houtan Park by Turenscape*; Wang 2013a; Wang 2013b). The green post-Expo network is complemented by "green axis" of Expo Boulevard, "green decorative spaces" between various facilities of the Expo or buffer belts between the Expo and the city, "green wedges" integrating the Expo's green space with the urban structure and "green chains" – the green areas by streets and roads (Lang and Min 2010). The Expo Park, Houtan and Bailianjing parks remained after the Expo on the revitalized Huangpu Riverside, connected into a linear system which acts as a giant reservoir of green areas in the city centre, serving as place of recreation, as well as eco-systemic services, ecological education and research. The Expo Park is utilized as a complementary post-Expo public space and hosts numerous cultural events, etc. Shanghai – the most vibrant and forward-thinking city of China – became a model example of "green" urban planning, delivering more and more pure air, modern public parks and green waterfronts, sustainable transport infrastructure and large-scale reservoirs of open green spaces (Enquist 2008: s. 258-267; Linden and Creighton 2008: chapt. VI; Un Tong 2011: 2-3, 9; Lang and Min 2010 : s. 2, 9, 74; de Dios Perez 2008: 152-159; *Expo 2010*; *2010 Shanghai*).

2.5. Symbolic legacy

Usually exhibition organizers ensured the Expo encompassed symbolical structures with distinct and memorable forms that related conceptually to the main theme or motto of the exhibition. Sometimes they were massive structures presiding over the exhibition areas and the city, shaping the original dominants or landmarks of its panorama. Among these structures was the Eiffel Tower, the fulfillment of Man's eternal dream of a tower taller than "1000 feet" and the symbol of the engineering capabilities of that era, Space Needle in Seattle – a spectacular manifestation of the technological jump and the conquest of space, or China Pavilion from Shanghai 2010, which constituted an expression of the Chinese desire to host a World Expo and many others. Sometimes the Expo's symbols were less scale structures – spatial installations, outdoor sculptures etc. – distinguished by their original and conceptual form as well as their exposed location.

Monumento de Colom 1888 Distinguishing landmark of Barcelona's landscape is the statue of Christopher Columbus, the symbol of the 1888 exhibition (by G. Buïgas, R. Atché), situated in a strategic point – at the crosspoint of important urban axes: the famous Rambla, Passeig de Colom – connected to the Ciutadella Park, and the Avenida del Parallel, leading to the foot of the Montjuic hill – the location of the 1929 exhibition. Standing on a high column, the majestic figure of the New World discoverer presides over the wharf and the old port, not only a witness to the 1888 exhibition, but also a symbol of a much broader meaning – the icon of Barcelona (Ellingham et alt. 1995: 174-176; Simonis 2008: 110-111, 118, 133-135; Sykta 2012b: 228-229, 231; Williams 2010: 20, 33, 58-60; *The end of the Century, the beginning of the Century. The 1888 exhibition*).

Trylon and Perisphere 1939 Unisphere 1964 The layout of the 1939 exhibition site was classical, composed of quadrangles filled with pavilions and axes coinciding in the Theme Centre with a complex of symbolical structures: the 186-metre Trylon spire alongside Perisphere, a sphere with a 55-metre radius (by W.K. Harrison, J.A. Fouilhoux) (Jackson 2008: 59-60; Mattie 1998: 198-199; Koolhaas 2013: 310; Olszewski 2012: 16-19; Nowakowska-Sito 2012: 25-26; Banham 1979: 388; Greenhalgh 2011: 181). According to R. Koolhaas, the Sphere and the Spire are direct references to the two opposite forms which defined Manhattan's architecture whose skyline was visible in the distance. Koolhas believes that separating those two structures signified a symbolic end to Manhattanism (Koolhaas 2013: 313). Trylon and Perisphere were dismantled after the exhibition, but to this day they are considered to be the most expressive and beautiful Expo symbols. The symbol of the 1964 Exposition was the sphere again – an openwork steel construction 36 m in circumference, representing the Earth with outlines of the continents – Unisphere (by Peter Muller-Munk Associates, G. Clarke), placed in the same location as Perisphere in 1939 (Cotter and Young 2004; Koolhaas 2013: 333; Mattie 1998: 220). "The Globe again, but ghostlike and transparent, with no contents. Like charred pork chops, the continents cling desperately to the carcass of Manhattanism" – so commented on this infelicitous work R. Koolhas (Koolhaas 2013: 332). Although, its pretentious construction ended in an aesthetic fiasco (Sykta 2007: 29; Sykta 2014b: 110-111, 120), this is just this sphere, placed in the center of the oval pool in the Flushing Meadows park, constituting its main attraction, indicating World's Expo, as the genesis of its creation.

Atomium 1958 The attraction of 1958 Brussels Expo was Atomium – an aluminum-coated gigantic model of an iron crystal molecule enlarged 150 billion times (by A. Waterkeyn). This "architectural monster" situated in the center of big plaza, rested on three legs and consisted of 9 steel spheres (Jencks 1989: 68; Mattie 1998: 202, 208). Atomium was criticized as a symbol of megalomaniac pathos: "Human proportions and needs were sacrificed... The absurd costs and technical acrobatics of the 'Atomium' will only vanish from memory when this architectural monster is demolished" (Mattie 1998: p. 208). Contrary to the expectations, Atomium has survived, becoming a lasting symbol of modern Brussels and significant landmark of city cultural landscape. The dark side of nuclear technology, professed by Atomium, did not discourage the organizers of the exposition, and the ambivalence of its reception was strengthened by its contrast with the Sputnik satellite in the Soviet Pavilion, a symbol of peace in the middle of the Cold War (Greenhalgh 2011: 43; Jackson 2008: 111-112; Sykta 2014b: 106, 107, 117, 118).

3. CONCLUSIONS

World exhibitions positively changed the landscape of host cities and significantly impacted their development – this is an obvious conclusion arising from the analysis of selected Expos and their heritage presented in this article. The cities benefited in terms of urban development, gaining attractive high-quality public squares and parks, new landmarks and uniquely formed architectonic features which carried great symbolism and meaning and with time came to serve the role of original logos for the cities. The cities also experienced ecological or environmental improvements – the parks which constitute the natural legacy of the Expos form a system of urban green areas, serve important eco-systemic functions and improve the quality of life of the residents. The post-Expo areas and objects, integrated with the city as part of a synergistic network of urban and natural links, benefit for many years after the exhibitions, as demonstrated by their position as "milestones" in urban development and their unfading popularity.

NOTES

[1]   The word 'bund' means embankment, waterfront or shaft.

[2]   'Shansui' means Mountain and Water.

BIBLIOGRAPHY

Banham, R. (1979). *Rewolucja w architekturze. Teoria i projektowanie w „pierwszym wieku maszyny".* Warszawa: Wydawnictwa Artystyczne i Filmowe

Blake, P. (1977). *Form Follows Fiasco. Why Modern Architecture Hasn't Worked*, Boston: Little, Brown & Company

Bolotin, N. and Laing, C. (2002). *The World's Columbian Exposition. The Chicago World's Fair of 1893.* Champaign Illinois USA: University of Illinois Press Urbana and Chicago

Bonta, J.P. (1975). *Anatomia de la interpretación en arquitectura. Resena semiotica de la critica del Pabellón de Barcelona de Mies van der Rohe.* Barcelona: Gustavo Gili

Capó, J. and Catasús, A. (2003). *Barcelona escultures.* Barcelona: Ediciones Polígrafa

Champigneulle, B. (1973). *Paris architectures, sites et jardins.* Paris: Seuil

Cotter, B. (2009). *Images of America. The 1939-1940 New York World's Fair*, [pdf] Charleston South Carolina USA: Arcadia Publishing. Available at: New_York_1939_book-sample-pages_Images of America The 1939-1940 New York World's Fair_Bill Cotter. Pdf [Access 12.04.2014]

Cotter, B. (2010). *Images of America. Seattle's 1962 World's Fair.* Charleston South Karolina USA: Arcadia Publishing

Cotter, B. and Young, B. (2004). *Images of America. The 1964-1965 New York World's Fair,* Charleston South Karolina USA: Arcadia Publishing

de Dios Perez, J. (2008). Shanghai Transforming. In: G. Iker, ed., *Shanghai Transforming. The changing physical, economic, social and environmental conditions of a global metropolis*, Barcelona: Actar, 152-155

Dutkowska, J. and Dutkowski, F. and Jankowska, A. and Siewak-Sojka, Z. and Sojka, L. (2007). *Hiszpania.* Bielsko-Biała: Pascal

Ellingham, M. and Fisher, J. and Kenyon, G. and Brown, J. (1995). *Hiszpania. Część wschodnia.* Bielsko-Biała: Pascal

Enquist, P. (2008). Chonming Island: Greening Shanghai in the Twenty-First Century. In: G. Iker, ed., *Shanghai Transforming. The changing physical, economic, social and environmental conditions of a global metropolis*, Barcelona: Actar, 258-265

Environmental Transformation. (2008). In: G. Iker, ed., *Shanghai Transforming. The changing physical, economic, social and environmental conditions of a global metropolis*, Barcelona: Actar, 218-255

Expo 2010 Shanghai China. (2010). *GA Dokument*, 112 China Today. (A.D.A. EDITA Tokyo), 8-19

Giedion, S. (1968). *Przestrzeń, czas i architektura. Narodziny nowej tradycji.* Warszawa: Państwowe Wydawnictwo Naukowe

Greenhalgh, P. (2011). *Fair World. A History of World's Fairs and Expositions from London to Shanghai 1851-2010*, Great Britain: Papadakis

Haduch, B. and Haduch, M. (2012). *Architectourism. 01. Hiszpania.* Kraków: ZOCO

Hintzen-Bohlen, B. (2008). *Andaluzja. Sztuka i architektura*, Ożarów Mazowiecki: Wydawnictwo Olesiejuk

Jackson, A. (2008). *Expo. International Expositions 1851-2010.* London: V&A Publishing

Jellicoe, G. and S. (2006). *The Landscape of Man.* London: Thames&Hudson

Jencks, C. (1989). *Architektura późnego modernizmu i inne eseje.* Warszawa: Arkady

Jing, L. and Xiangming, Z. (2010). *From "Green Expo" to "Harmonious City": Sustainable Principles of the Planting Design in the World Expo Park of Shanghai.* [pdf] In: The 47th IFLA World Congress, Harmony and Prosperity – Traditional Inheritance and Sustainable Development. Suzhou: IFLA and CHSLA

de Jong, C. and Mattic, E. (1994). *Architectural Competitions 1792 – Today,* Köln: Taschen

Jun, D. and Nannan, D. (2010). *Shanshui Concepts in Landscape Planning and Design of the Expo Park in Shanghai.* [pdf] In: The 47th IFLA World Congress, Harmony and Prosperity – Traditional Inheritance and Sustainable Development. Suzhou: IFLA and CHSLA

Koolhaas, R. (2013). *Deliryczny Nowy Jork. Retroaktywny manifest dla Manhattanu.* Kraków: Karakter

Lang, Z. and Min, C. (2010). *Space Planning of the World Expo Area in Shanghai*. [pdf] In: The 47th IFLA World Congress, Harmony and Prosperity – Traditional Inheritance and Sustainable Development. Suzhou: IFLA and CHSLA

Lasiewicz-Sych, A. (2015). Strategia tworzenia miejsc – szkic o architekturze Seattle. Strategy of Placemaking – an Essay on Seattle Architecture. *Czasopismo Techniczne. Technical Transaction*, Architektura. Architecture ROK 2015 (112), Zeszyt / Issue 3-A (3), 97-125

Linden, G. and Creighton, P. (2008). *The Expo Book. A Guide to the Planning, Organization, Design & Operation of World Expositions*. [pdf] Milwaukee Wisconsin USA: Inside Parks & Musuems IPM Magazine. Available at: http://theexpobook.com/TheExpoBook-ch4.pdf [1 Jun 2016]

Lynch, K. (2011). *Obraz miasta*. Kraków: Archivolta

Mattie, E. (1998). *World's Fairs*, New York: Princeton Architectura Press

Milan World's Fair 2015. Guide to the Expo in and around the City. (2014). New York: Rizzoli

Miralles, R. and Sierra, P. (2007). *Barcelona. Contemporary architecture. 1979-2010*, Barcelona: Edicions Poligrafa

Nowakowska-Sito, K. (2012). Inżynierowie maszyn i dusz: nowojorska wystawa światowa 1939 roku a modernistyczna utopia lat trzydziestych. In: J.M. Sosnowska, ed., *Wystawa Nowojorska 1939. Materiały z sesji naukowej Instytutu Sztuki PAN Warszawa, 23-24 listopada 2009 r.* Warszawa: Instytut Sztuki Polskiej Akademii Nauk, 25-36

Olszewski, A.K. (2012). Wystawa nowojorska w 1939 roku. Program i realizacja. In: J.M. Sosnowska, ed., *Wystawa Nowojorska 1939. Materiały z sesji naukowej Instytutu Sztuki PAN Warszawa, 23-24 listopada 2009 r.* Warszawa: Instytut Sztuki Polskiej Akademii Nauk, 15-24

Simonis, D. (2008). *Barcelona*, G+J RBA National Geographic

Spencer-Jones, R., ed. (2008). *1001 ogrodów, które warto w życiu zobaczyć*, Warszawa: Muza S.A.

Sykta, I. (2007). *Znaczenie wyróżniających się, kontrowersyjnych obiektów architektury współczesnej dla kształtowania i percepcji krajobrazu miejskiego*. Phd thesis. Cracow University of Technology

Sykta, I. (2012a) Parki Barcelony – od stylu modernisme po współczesne krajobrazy tworzone „od-nowa". *Architektura krajobrazu. Studia i Prezentacje*, 1(34) 2012, 106-120

Sykta, I. (2012b) Przestrzenie kommemoratywne w krajobrazie Barcelony. „Ogrody pamięci" w sztuce ogrodowej i architekturze krajobrazu. *Czasopismo Techniczne. Technical Transaction*, Architektura. Architecture ROK 2012 (109), Zeszyt / Issue 2-A (7), 227-239

Sykta, I. (2014a) Ewolucja idei postępu i wizji miast przyszłości zapisana w krajobrazach, obiektach i pokazach wystaw światowych – od Londynu 1851 do Nowego Jorku 1939. Evolution of the idea of progress and visions of future cities encoded in the landscapes, architectural structures and shows of world exhibitions – from London 1851 to New York 1939. *Przestrzeń i Forma*, 21/2014, 353-376.

Sykta, I. (2014b) Ewolucja idei postępu i wizji miast przyszłości zapisana w krajobrazach, obiektach i pokazach wystaw światowych – od Brukseli 1958 do Osaki 1970. Evolution of the idea of progress and visions of future cities encoded in the landscapes, architectural structures and shows of world exhibitions – from Brussels 1958 to Osaka 1970. *Przestrzeń i Forma*, 22/2015, 103-122.

Sykta, I. (2014c) Wystawy międzynarodowe i ich wpływ na kształtowanie krajobrazu miast – próba retrospekcji i współczesnej oceny skutków krajobrazowych. The international exhibitions and their impact on the city landscape – an attempt of retrospection and contemporary valorization of their influence on countryside. *Teka Komisji Architektury, Urbanistyki i Studiów Krajobrazowych*, X/4 (O/Lublin PAN), 5-34.

Szolginia, W. (1985). *Cuda architektury*. Warszawa: Krajowa Agencja Wydawnicza

Szyma, M. and Michalec, B. and Petryszak, G. (2007). *Włochy. Praktyczny przewodnik*, Bielsko-Biała: Pascal

Trancik, R. (1986). *Finding Lost Space: Theories of Urban Design*. New York: J. Wiley

Un Tong, L. (2011). *World Expo 2010 Shanghai China. An Analysis of the possible impacts of World Expo 2010 Shanghai on the tourism development*. Saarbrucken Germany: LAP Lambert Academic Publishing,

Villa, F. (2015). *Spacerem po Mediolanie.* Warszawa: National Geographic

Williams, R. (2010). *Barcelona. Step by step.* Warszawa: Berlitz

Żórawski, J. (1973). *O budowie formy architektonicznej.* Warszawa: Arkady

web sources

Wang, L. (2013) a Houtan Park. [online] www.landscapevoice.com. Available at: http://landscapevoice.com/houtan-park-%e5%90%8e%e6%bb%a9%e5%85%ac%e5%9b%ad/ [Access 14 Jun 2016]

Wang, L. (2013) b Houtan Park Shanghai. [online] www.land8.com. Available at: http://land8.com/profiles/blogs/houtan-park-shanghai-china [Access 14 Jun 2016]

www.barcelona.cat. Barcelona escultures. *The end of the Century, the beginning of the Century. The 1888 exhibition.* [online] Available at: http://www.bcn.cat/publicacions/Bcn_escultures/info/chapter1.html [Access 15 Jun 2016]

www.barcelona.cat. Barcelona escultures. *The era of the 1929 Internacional Exhibition. The first third of the 20th century* [online] Available at: http://www.bcn.cat/publicacions/Bcn_escultures/hometext.html [Access 15 Jun 2016]

www.barcelonalowdown.com. *Laribal Gardens – Montjuïc.* [online] Available at: http://www.barcelonalowdown.com/laribal-gardens-montjuic/ [Access 14 Jun 2016]

www.bie-paris.org. *2010 Shanghai.* [online] Available at: http://www.bie-paris.org/site/en/expos/past-expos/expo-timeline/2010-shanghai [Access 15 Jun 2016]

www.bie-paris.org. *World Expo Museum.* [online] Available at: http://www.bie-paris.org/site/en/world-expo-museum [Access 15 Jun 2016]

www.chicagoparkdistrict.com. *Jackson Park.* [online] Available at: http://www.chicagoparkdistrict.com/parks/jackson-park/ [Access 10 Feb 2016]

www.chicagoparkdistrict.com.*Midway Plaisance Park.* [online] Available at: http://www.chicagoparkdistrict.com/parks/Midway-Plaisance-Park/ [Access 10 Feb 2016]

www.en.wikipedia.org (2003). *Alaska–Yukon–Pacific Exposition.* [online] Available at: https://en.wikipedia.org/wiki/Alaska%E2%80%93Yukon%E2%80%93Pacific_Exposition [Access 23 May 2016]

www.en.wikipedia.org (2004). *Expo 2010.* [online] Available at: http://en.wikipedia.org/wiki/Expo_2010 [Access 15 Jun 2016]

www.en.wikipedia.org (2004). *Jackson Park (Chicago).* [online] Available at: https://en.wikipedia.org/wiki/Jackson_Park_(Chicago) [Access 10 Feb 2016]

www. en.wikipedia.org (2005). *Midway Plaisance.* [online] Available at: https://en.wikipedia.org/wiki/Midway_Plaisance [Access 10 Feb 2016]

www.en.wikipedia.org (2006). *Poble Espanyol.* [online] Available at: http://en.wikipedia.org/wiki/Poble_Espanyol [Access 15 Jun 2016]

www.en.wikipedia.org (2002). *World's fair.* [online] Available at: http://en.wikipedia.org/wiki/World's_fair [Access 5 Jun 2016]

www.es.wikipedia.org (2003). *Modernismo catalán.* [online] Available at: http://es.wikipedia.org/wiki/Modernismo_catal%C3%A1n [Access 15 Jun 2016]

www.expo2010.cn (2010). *A Preliminary Tour of the Expo Site.* [online] Available at: http://www.expo2010.cn/expo/expo_english/documents/em/node2524/userobject1ai52529.html [Access: 20 Nov 2014]

www.homedsgn.com (2011). *Shanghai Houtan Park by Turenscape.* [online] Available at: http://www.homedsgn.com/2011/05/02/shanghai-houtan-park-by-turenscape [Access 2 Jun 2016]

www.mediolan.pl. *Park Sempione.* [online] Available at: http://www.mediolan.pl/sport-i-wypoczynek/parki/park-sempione/ [Access 14 Jun 2016]

PLANNING AND MANAGING CHANGES IN RURAL LANDSCPAE CONSERVATION. THE CASE OF JIANAN IRRIGATION CULTURAL LANDSCAPE IN TAIWAN

Chun-Hsi Wang
Graduate Institute of Folk Art and Cultural Heritage, National Taipei University, Taiwan

ABSTRACT

A rural landscape is comprised with various dynamic elements and is a ever changing process. It may be considered with cultural heritage value which is worth to be preserved. However, conservation methods of the landscape are quite different to those of monuments. It needs not only conventional preservation method, but also planning tools in landscape scale; it also needs reflection on life of people in the cultural landscape, and consideration on possible and ongoing changes in the landscape. In reality, a living cultural landscape cannot and should not be frozen in a specific state, guiding, managing and monitoring change through planning process, which integrate the needs, wishes and imaginations of people in it, is essential for conservation.

An irrigation system with rural lands could be considered as a continuing evolving cultural landscape. Jianan Irrigation System, built in 1920 by the Japanese Colonial Government and is still working, was registered as legal cultural landscape with cultural heritage value in 2009 for its importance in Taiwan's engineering and agricultural history. The conflict and dilemma of conservation in this case may have further consideration on managing changes and overall policy making.

Keywords
cultural landscape, cultural heritage, changes, irrigation landscape

1. INTRODUCTION

1.1. Rural landscape with cultural heritage value

There are various elements in a rural landscape. For instance, farms, buildings, natural plants and crops, all comprise the scenery we see today. However, what we see is the result of continuing operation by people. It may include agricultural process through time, construction due to the basic need of people, and the ritual and activities accompanied with the group life of people. These tangible and intangible elements may be connected with the history and culture of people through time which may become part of self-identity of local people and need to be preserved. In this sense, a landscape area may become a place with cultural heritage value, which is also considered as a cultural landscape.

The cultural landscapes represent the "combined works of nature and of man". More than 100 sites were nominated as World Heritage cultural landscape. A rural landscape could be considered as an organically evolved – continuing landscape. However, the protection of a landscape with the viewpoint of cultural heritage is different from those of monument and buildings. It will be a new challenge to the protection objects, scale, and methods. After the amendment of the Cultural Heritage Preservation Act in 2005, the category of the Cultural Landscape had been added to the Act. The landscape site with cultural heritage value man is protected under the Act.

1.2. Research objective and method

An empirical research method is used in this study, which includes a literature review and site observation. Discussions will focus on the Jianan Irrigation System, an historical irrigation cultural landscape in Taiwan, registered as a cultural heritage site of Taiwan in 2009. The research objective of this paper may be as follow: firstly, to explore the dilemma and conflict between a dynamic and ever changing landscape and the preservation principle of cultural heritage; secondly, to analyze the concept of "managing change" through planning process which is the possible way of functional-based conservation in a cultural landscape; finally, to review experiences and problems in the case of the Jianan Irrigation System Cultural Landscape in Taiwan.

1.3. Jianan Irrigation System Cultural Landscape

The southern part of Taiwan is a relatively flat area. However, before the Jianan Irrigation System was built there were only local irrigation systems in the rural areas. These were dependent on the occasional rain-water. In 1920, the Japanese Colonial Government decided to build an irrigation system to improve the agricultural productivity of these plains. Construction began in 1920, and finished in 1930. More than 150,000 hectares of dry farmland that, in the past could only depend on inconsistent rainfall, were transformed into productive paddy fields. The system, stretching over 160,000 km. consists of a reservoir, waterways, water gates, tunnels, aqueducts, inverted siphons and other facilities, and also an irrigation system and management organization that is still functioning to this day (Fig.1, Fig. 2).

The Jianan Irrigation Association was also founded in 1920 to operate the system. This association, still functioning to this day, controls, operates, and manages the system, according to water demand. The maintenance of the system is also the Association's responsibility. These include the renovation of relevant facilities and repair of the waterways. However, the main structure and important elements of the system, such as the reservoir, main waterways and aqueducts, are still in their original state (Fig.3).

Fig.1. The operation map of the Jianan Irrigation System (Taiwan Water Conservancy Bureau 1965).

Fig.2. The agricultural process shows the dynamics of a landscape, author: Chun-Hsi Wang.

Fig.3. The agricultural process shows the dynamics of a landscape, author: Chun-Hsi Wang.

From an historical point of view, this system was an important mile-stone in Taiwan's agricultural development. From the technological point of view, the construction and operation of the system represents human ingenuity. From the landscape point of view, the system created a harmonious rural landscape, with elements of the system integrated into it. From the heritage point of view, it can be seen as an organically evolving cultural landscape. Important elements of the system represent human evolution under the influence of physical constraints and/or opportunities presented by the natural environment.

After the 2005 amendment to the Cultural Heritage Preservation Act, a Cultural Landscape category was added to the Act. In 2009, the System was registered as one of Taiwan's legally cultural landscapes.

2. CHANGES AND CULTURAL LANDSCAPE

2.1. The change through time

A cultural landscape is comprised with various elements. Wang (2014) argued that a cultural landscape should be reviewed from six basic factors: theme, people, function, environment, object, and time. The facet of "time" may have an important meaning. A cultural landscape may be interpreted as functioning process made by people, at the same time some objects are made in the natural environment, while it is a dynamic and changing process through time by which the historicity also accumulated. A cultural landscape has become the "Text" of a site, accompany with other components, which may describe the development history through time. In this sense, all elements in a cultural landscape must be changing through time, and also a dynamic process which will be continuing changing. Even the changing process may be stopped in the past, the influences should be still recognizable in the present. What we see and perceive "now" must be connected with the "past", more or less. If the "time" is missing in the heritage, and the various information and evidences accumulated through time is also missing, then the people, function, environment, and object could be observed in the single point of "past" time. These evidences may be only existed in the past "memory", while the landscape now is seldom influenced.

Thus, landscape itself is an ever changing space. It is due to people's intervention and different usage in it through time. Landscape and culture are dynamic, undergoing changes, sometimes slow, sometimes fast (Haber, 1995: 39). Landscape is time materialized. Or, better, Landscape is time materializing: landscapes, like time, never stand still. (Bender 2002: S103). Humans have always adapted their environment to better fit the changing societal needs and thus reshaped the landscape(Antrop 2005: 32).

2.2. Dynamic in a cultural landscape

The dynamic in a cultural landscape means even a "stable" landscape is comprised with consecutive minor changes. These changes do not make intentionally, but the nature of a cultural landscape. The "dynamic" is scenery viewed in a micro scale and short time period, which reflects a situation of continuous working. Elements in a cultural landscape are not always the same and stable, while the appearance and context are composed of through these dynamic process of working and intervention. Thus, the growing of plant, people's usage and related ritual and etc. should be considered as part of a cultural landscape which reflects the dynamic situation. Facing changing economic and environment conditions, it is important to conservation and management of a landscape that dynamic process should be protected through sustaining its general character, rather than preserving its every detail (Phillips 2002: 46). Rather than protect the *status quo*, the conservation objective of a cultural landscape should be to identify, understand and manage, in a responsible and sustainable manner, the dynamics of those processes that influence their evolution (Engelhardt 2012: 320).

On the other hand, change in a cultural landscape is an inevitable result. In a landscape, there are many people involved in it, which is usually spread on numerous patches owned by different people. In this sense, it is very difficult to control each stakeholder that deal with the private own property. Strictly planned landscapes with controlled management only occur in completely artificial landscapes such as gardens, parks and urban sites, although even then the development is far from completely determined (Antrop 2005: 31).If it is an evolution through a long time period, the change of landscape may be more obvious. In a working landscape which features recording history of a site, there should be marked with evidences of every period. Thus the change in a historical cultural landscape should be considered neutrally, since it may be conflict to the nature of preservation of a cultural heritage, especially monumental-based heritage.

However, even the change is part of feature of landscape, and it should be accepted in the management work, the physical evidence with heritage and historical value in the landscape is still altered and facing major change possibly. In this case, the conflict may occur for the cultural heritage context thinking. Although the present landscape is the result of the changes accumulated in the past, and we may accept possible changes in the future management process and concepts, it is argued that there is some limit for the changes, if one is to retain the values of the landscape, and sustain their authenticity and integrity over time (Mitchell, Rössler and Tricaud 2009; Phillips 2002). For the cultural landscape with cultural heritage value, on the one hand we should try to keep its feature already exists which comprises the scenario of cultural heritage and the components of "environment" and "object"; on the other hand, the ever changing process of a cultural landscape faces the fundamental difference of preservation concept expected in the field of monument cultural heritage. The concept of "managing change" should be utilized to keep the balance between preserving physical evidence and the inevitable changing process. This conflict may be most obvious in the case of organically evolved landscape – continuing landscape, in which the conservation of traditional value and feature must be responded to the change due to overall social, economic, and environmental situation.

3. CHANGES AND CONSERVATION

3.1. The limit of change

Smith (1999: 116-118) argued three different levels of change which could be considered only if the historic environment has no permanent damage, and the decision must be made on the best possible information: critical assets must be conserved at all cost, constant assets could be changed while retaining their overall character, and tradable assets could be exchanged for other benefit. From this point of view, critical assets in a cultural landscape are important physical elements which may reflect the character of the "theme" of the cultural landscape and should not be changed. These elements should be preserved under conventional monumental-based preservation method from keeping changing. As for constant assets, to maintain the primary feature and value of a continuing landscape, the change should be allowed under management by which balance between the impact due to change and the scenery tried to be maintained is kept. Tradable assets should be freely changed without limitation if the value and "theme" of the cultural landscape are not influenced.

3.2. The dilemma of change

Conservation concepts and methods of a cultural landscape with cultural heritage value may usually far beyond conventional concepts of cultural heritage which are based on objects and architecture. The conservation of cultural landscape which may face various elements in different categories, which is usually unfamiliar to the field of conventional monument-based cultural heritage. This may conflict with the "preservation" concept which mostly means keeping things and objects from change.

Different to the method of "restoration" usually used in monumental cultural heritage conservation, the landscape requires different way. For those cultural landscapes in countryside, even were there sufficient labor and money, the entire countryside cannot be made into a museum of ersatz landscapes where the long term agricultural technological progress is abandoned and traditional techniques frozen forever (Green and Vos 2001: 144). Changes are inevitable for some traditional technology and progress, where the landscape is also changed a little bit. Even more, the changes in technology, culture and economy are threatening traditional landscapes, including the biodiversity on which they are based, but also the structure of rural society (Agnoletti 2006: XIII–XIV). Thus, although the change is inevitable, the feature and characteristic of cultural landscape with cultural heritage value will eroded due to excessive and uncontrolled changes. The dilemma of change makes it difficult to manage change.

3.3. Planning and conservation in landscape

The object of management should reflect the expectation of the conservation of a cultural landscape with cultural heritage value. The concept of protection should be embedded in the regional planning where the cultural landscape located. The site where the landscape located is the result of long term operation, which may come from the planning established in the past. Once the landscape is cherished with its cultural heritage value, it should be avoided that abandoning the original planning project totally due to the new title of "cultural landscape". On the contrary, it should be added in the planning that the thinking and mechanism which may protect and maintain the landscape. In this way, the "theme" and "function" may continuous operate in the cultural landscape through the amended planning.

For managing changes in a cultural landscape with cultural heritage value, tools and mechanism used are not limited to the field of cultural heritage and land usage. It should define suitable encourage and limitation means according to the "theme" and operation in each cultural landscape case. The concept of cultural heritage should be added in the land use code in planning, which may have minor limits compare to general usage while still respect necessary and continuous dynamics and change in the landscape.

In a more broad scale, the land use planning is closely connected to the economic and industry plan of an area. For instance, the decision of compulsory purchase large area land for industrial or commercial usage by government will totally change the landscape of agriculture which is considered a direct change and erosion. Although the landscape may be change through time in its nature, it should only allowed in a long term and slow process, and the dynamic in an internal system. The short term, broken, and severe change will destroy the cultural heritage value in a cultural landscape totally due to the feature and characteristic of the landscape disappear.

4. CONSERVATION SITUATION IN JIANAN IRRIGATION SYSTEM

4.1.Monumental-based and functional-based conservation

In Jianan Irrigation System Cultural Landscape, what treasured in the past were buildings and structures directed related to the irrigation process, such as the reservoir, spill way, aqueducts, and etc. The preservation of these facilities were also considered in a monumental based concept, which inherited from the thinking of preservation and conservation of cultural heritage should only focus on the physical elements, building, and facilities through the designation or registration and successive repair and restoration which may ensure the form and appearance. However, the restriction on monumental-based conservation which usually facing the argument of preservation of form and appearance, and the conflict between original parts and on-going operation, has led more and more public and private institutes into hesitating on conservation work of cultural heritage which may further destroy original elements with heritage value.

It would be an immense damage to monuments and other cultural heritage if lacking an integral cultural landscape context. In Jianan Irrigation System, the aqueduct crossing Tseng-wen River designated as a monument under the Act which is the longest aqueduct of the system and has transferred water since 1920s. In 2014, a new, parallel aqueduct was built, and the old one was disconnected from the irrigation system which now became a true but isolated "monument". Even from the monument point of view the object of this aqueduct was well preserved, it is de-contextualized from the function and cultural landscape point of view. The aqueduct now just likes a frozen fossil, which may not be seen as part of true history once it was deteriorated, or moved or destroyed from the original site (Fig. 4).

Fig.4. The aqueduct crossing Tseng-wen River which was cut-off, author: Chun-Hsi Wang.

What is more important in the conservation of cultural landscape is the mechanism of functional-based conservation. The operation and the scenery due to the operation may be conserved through the functional-based mechanism. The irrigation facilities in the Jianan Irrigation System Cultural Landscape, such as water gates, control valves on transfer tubes, are key elements to the irrigation works. These elements should be allowed to be repaired or replaced with similar parts in functions and/or shape once they were broken. Even it may have minor change, the restriction from emotional or nostalgic reasons should be avoided.

4.2. Regional planning

In the area where the Jianan Irrigation System Cultural Landscape located, the regional planning has been established for more than 30 years. A large area of agricultural zone for cultivation, and village zone next to the agricultural area were planned in the planning according to long term land usage in the past 50-60 years, which reflected the interaction between rural village and agricultural process. However, the real usage on the land has changed through time due to the agricultural technology and the industrialized on agriculture, which may be seen on the changes of greenhouse and potting in farms. In the Jianan Irrigation System Cultural Landscape, some farms originally used for sugarcane planting were changed as technology area for orchid. Although it is still used as "agricultural" zone, the new type of land usage seems irreversible since the original land is covered by concrete and greenhouse which may be considered a long-term damage to land, landscape, and agriculture from the cultural heritage point of view (Fig.5).

Although the mechanism from regional planning is still the major protection means to the Jianan Irrigation System Cultural Landscape, the substantial revision on the planning is not necessary. The area required further protection is around 40,000 hectares which spread widely and had various usages (Ping-Sung Wu (PI), 2015: 224–237). What is important is how to protect the landscape through maintaining long-term usage which has become the characteristic of the cultural landscape. In this sense, the agricultural zone should not be easily changed separately while detail regulation may be reviewed and amended for conservation purpose. However, the cultural affair authorities should be involved in the investigation process of large scale change project.

Fig.5. The orchid greenhouse which is irreversible to land usage, author: Chun-Hsi Wang.

4.3. Agricultural policy

The agricultural policy affected the Jianan Irrigation System Cultural Landscape eventually. The overall industrial policy may become the most influential factor to the preservation and conservation of cultural landscape with cultural heritage value. In the case of Jianan Irrigation System, some large scale farms were changed as science and technology area or industrial area. Besides, due to the consideration of transportation, wholeness of land, and budget, the land and farms of government owned company were chosen for compulsory purchase which has further scattered the wholeness of farming area. On the other hand, some buildings are built on the farm lands: some are legal facilities related to agriculture production, however some are illegal houses built as "second house" of people from cities. It may be due to continuous agricultural declining and urban sprawl (Fig. 6).

The situation mentioned above should be reconsidered through the policy debate: is the industrial development the only way for future? Has the intangible value of agriculture on social aspect been noticed and valued? Is it suitable to view the farm land as real estate? From past experiences, although the Jianan Irrigation System was considered as a collection of irrigation facilities, the kernel issue in it is the farming process. Once the farming process stops, the channel will be changed as drainage since there is no necessary to irrigate through these structures. On the other hand, if the value of agriculture process is treasured, the whole system may be preserved and conserved due to the farming is inseparable from irrigation (Fig. 7).

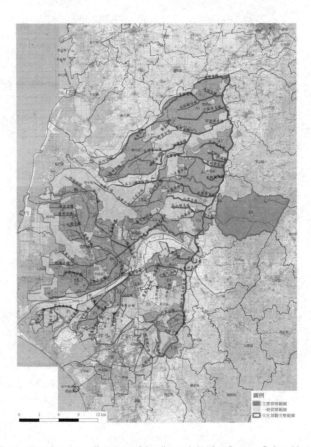

Fig.6. The proposed conservation area of the Jianan Irrigation System Cultural Landscape,
after: Chun-Hsi Wang.

5. CONCLUSIONS

In a rural landscape, it is a dynamic process from the micro and short-term point of view. Once the landscape is expected to be preserved with its cultural heritage value, it may face the conflict due to conventional cultural heritage conservation concepts which the form and physical appearance are essential. Because of the landscape with its nature of change and dynamics, the conservation works require adjustment and transformation on the concepts inherited from cultural heritage. The principle of managing change through planning process may guide a changing and dynamic landscape with the integral concepts within

Fig.7. The houses in the farmland show the problem of agricultural policy, author: Chun-Hsi Wang.

the scope of cultural heritage conservation. The principle of functional-based conservation may provide different possibility for the operation of "theme" and "function" in a cultural landscape.

In the Jianan Irrigation System Cultural Landscape in Taiwan, it is facing various challenges of conservation and preservation. Although the cultural heritage value of physical facilities and structures have been noticed, the key factor of continuing operation, agricultural process, has been neglected. With the concept of functional-based conservation, it is expected that the agricultural process will be maintained, while the preservation and conservation measures of cultural heritage are not excluded, by which irrigation facilities for the agricultural process may be conserved under the principle of managing change through the planning. However, it may be the most critical challenge to the conservation of a rural landscape with cultural heritage value that the overall future industry policy since it is usually the most serious threat which may change the function and scenery of landscape in the largest scale.

BIBLIOGRAPHY

Agnoletti, M. ed. (2006). *The conservation of cultural landscapes*. Wallingford, UK ; Cambridge, MA: CABI.
Antrop, M. (2005). Why landscapes of the past are important for the future? *Landscape and Urban Planning*, *70*(1-2), pp. 21–34.
Bender, B. (2002). Time and Landscape. *Current Anthropology*, *43*(54), pp. 103–S112.
Engelhardt, R. (2012). The Hoi An Protocols for Best Conservation Practice in Asia – Application to the safeguarding of Asian cultural landscapes. In K. Taylor and J. Lennon, eds, *Managing Cultural Landscape*. London; New York: Routledge, pp. 309–324.
Green, B., and Vos, W. (2001). Managing old landscape and making new ones. In B. Green and W. Vos eds, *Threatened landscapes: conserving cultural environments*. London; New York: Spon Press, pp. 139–149.
Haber, W. (1995). Concept, Origin and Meaning of "Landscape." In B. von Droste, H. Plachter, and M. Rössler eds, *Cultural Landscapes of Universal Value: components of a global strategy* Stuttgart and New York: Gustav Fischer Verlag, pp. 38–41.
Mitchell, N., Rössler, M., and Tricaud, P.-M. eds. (2009). *World Heritage Cultural Landscapes – A Handbook for Conservation and Management*. Paris: UNESCO World Heritage Centre.

Phillips, A. (2002). *Management guidelines for IUCN category V protected areas: protected landscapes/ seascapes*. Gland, Switzerland and Cambridge, UK: IUCN.

Ping-Sung Wu (PI) (2015). *The Management Plan of Wushantou Reservior and Jianan Irrigation System Cultural Landscape*. Tainan, Taiwan: NCKU Research & Developemnt Foundation.

Smith, K. (1999). Sustainable landscape management: Peak practice and theory. In J. Grenville ed., *Managing the historic rural landscape*. London; New York: Routledge, pp. 111–121.

Taiwan Water Conservancy Bureau (1965). *Irrigation Maps of Taiwan*. Taiwan Water Conservancy Bureau.

Wang, C.-H. (2014). *The Conservation and Management of "Cultural Landscape" within the Scope of Cultural Heritage* (Unpublished Dissertation). National Cheng Kung University, Tainan, Taiwan.

CITY LANDSCAPE. PRESENT STATE AND PROBLEMS WITH PROTECTION OF POST-WAR SINGLE FAMILY HOUSE COMPLEXES FROM UNCOTROLLED MODERNIZATIONS

Elżbieta Przesmycka, Zuzanna Napieralska
Wrocław University of Technology, Faculty of Architecture

ABSTRACT

In Wroclaw, as well as in other Polish cities, post war buildings are a significant part of the existing urban space. Its modernization creates specific problems in the field of residential buildings, both multi-family and single-family. While the discussion about renovation of multi-family 'big slab' constructions is relatively often undertaken, the subject of renovating single- family, post war architecture is very rare. We have not yet created the standards and criteria describing correct and efficient methods of modernizing post-war single-family house settlements that would defend the urban context. This problem has been left to house owners. The article presents the current state of Wroclaw post-war single family house estates, showing deformities of the original project and other consequences of uncontrolled extensions and modernizing. Selected house complexes have been originally well planned with regular urban layout and clear street network. Numerous, uncontrolled interferences with the volume of the houses irreversibly change the character of those settlements. House owners often fail to realize that the potential and the full value of their estates are in the whole urban complex, which shows the full attractiveness of the architecture and urban planning.

Keywords
Urban order, modernizing, post-war architecture, single-family house, settlements

> *Spatial order is a state of spatial organization that meets the quality requirements of social life, culture, economy and sustainable environment. It is "an arrangement of space that creates a harmonious whole, and takes into account all the modalities and functional, socio-economic, environmental, cultural, compositional and aesthetic requirements in structured relationships".[1]*

1. INTRODUCTION – CITY LANDSCAPE

The essence of the urban landscape is its continuous transformation. It is like a living organism that is not limited to permanent, physical structures of buildings, but interconnected cause and effect relationships. Landscaping in the city is operating on elements which undergo changes over time and are not entirely predictable – as cited in Jean Nouvel: "in the city, things are in a state of continuous processes of formation and disintegration. We need to discover this evolutionary process to evaluate changes, interact with them, or act against them. (...) This means the end of long-term planning, standard drawings and zoning".[2] In the perception of the city as a space, it is essential to accept its changeability, remembering that it is the common good. All users of the landscape should take responsibility for the environment in which they live and co-create.

The same problem translated into a smaller urban scale also applies to single-family housing units and social communities that inhabit them. Imprecise so far in Poland legal regulations concerning building transformations result in uncontrolled deformities of the initial urban assumptions of single-family housing settlements. Often the value of the building plot depends on what is happening in the neighboring areas. None of the owner's actions is detached from the interests of the entire community; moreover, they should be controlled by this community and accepted. This means a new way of thinking that starts with the analysis of common and public good and owners' rights. Spatial planning cannot be reduced to creating conditions for efficient building on areas in accordance with owners' expectation, but it should protect the most precious value of space to achieve the best possible functional, aesthetic and social effects.

2. PRESENT TRANSFORMATIONS OF POST-WAR SINGLE-FAMILY HOUSE SETTLEMENTS. EXAMPLES FROM WROCŁAW

For several years, we can observe the phenomenon of widespread modernization of many single-family houses within existing assumptions of housing estates from the 1960s to 1980s. Lack of good practices in terms of the modernization of post-war architecture and no precise provisions in the Local Development Plan governing individual renovation and modernization of such housing result in its steadily losing its original character. Modernist "cubes" undergo such transformations of their bodies that it is difficult to identify the design pattern, according to which they were created. Once uniformly designed components in terraced development transform into buildings that are chaotic and architecturally incompatible.

Renovations and upgrades are inevitable, but it is possible to avoid bad decisions the consequences of which will be experienced over the next years.

Currently, it is possible to determine three main problems that occur in post-war detached housing estates:

- problems associated with the poor technical condition of the building and the need to adapt it to contemporary requirements.
- social problem, ·
- problem of legislation governing the modernization of the development.

Poor technical condition affects most of the buildings with post-war heritage. Unfortunately, during Poland under the communist regime housing was characterized by the use of cheap and poor construction materials, which today results in their excessive degradation and unsightly aging of buildings. Improving thermal standards is currently the basis of decisions concerning heat insulation of buildings, which increases the comfort of the apartment. At the same time functional and spatial building systems no longer correspond to modern users. Dividing houses into small spaces that are often incommodious, with badly designed communication zones, are the cause of extension or construction of superstructures in small houses by investors. However, this entails the risks associated with maintaining original form and character of the building. This results in the change of proportions and shape of the body which is not always noticed by investors and authors of extension projects. Another problem is low awareness of the inhabitants of the settlements of the space, in which they live, and above all the fact that their house is an integral part of the larger urban complex. Thus, it is essential that current owners are willing to preserve and expose the architect's original concept. Renovations or upgrades undertaken by them should not conceal and completely change the character of the buildings. Unfortunately, a theory still lingers that socialist architecture has no aesthetic qualities.

A social phenomenon is the present generational change in post-war housing estates. New, young owners often choose comprehensive house renovations, and the current trend of communist era design among the generation of 20- and 30-year-olds gives hope that they will want to maintain or – in some cases – restore the original character or design of the building. It seems that within the next decade this type of single-family housing units will undergo fundamental changes forced by the change in ownership of buildings and generational change in housing estates.

2.1. "Budowlani" settlement in Wrocław

In 1968, the "Budowlani" housing estate – an interesting and comprehensively developed single-family settlement – was opened. Architecture and urban project of this settlement in Ołtaszyn district, in the southern part of the city, was developed by architects Witold Molicki and Ryszard Spławski. It is possible to distinguish there retail and trade facilities and a primary school that was created in 1964. The advantage of this housing estate is undoubtedly its location. It is situated in a quiet and green part of the city. It is adjacent to allotment gardens and located in the vicinity of Południowy (South) Park. Designers also took care of the central point, which is also a landmark – a square with a bus terminal.

Flat, minimalist facades originally only added variety to the geometric divisions of the windows, (still preserved in some of the buildings), and terraces on upper floors. Today, despite their still visible project concept, buildings are modernized and extended in a random manner.

Two-storey, semi-detached houses without basements had little usable space of 130 sq. m (including a garage). No basement was quite a rare solution, a significant portion of the conventional single-family housing in Poland had underground level. In the basement, mostly all the utility rooms and garages were located. The authors of the "Budowlani" housing estate designed garages on the ground floor, including them in the blocks of the buildings. The layout of the ground floor of the majority of the buildings located in the presented housing estate features a kitchen – 10.9 sq. m, toilet – 1.8 sq. m, a living room – 29.5 sq. m and a hall – 5.2 sq. m, which in total offers a space of 47.36 sq. m. On the first floor, there are three rooms with an area of 14.0 sq. m, 15.1 sq. m and 10.0 sq. m with a dressing room and a bathroom – 4.00 sq. m.

Over the years, the "Budowlani" housing estate has undergone numerous renovations and reconstructions of buildings. Homeowners have tried to eliminate the functional and operational inconvenience of the buildings with varying degrees of success.

The main drawback of the development is its small usable area. Currently it is possible to notice numerous cases of constructing extensions and superstructure in original buildings, changing the architectural expression of the entire housing estate (examples of such implementations are depicted in Figures 1 and 2).

Another way to increase the usable area is the conversion of a garage into a living space. This is repeated in several buildings. However, it does not introduce significant changes to the original structure.

Another problem faced by the residents of the housing estate is the location of the main entrance to the house on the side elevation. Homeowners solve this problem by constructing a small vestibule and locating entrance from the street.

Fig.1. Extension of a semi-detached building, "Budowlani" housing estate, source: Zuzanna Napieralska.

Fig.2. Construction of a superstructure in one segment in a semi-detached building, "Budowlani" housing estate, source: Zuzanna Napieralska.

Fig.3. Adaptation of a garage into a living space, "Budowlani" housing estate, author: Zuzanna Napieralska.

Fig.4. Adaptation of a garage into a living space, "Budowlani" housing estate, author: Zuzanna Napieralska.

Fig.5. Adding a vestibule and moving the main entrance to front of the building, "Budowlani" housing estate, author: Zuzanna Napieralska.

2.2. House complex at Kwiska street, Wrocław

Another example of an organized single-family housing in Wroclaw is the "mixed" building pattern at Kwiska street. It was designed by Maria Wolcendorf-Łukaszewicz and created on the basis of a detailed development plan drawn up before the liquidation of a civil airport at ul. Lotnicza. The final housing estate was not implemented in its original form. "Moving the airport to the Strachowice region resulted in suspending further implementation of single-family housing in the housing estate and allocating the remaining, undeveloped land between the streets Kwiska, Kłodnicka, Bystrzycka and Na Ostatnim Groszu for a "big slab" multi-family housing".[3]

The single-family residential complex includes 37 semi-detached buildings, 10 series of terraced houses, consisting of 7-10 segments in one series, and 24 detached houses. An important aspect of the complex is its compact, energy-efficient building arrangement. Additional values are intimate space of the settlement with high greenery, clear street network and location in the city center (in the vicinity of Legnicka street).

Terraced buildings are located on plots with an area not exceeding 115.0 sq. m (22.0 m length by 5.0 m width). A housing segment occupies an area of approx. 55.0 sq. m, on the front there is a small entrance area with a parking space of approx. 5 x 5 m, while at the back of the house there is a 5 x 6 m garden. Buildings have three storeys. A terraced house segment has an area of approx. 108 sq. m (with a vertical communication), basement level with the area of approx. 50.00 sq. m. Originally, a garage and a utility room were located in the basement level. The high ground floor housed a hall, a kitchen, a toilet and a large living room. Three bedrooms with dressing room and bathroom were located on the first floor. It should be noted, however, that there was some freedom in designing the functional layout of the apartment and ultimately not all segments were implemented according to the design. The disadvantage of these buildings is their little usable space. Created in the form of compact building arrangement, small terraced segments failed to offer a comfortable living space. Today, one can observe the interference in the structure of the building aimed at increasing the usable space. The most common way to increase the area of the building is creating the entrance retracted relative to the facade in the building. The original solution of the entrance zone can be still found in many buildings. In some segments, there is an added vestibule that extends beyond the outline of the building. Below are illustrations presenting this type of a superstructure.

Also in this building complex, owners convert garages into living areas.

Fig.6 and 7. Adding a vestibule, single-family house complex, Kwiska street, author: Zuzanna Napieralska.

Fig.8 and 9. Adaptation of a garage and basement level into living areas, Kwiska street,
author: Zuzanna Napieralska.

2.3. House complex in Oporów "Osiedle Młodych" housing estate –
a colony of houses for 91 families, Wrocław

An interesting complex of the post-war single-family housing arrangement are the buildings located between the streets Trentowskiego and Morelowskiego in Wroclaw. The project was completed in 1977 and it is the result of the continuation of working on an affordable and functional one-family house, initiated in the SARP competition in 1972. Despite the outcome of the competition and selection of the winning design by Leszek Konarzewski and Andrzej Poniewierka, the implementation failed to take place. Leszek Konarzewski, co-creator of the project took the initiative to design a housing estate in a similar architectural arrangement, but the buildings had a conventional construction rather than those from lightweight prefabricated elements which had been shown at the competition stage.

Despite the requirement of compact building arrangement, the designer wanted to offer the residents an intimate space. Residential buildings are clustered around small squares at the end of access roads (from 5 to 9 segments per one square). As a result, they created spaces accessible only to residents and traffic in the immediate vicinity of the house is minimized.

Common green area per several segments of the building arrangement is well-maintained. Another important element of this space is the design of parking by access roads. This results in minimizing the number of cars within the common area of the square.

In the 1990s, the designer presented a draft of the superstructure of the existing building segments, so that there is no uncontrolled interference in the original block of the buildings.[4] Designed superstructures were implemented in most houses.

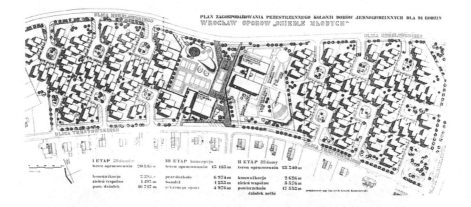

Fig.10. The urban plan of the house complex in Oporów, source: Designer's archives.

Fig.11. One of the common spaces in the residential complex; author: Zuzanna Napieralska.

3. METHODS OF EVALUATION AND ANALYSIS OF THE PUBLIC SPACE IN POST-WAR HOUSING ESTATES

Due to the far-reaching and difficult to control transformation of the post-war architecture, especially residential architecture, plenty of research papers have already been created that specify the manner and degree of impact of these transformations in the urban space.

An example of one of them is a method for the analysis of deformity of the public spaces in the housing estates, developed by Adam Zwoliński, called the Pattern of Deformation Factors.[5]

The analysis is carried out in four phases:

Phase I – Evaluation – direct registration of space in the form of numerical and percent values

Phase II – Occurrence of Deformation – this is determined on the basis of the analysis and processing the evaluation results on the basis of determining a positive or negative value for the occurrence of the evaluated deformation. Assigning this value takes place on the basis of the individually defined Condition for the Occurrence of Deformation. The occurrence of deformity is a phase, through which the COD criteria are selected. The criteria with a negative value are eliminated – this value indicates that there is no particular deformity in the specified area. A positive value indicates the occurrence of deformity and the introduction of criteria for the next COD phase.

Phase III – Scale of Deformation - in this phase, selection criteria are scaled individually based on the analyses of the existing situation. The essence of this phase is to choose such a scale of deformity that its use makes it possible to determine the severity of the particular deformity in the evaluated area. Scaling is individual for each criterion under evaluation, but the condition of correct analysis of this evaluation phase is the homogeneity of the Scale of Deformity, understood as the same number of equal intervals, adopted for all COD criteria.

Phase IV – Deformation Mapping – this consists in a synthetic, parametric and graphic mapping of spatial deformity. Data from the phases of Occurrence of Deformations and Scale of Deformation are transferred to the Deformation Parameters Index, which lists the occurring deformity and their location in the specified area.

The matrix of evaluation of the Deformation Parameters Index consists of a text part that includes the first three phases of the evaluation, and a graphic part with a map of the location of deformity in the area.

The next step of the COD method is the interpretation of the results. The author presents four types of interpretation: general, individual, problem- and location-based.

General interpretation is a comprehensive analysis of the results, individual interpretation aims to analyze the deformity registered in individual areas. Individual interpretation is aimed at showing the arrangement and the balance of deformities in public spaces of each evaluated housing complex. The problem-based interpretation relies on the analysis of the results for each COD criterion. The criteria define the evaluated problem - deformity that occurs in the evaluated area. This interpretation is aimed at problem-based approach to designate actions aimed at improving public spaces in evaluated areas of the city. Location-based interpretation shows the relationship between the occurrence and severity of deformities in the evaluated areas and the physical location of these places in the space of the housing estate.

Another proprietary method for evaluation of the quality of spatial solutions applied in single-family housing estates is the correct definition of space requirements by using certain criteria. In his research paper, author Waldemar Szeszuła[6], drew attention to the influence of the spatial configuration in the single-family housing arrangement on the social sphere of the housing environment. He proposed eight criteria that in a measurable way judge the space of the housing estate and allow its comparative analysis:

- compositional clarity of the complex,
- the possibility of the occurrence of synergistic landscape and spatial effects
- the presence of a safe space,
- the presence of a socially integrating space,

- the complexity of space,
- the ability to identify and annexation of semi-public space for a certain group of residents,
- the criterion of the occurrence of conflicts of public and private spaces.
- the criterion of spatial order with particular emphasis on the needs of self-determination and autonomy.

The cited selected examples of methods may be helpful in evaluating the state of transformation taking place in Polish housing estates, particularly in single-family housing arrangement.

The set of criteria presented by the authors makes it possible to evaluate both projects and ready urban solutions with full regard to the requirements of residents.

4. CONCLUSIONS

Standardized and inscribed in the norms, the post-war architecture is undoubtedly a problem of modern cities. However, most of these projects have values and architectural concept. Among many similar buildings, there are also interesting projects or urban complexes, which – despite having been implemented in so difficult for creative architectural thinking, post-war era – must be protected against uncontrolled changes. When searching for the causes of the current chaos in the city, including in settlements and smaller residential complexes, we can distinguish some fundamental causes:

- lack of understanding for the value of space by the residents and politicians;
- imperfection in the operation of the Polish system of space management;
- deregulation of the space management system in the name of economic liberalism;
- lack of respect for copyright;
- lack of regulations required for the formation of integrated spatial concepts.[7]

"Housing problems" include both the right to decent living and the right to live in a good environment – understood as the right to a good arrangement of space not only in terms of physical access to air, light and nature, but also to public space organized in a harmonious and aesthetically valuable manner. Currently, the integrity and modernistic character of the post-war housing estates of detached houses is put into question. Numerous upgrades of existing single-family housing buildings, triggered by generational change, changing homeowners or simply individual needs, not only translate into an irreversible change of the character of individual buildings, but – as a consequence – into entire urban concepts.

NOTES

[1] Polish Resolution on Planning and Spatial Development of 27 March 2003. Polish Parliament, Warsaw

[2] Dubost, J.-C., Gonthier, J.-F. (1996), *Architecture for the Future*. Paris: Terrail

[3] Instytut Architektury i Urbanistyki Politechniki Wrocławskiej, Komunikat I-1/K-105/92, Wrocław 1992

[4] Przyłęcka D. (2012). *Nie od razu Wrocław odbudowano. Plany zagospodarowania przestrzennego, koncepcje oraz projekty urbanistyczne i architektoniczne a ich realizacje w latach 1945-1989*. Wrocław: Oficyna Wydawnicza ATUT. The author, together with architect Bogusław Łaciak, are the designers of the big slab, multi-family residential complex for approx. 10 thousand residents.

[5] The method was developed as a part of the author's PhD thesis entitled: Wyznaczniki urbanistycznej transformacji zespołów mieszkaniowych w oparciu o parametry użytkowania przestrzeni publicznych. Na przykładzie wielkopłytowych osiedli mieszkaniowych miasta Szczecina. Thesis supervisor: Waldemar Marzęcki

[6] Author of the method, Waldemar Szeszuła, is an assistant professor at the Department of Urban and Spatial Planning at the Faculty of Architecture, Poznan University of Technology, currently the subject of his research is focused on the quality of space in detached houses.

[7] Polska Polityka Architektoniczna. Polityka jakości krajobrazu, przestrzeni publicznej, architektury Polska Rada Architektury, SARP, TUP, Izba Architektów RP, Warszawa 2011

BIBLIOGRAPHY

Adamczewska-Wejchert, H. (1985). *Kształtowanie zespołów mieszkaniowych*. Warszawa: Arkady.

Basista, A. (2001). *Betonowe dziedzictwo. Architektura w Polsce czasów komunizmu*. Warszawa-Kraków: PWN.

Brukalska, B. (1948). *Zasady społeczne projektowania osiedli mieszkaniowych*. Warszawa: Wydawnictwo Ministerstwa Odbudowy.

Chmielewski, J.M. (2001). Teoria *urbanistyki w projektowaniu i planowaniu miast*. Warszawa: Oficyna Wydawnicza Politechniki Warszawskiej.

Chwalibóg, K. (ed.) (2011). Polska polityka architektoniczna. Polityka jakości krajobrazu, przestrzeni publicznej, architektury. Warszawa: SARP [online]. Available at: http://www.sarp.org.pl/pliki/ppa.pdf [Access 15 Dec. 2015]

Czarnecki, W. and Ullman J. (1985). Zabudowa niska – kierunki poszukiwania optimum na przykładzie budownictwa mieszkaniowego. *Zeszyty Naukowe Politechniki Białostockiej*, seria "Architektura" nr 2.

Goljaszewska, B. (1984). *Zabudowa jednorodzinna a koncepcje urbanistyczne*. Warszawa-Łódź: Wydawnictwo PWN.

Orchowska, A. (2002). *Aspekt urbanistyczny i architektoniczny odnowy zespołów mieszkaniowych II połowy XX wieku*. PhD thesis. Cracow University of Technology.

Przyłęcka, D. (2012). *Nie od razu Wrocław odbudowano. Plany zagospodarowania przestrzennego, koncepcje oraz projekty urbanistyczne i architektoniczne a ich realizacje w latach 1945-1989*. Wrocław: Oficyna Wydawnicza ATUT.

Sepioł, J. (ed.) (2014). Przestrzeń życia Polaków. Raport. Warszawa: SARP [online]. Available at: http://www.sarp.org.pl/pliki/1908_53fdc64bb3140-pzp_spistresci_1.pdf [Access 15 Dec. 2015]

Szeszula, W. (2010). *Kryteria oceny rozwiązań przestrzennych zespołów zabudowy jednorodzinnej*. [pdf] Architecturae et Artibus 1/2010, p. 76-84. Available at: http://wa.pb.edu.pl/uploads/downloads/11--Kryteria-oceny-rozwiazan-przestrzennych-zespolow-zabudowy-jednorodzinnej.pdf [Access 15 Dec. 2015]

Wallis, A. (1978). *Społeczne aspekty zespołów mieszkaniowych. Studia nad osiedlami*. Warszawa: ZW CZSR.

Wojtkun, G. (2010). *Wielorodzinne budownictwo mieszkaniowe w Polsce. W cieniu wielkiej płyty*. [pdf] Przestrzeń i Forma, 14/2010, p. 175-194. Available at: http://www.pif.zut.edu.pl/pif-10_pdf/016%20WOJTKUN%20Grzegorz%20XX.pdf [Access 15 Dec. 2015]

Zwoliński, A. (2009). *Determinations of Urban transformation of housing areas on the basis of spatial parameters of public spacer. The case of LIPS's (Large Panel System) housing in Szczecin. Summary of doctoral thesis – part 2: Introduction to the method*. [pdf] Przestrzeń i Forma, 12/2009, p. 397-414. Available at: http://www.pif.zut.edu.pl/pif-12_pdf/C-09%20Zwolinski.pdf [Access 15 Dec. 2015].

THE ANCIENT HARBOUR OF AMATHUS:
CURRENT PERCEPTIONS AND FUTURE PROSPECTS
OF A SUBMERGED LANDSCAPE

Maria Ktori
University of Cyprus

ABSTRACT

The ancient harbour of Amathus is located in the south coast of Cyprus, situated at the west of Ayios Tychonas village in Limassol District. The outer harbour lies at a depth of 4 metres, expanding for 100 metres from the shore and is dated in the 4th-3rd century B.C.. The underwater investigations in the outer harbour were conducted in the 1980s by an archaeological team led by Dr. Jean-Yves Empereur. Several years later, in 2005, the Department of Fisheries and Marine Research published a report on creating an artificial reef that would include the ancient harbour. Ten years have passed since then and the reef was established but imposed great stress on the site. The current difficulties faced and the possibilities of turning the harbour into an underwater park or preserve are discussed, based on underwater heritage management developments. In that regard, the relationship between sustainable development, the stakeholders, the submerged landscape treatment and management were considered to establish the management possibilities and future prospects of the site.

Keywords
maritime landscape, submerged heritage, management plan, marine protected area, Amathus

1. INTRODUCTION

Limassol district is rich in archaeological remains dating to various periods, reflecting its past. One of them is the archaeological site of Amathus, situated on two coastal hills west of Ayios Tychonas village. Amathus had been inhabited since 1100 BCE and by the 5th – 4th century BCE, the Classical kingdom had flourished there (Aupert 1997: 21; Iacovou 2002: 101-122; Catling 1996). The Department of Antiquities and the French mission of the French School of Athens began excavating the site in the 1960s and 1970s respectively, while the submerged harbour was investigated in the 1980s.

1.1. Remarks / Methodology

The research carried out for this paper was based on the available archaeological data and the site assessment carried out by the author. The underwater investigations in the 1980s and the excavation at the coastal basilica in the 1990s were the focal points, followed by a terrestrial and underwater assessment survey in autumn 2015 to contextualise everything and evaluate the current situation.

This elucidated several aspects of the project: a)assessing the possibilities for a submerged heritage site such as the Amathus harbour, b)linking the maritime landscape with the evolving urban setting, and, c)ways to promote maritime culture to the public. The above-mentioned points can only be implemented through the establishment of a management plan. The ancient harbour is part of a marine reserve since

2011, thus the proposed plan incorporates it as it is part of the maritime landscape. Although there are international examples of submerged landscape management, this has not been attempted yet in Cyprus and there is no national management framework regarding submerged cultural heritage. Therefore, the author reviewed current international practises before suggesting the most suitable.

2. LINKING THE MARITIME LANDSCAPE AND THE EVOLVING URBAN SETTING

Landscape is a term first used in the late 16th century by Dutch painters, describing many aspects of Archaeology since the 1980s. David and Thomas (2008: 27) argue that this shift denotes a significant change of perspective, as landscape is treated as a field of investigation in its own right. This is evident in the culmination of the field of Landscape Archaeology, which shares an intrinsic connection with the evolution of the theoretical framework of each Archaeology strand (Seibert 2006: xvi). Issues such as urbanism, population changes and economic development have been studied since the early 20th century, with researchers employing different theoretical approaches and methodologies. It has also been argued that *Landscape Archaeology* is the best approach to analyse and interpret these phenomena in regards to settlement transformation patterns (Bintliff 1999).

Landscape Archaeology has undeniably evolved over the years; human historical landscapes were initially treated as environmental landscapes and archaeologists aimed to understand the social and community organisation (David and Thomas 2008: 28). This changed later, as the development of Cultural Resource Management (CRM) in the late 1960s helped the shifting towards social landscapes (David and Thomas 2008: 33-35). Ford (2011: 1-2) considers that the landscape exists when culture intersects space, and therefore numerous disciplines study it with varying research questions, methodologies and results. Landscape is inextricably connected to the physical environment. Furthermore, any coastal setting is studied in Maritime Archaeology as a coastal landscape, or a maritime landscape which is a broader concept (Ford 2011: 4).

The term *maritime cultural landscape* was coined in the 1970s by Westerdahl and refers to both terrestrial and submerged remnants of maritime culture (Westerdahl 1992: 5; Westerdahl 2011: 733). Such a landscape is complex and includes all the activities that are associated to the coast and the sea, whether those were considered to be close-ranging (e.g., lighthouse maintenance) or far-ranging (e.g., fishing). Westerdahl's seminal studies defined such landscapes as multi-faceted, cognitive, varied, with a profound action radius, and chronologically multi-layered (Westerdahl 1992: 5-6; 2011: 736). His approach includes maritime history and ethnography, which ultimately extends Maritime Archaeology itself beyond the ship or shipwreck with diverse applications and results and includes both tangible and intangible heritage (Flatman 2011: 312-313; Ford 2011: 5-6).

2.1. The Amathus maritime landscape

Amathus is located on two coastal cliffs along the southern coastline and its foundation must be related to the natural harbour located directly south of the cliffs (Hermary, 1999) (Fig. 1). The location offered advantages when defending the site from the acropolis, which served as a landmark for mariners (Péchoux 1996: 9-10). The proximity to the Kalavasos mines was another benefit; after the Kalavasos-*Ayios Dimitrios* and Encomi centres disappeared in the 12th c. BCE, Amathus could expand its area of influence and even control them (Aupert 1997: 22-23; Iacovou 2008: 638).

The systematic excavations of the French mission and the Department of Antiquities revealed extensive parts of the settlement that was established by the beginning of the Cypro-Geometric Period (1050-750 BCE) (Aupert, 1996a: 23-26, 99-107; Satraki, 2012: 269-270). In the 6th c. BC.Cyprus becomes part of the Achaemenid Empire and the Cypriots were required to join the Phoenician fleet against the Greeks during

Fig.1. Southeast view of the Amathus coastal hills (photo Maria Ktori).

the Ionian Revolt (Briant 1996: 61-64; Stylianou 1989: 410-411, 421-422; Christodoulou 2006). Despite the Cypriots' anti-Persian feelings, Amathus did not participate in the 499 BCE revolt against them and continued to develop (Stylianou 1989: 434-436; Demetriou 1993: 57; Briant 1996: 160). By the end of the Cypro-Classical Period (450-325 BCE) it had three necropolises, a defence wall, a sanctuary at the acropolis and an inner harbour (Aupert 1984: 19-21; Satraki 2012: 202-204, 282-283; Aupert and Leriche 1996: 89-98, 110-130).

Another failed revolt followed in 351 BCE and despite that, the Salaminian king Pnytagoras cooperated with Alexander the Great in the battle at Tyre. It was a key move, resulting in the integration of Cyprus into Alexander's empire by 321 BCE. Regardless of Demetrius Poliorcetes' later intervention and the installation of an Antigonid garrison at Amathus (Petit 2007: 97), the Ptolemies were able to regain full control of Cyprus by 295 BCE. Although this signified the end of the Cypriot kingdoms, the urban centre of Amathus develops further as stoas were added to the agora and a *balaneion* was built (Prête 2007).

At that point, Amathus had been established for about 700 years and its coastal hills are focal to the architectural activity of the polity. The buildings and mainly the acropolis, are landmarks that shape the coastal landscape, while the construction of the artificial harbour in the Hellenistic Period further enhanced the city's maritime connections with the Levantine coast (Theodoulou 2006: 98). Although the harbour was short-lived and possibly never completed (Raban 1995: 160-161; Empereur and Verlinden 1987: 8, 15), it forms a dynamic maritime landscape when paired with the road system of southern Cyprus. Specifically, the only natural road connecting east and west Cyprus lies along the narrow coastal plain. Bekker-Nielsen (2004: 194-195) comments that both the modern and ancient road used the natural corridor. The ancient road ran close to the *agora* and possibly curved along the western coastal cliff, exited through the west gate and continued towards Kourion to the west (Bekker-Nielsen 2004: 196) (Fig. 2).

The road network developed further in the Roman Period (58 B.C.- 395 C.E.), reflecting the mobility in Cyprus while adding another layer of complexity in the maritime landscape of Amathus. Amathus was connected to Kourion in the west, Kition in the east, and Tamassos in central Cyprus (Bekker-Nielsen 2004: 194-201). The road connecting to Tamassos is attested in *Tabula Peutingeriana*. It is considered to have existed since the Cypro-Archaic Period and used until the end of the Roman Period, in connection to the trade of metals and timber (Bekker-Nielsen 2001: 252-253).

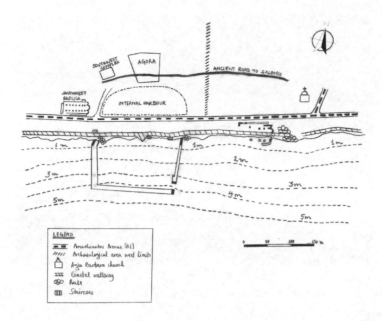

Fig.2. Map showing part of the Amathus coast (map after: Maria Ktori, modified after Aupert, 1996).

Amathus declines with the shift of the administrative centre to Nea Paphos in the Roman Period. It is affected by a series of earthquakes but flourishes sporadically in Late Antiquity and early Byzantine Period (Aupert 1996a: 58-59; Theodoulou 2006: 146). These episodes are reflected in the architectural remains, namely the five Early Christian basilicas. From those, the three-aisled basilica southeast is partially submerged and close to the submerged harbour (Fig. 2, 4). It is the second largest after the basilica of Campanopetra in Salamis, and dates in the second half of the 5th c. C.E. Its destruction in 653/654 CE coincides with the second Arab raid which forced the inhabitants to permanently abandon Amathus (Prokopiou 1996: 164; Aupert 1996a: 66).

2.2. The harbour complex and the coastal basilica: a fragmented landscape

The underwater investigations conducted between 1984-1986 showed that the inner, circular basin located at the southernmost part of the lower city was connected to the submerged harbour complex (Hermary et al., 1985: 984; Empereur and Verlinden 1987: 7) (Fig. 2). This discovery confirmed the 1976 geophysical survey results (Aupert and Hermary 1980: 221). The French team excavated to a depth of 2.5m in the centre of this basin, finding a layer of mud and sea shells that could be dated in the 4th – 3rd century B.C. and corroborated its use until it completely silted by the end of the Cypro-Classical Period (Aupert 1979; Aupert 1996b: 168-169).

Theodoulou suggests that the basin could actually be part of the greater harbour complex. As it had silted, the need for constructing an artificial harbour was even more important as it would facilitate the military forces of the era (Theodoulou 2006: 149, 230-250). The remains of the submerged outer harbour are still visible today (Fig. 3). The three moles form a quadrilateral basin, with an approximately 20m wide entrance located at the north-eastern corner of the east mole. The east and west moles are 100m long while the connecting north mole is 180m long. As the city walls extend over the moles, the harbour is actually enclosed, a *limen kleistos* (Raban 1995: 161) (Fig. 5).

Fig.3. Southwest view of the western semi-submerged mole (photo: author).

Fig. 4. Southeast view of the coastal basilica (photo: author).

This comes in direct contrast to the medieval writers' perspective, as expressed in written descriptions, watercolours and engravings. The 16th century travellers, Florio Bustron and Étienne de Lusignan had visited Amathus and both described it as majestic, noble and charming. All these elements are directly related to the untainted landscape the two travellers had encountered. In his brief description of the coast, Bustron mentions the ruins of the west mole, mosaic fragments that are related to buildings situated close to the foothills. Similarly, Étienne de Lusignan describes the abundance of ancient relics across the coastal landscape, which formed a coherent unit (Hellmann 1984: 79-80). Several more travellers visited Amathus in the following centuries, and their published notes on the visible archaeological remains reflect the original coherence of the landscape, as depicted by Luigi Mayer (Fig. 6).

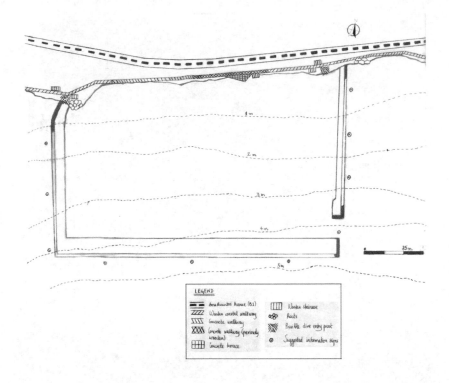

Fig. 5. Map of the harbour area (map Maria Ktori, modified after Aupert, 1996).

Fig.6. Luigi Mayer, Roadstead in the island of Cyprus showing the ramparts of Amathounta and the town of Limassol. 1792, watercolour 36 x 50 cm (Costas and Rita Severis Foundation).

2.3. A submerged landscape in an urban context: problems and prospects

The archaeological evidence from Amathus show that coastal landscapes are areas of intense activity. Any coastal area is a boundary place that attracts humans as it offers more than practical solutions for survival. It broadens the horizon of opportunities and options, which is evident by the development of the modern urban centre of Limassol. The city has expanded significantly and its eastern suburbs are situated as far as Amathus. The urban landscape is connected with the city's history and its post-1974 war economic development. To facilitate the commercial and other needs, a new port was constructed in 1973 and an industrial zone developed between the old and the new port. The industrial zone is also the hub for the leading local wineries such as KEO, ETKO, SODAP and LOEL. Its coastal location enabled Limassol to develop as the island's greatest seaport and tourist resort. This gave another impetus to urban development, while more recently sustainability has become a prominent feature in various projects (Gerasimou and Georgoudis 2011: 112). Considering all the above, and the extensive construction development across the coastline, several issues arise.

Limassol district is very rich in archaeological remains and sites of cultural significance. The development of the city and its suburbs, however, has imposed great stress, especially after the post-1974 war era when Cypriots were trying to recover and rebuild their country. From the mid-2000s onwards, sustainability expanded beyond construction projects into urban development, with a holistic approach that includes the natural and cultural resources of the district.

In an effort to protect the marine resources, the Department of Fisheries and Marine Research published a report regarding the establishment of a Marine Reserve in the Amathus coastal area. The reserve would include the ancient harbour, the *posidonia oceanica* meadows and an artificial reef (Ramos-Esplá 2005: 1). Its main purpose is the preservation, study and protection of the coastal zone marine bottom communities, as well as attract recreational divers.

The design and implementation of the artificial reef focused on the establishment of different protection zones covering a total of 284 ha (Ramos-Esplá 2005: 86-90). According to the proposed plan, all activities at the area should be monitored and regulated; in the case of scuba diving, a permit and quotas should be necessary prior to any diving activities in the artificial reef (Ramos-Esplá 2005: 90).

The implementation of the artificial reef intensified the need for a complete management plan. The absence of legal frame on submerged cultural remains is a problem, and the possibilities presented here are based on the UNESCO 2001 Convention of Underwater Cultural Heritage. However, the *posidonia oceanica* meadows are located at the harbour and complicate the matter, being an important, rare and vulnerable habitat of the Mediterranean Sea (Ramos-Esplá 2005: 25) (Fig. 7).

Fig.7a-b. The posidonia oceanica meadows on the harbour structures (photo: author).

As the ancient harbour was never fully excavated, the first step would be to perform a full-scale survey in the harbour area and identify any features of interest. This will ensure that any archaeological features will be documented, excavated and preserved *in situ* prior to opening the site to the public. Thus, the project has the survey and harbour excavation as pre-requisites.

Such activities can take place as early as April, whereas any retrieved will be transferred to the Conservation Laboratory for Underwater Antiquities (Rule 24). The post-fieldwork analysis of the data will provide the project director the necessary information to finalise the proposed management plan. The pending construction of a wooden quay along the harbour remains is another issue that needs to be addressed (Schmidt and Hadjisavva), because it will only damage them.

Several countries have created diving trails, underwater parks or preserves (Cohn and Dennis 2011). Diving trails can always be incorporated in the latter, leading visitors from one area of interest to another and promoting cultural heritage. It could be implemented in the harbour area and provide information to recreational divers. The information offered along the trail should not be limited to the archaeological aspect of things; the harbour has been part of a Marine Reserve for almost a decade now, and all divers should be made aware of the local marine ecology. The promotion of public access to an underwater archaeological site can be achieved with enforcing the appropriate regulations (Rule 7). Hence, the creation of an underwater park would be the ideal solution, given the importance of the site and the sensitivity of the marine environment.

Such integrated approaches have been implemented before, as in the case of Sebastos harbour in Caesaria Maritima. As Raban (1992: 27) notes, the creation of an underwater park was the natural culmination after 15 years of terrestrial and underwater research at Sebastos harbour. The Sebastos underwater park gave significant impetus to the local diving community and enabled the locals to be actively involved in the promotion and safeguard of their cultural heritage (Raban 1992: 27-28). The received feedback allowed them to make the necessary adjustments to successfully establish a 'self-guided and annotated underwater tourist-diver park' (Raban 1992: 35). The Sebastos example is the most relative to Amathus, as the submerged cultural site is in both cases a harbour. Its value lies in the investigation process prior the creation of the park and the later improvements. Cohn and Dennis (2011: 1072-1073) consider it a very effective example because it expands tourism opportunities into one may term as maritime heritage tourism.

The creation of an underwater park is a time-consuming affair both in terms of design and implementation; establishing a dive trail could be a preliminary solution until such a park is established. In autumn 2015, measurements and photos were taken, to explore this possibility further. As seen on the map, there are two possible dive entry points from the beach accessible via wooden staircases (Fig. 5). Divers can always opt for a boat dive along the northern mole. The dive trails can regulate diving traffic and alleviate any stress imposed on the submerged remains. They allow divers to either view the harbour moles externally or explore the basin internally.

Although the coastal walkway adds another layer of fragmentation to the archaeological area, it can be used as a terrestrial trail connecting the harbour and the coastal basilica. Secondly, it can connect the coastal archaeological zone to the greater Amathus archaeological site. A starting point would be the coordinated placement of information signs along the terrestrial and underwater routes, which should be adapted to the different age groups that may use them. There can be several thematic categories: a) brief historical outline of the flourish and decline of Amathus, b) the harbour history, c) the coastal basilica in the early Christian Period, d) the excavations conducted in the two monuments, e) marine biodiversity of the harbour area and the Marine Reserve, f) future plans. One may reasonably argue that the proximity of the two monuments expands the management possibilities exponentially and makes the Amathus coastal archaeological zone unique and very diverse.

2.4. Connecting the dots: from maritime landscape to cultivating 'maritime consciousness'

Raising local and public awareness is crucial in any management plan. Once the underwater survey and excavation conclude, one should consider the promotion of the harbour and its use as an education tool (Rule 35). The harbour can be a teaching tool for primary and secondary school teachers. The use and implementation of Archaeology in a History class makes the class more interesting and helps students contextualise various concepts, understand and use evidence, and develop historic awareness.

There are two different examples developed by Cypriot educators, one focusing on an archaeological collection (Makriyianni *et. al.* 2011a; Makriyianni *et. al.* 2011b), and another focusing on a city as a great archaeological site (Tuğberk, Pachoulides and Makriyianni 2009). The Amathus harbour combines these two approaches, as it is a site where artefacts have been retrieved from. It would be interesting to develop educational material by merging the approaches on one hand, and offering a rather simplified version of that material to be used by divers. This would be a step forward towards cultivating 'maritime consciousness', starting from a young age and resulting to adults respecting and protecting their submerged cultural heritage.

The educational material should include information on the maritime landscape, its original form and explain its current fragmentation. It is also important to convey the evolution process encountered in such a dynamic coastal environment, so the students will further contextualise the tangible and the historical evidence. As a result, *landscape literacy* is integral to the learning process and it will certainly give the educational material a different dimension.

3. CONCLUSIONS

The importance of Amathus makes the ancient harbour a high-profile site by association, while the sensitivity of the marine environment of the area is an additional sign to tread carefully, in the efforts to establish a cultural management plan for the area. Before such an implementation, the full investigation and assessment of the harbour area should be mandatory and the pending problems resolved.

In regards to the future management plan itself, three different practices were examined: underwater parks, underwater preserves and diving trails. There are several international examples promoting each practice, but establishing a regulated underwater park with incorporated diving trails appears to be the optimum solution. The establishment of an underwater park has never been attempted in Cyprus before, and the ancient harbour can be an ideal starting point towards that direction.

The proposed plan should include ways of promoting the site and educating the public. Using the harbour as a teaching tool by both primary and secondary school teachers would be an excellent way of establishing and cultivating a nucleus of 'maritime consciousness,' primarily amongst the youngest members of the society. Other target groups can of course be considered, while the appropriate information material should be prepared accordingly.

The ancient harbour of Amathus deserves attention and promotion at a local and international level. This paper offers a general overview of the current situation and problems and aims to offer alternative solutions and insight to what could later transform into the basis for a complete management plan.

BIBLIOGRAPHY

Aupert, P. (1979). Rapport sur les travaux de la Mission Française à Amathonte en 1978. Les activités sur le terrain. Le port d'Amathonte. *Bulletin de Correspondance Hellènique*, 103, pp. 725-728.

Aupert, P. (1984). Les auteurs anciens. In: Aupert, P. and Hellmann, M.-C., eds., *Amathonte I, Testimonia*

1: Auteurs Anciens, Monnayage, Voyageurs, Fouilles, Origines, Géographie (Etudes Chypriotes IV). Paris: Editions Recherche sur les Civilisations – Ecole Française d'Athènes, pp. 11-56.

Aupert, P. (1996a). Histoire de la ville et du royaume. In: Aupert, P. ed., *Guide d'Amathonte* (Sites et monuments XV). Paris: De Boccard, pp. 17-69.

Aupert, P. (1996b). Le port interne. In: Aupert, P. ed., *Guide d'Amathonte* (Sites et monuments XV). Paris: De Boccard, pp. 168-169.

Aupert, P. (1997). Amathus during the First Iron Age. *Bulletin of The American Schools of Oriental Research*, 308, pp. 19-25.

Aupert, P. and Hermary, A. (1980). Rapport préliminaire sur les travaux de l'Ecole Française d'Athènes (1975-1979). Cinq années de recherche: topographie et chronologie du site. *Report of the Department of Antiquities Cyprus*, 217-238.

Aupert, P. and Leriche, P. (1996). La muraille sud-ouest et la porte occidentale. In: Aupert, P. ed., *Guide d'Amathonte* (Sites et monuments XV). Paris: De Boccard, pp. 89-99.

Bekker-Nielsen, T. (2001). The ancient road between Amathous and Tamassos. *Report of the Department of Antiquities, Cyprus*, pp. 247-254.

Bekker-Nielsen, T. (2004). *The Roads of Ancient Cyprus*. Copenhagen: Museum Tusculanum Press and University of Copenhagen.

Bintliff, J. L. (1999). Regional field surveys and population cycles. In: Bintliff, J. L. and Sbonias, K. eds., *Reconstructing Past Population Trends in Mediterranean Europe (3000 BC - AD 1800)* (The Archaeology of Mediterranean Landscapes 1). Oxford: Oxbow Books, pp. 21-34.

Briant, P. (1996). *Histoire de l'Empire Perse de Cyrus à Alexandre*. Paris: Fayard.

Catling, H. (1996). Amathus. In: Hornblower, S. and Spawforth, A. eds., *Oxford Classical Dictionary*, 3rd ed. Oxford: Oxford University Press.

Christodoulou, P. (2006). La place de Chypre dans le conflit entre le monde Grec et la Perse (500-449 av. J.C.). *Επετηρίδα του Κέντρου Επιστημονικών Ερευνών*, 32, pp. 9-43.

Cohn, A. B. and Dennis, J. M. (2011). Maritime Archaeology, the dive community, and heritage tourism. In: Catsambis, A., Ford, B. and Hamilton, D. L. eds., *Oxford Handbook of Maritime Archaeology*. Oxford: Oxford University Press, pp. 1055-1081.

David, B. and Thomas, J. (2008). Landscape Archaeology: introduction. In: David, B. and Thomas, J. eds., *Handbook of Landscape Archaeology* (World Archaeological Congress Series 1). Walnut Creek: Left Coast Press, pp. 27-43.

Demetriou, A. (1993). The 5th-4th century B.C. history of Cyprus. Need for revision? *Κυπριακαί Σπουδαί*, ΝΣΤ', pp. 57-68.

Empereur, J.-Y. and Verlinden, C. (1987). The underwater excavation at the ancient port of Amathus in Cyprus. *The International Journal of Nautical Archaeology and Underwater Exploration*, 16.1, 7-18.

Flatman, J. (2011). Places of special meaning: Westerdahl's comet, "agency," and the concept of the "Maritime Cultural Landscape". In: Ford, B. ed., *The Archaeology of Maritime Landscapes*. New York: Springer-Verlag, pp. 311-329.

Ford, B. (2011). Introduction. In: Ford, B. ed., *The Archaeology of Maritime Landscapes*. New York: Springer-Verlag, pp. 1-9.

Gerasimou, S. and Georgoudis, M. (2011). Sustainable Mobility in Cyprus: the city of Limassol. In: Pratelli, A. and Brebbia, C. A., eds. *Urban Transport XVII. Urban Transport and the Environment in the 21st Century* (WIT Transactions on the Built Environment). Wessex: WIT Press, pp. 109-116.

Hellmann, M.-C. (1984). Les voyagers. In: Aupert, P. and Hellmann, M.-C., eds., *Amathonte I. Testimonia I. Etudes Chypriotes IV*. Paris: De Boccard, pp. 77-99.

Hermary, A. (1999). Amathous Before the 8th Century BC. In: Iacovou, M. and Michaelides, D. eds., *Cyprus: The Historicity of the Geometric Horizon*. Nicosia: University of Cyprus, pp. 55-59.

Hermary, A., Saulnier, J.-M., Queyrel, A. and Empereur, J.-Y. (1985). Rapport sur les travaux de l'Ecole

française d'Athènes à Amathonte de Chypre en 1984. *Bulletin de Correspondance Hellénique*, 10 969-989.

Hermary, A., Schmid, M., Pralong, A., Saulnier, J.-M., Empereur, J.-Y. and Verlinden, C. (1987). Rappo sur les travaux de la mission de l'Ecole Française à Amathonte en 1986. *Bulletin de Correspondan Hellénique*, 111.2, 735-759.

Iacovou, M. (2002). Amathous, an early Iron Age polity in Cyprus: the chronology of its foundation. *Repo of the Department of Antiquities*, pp. 101-122.

Maarleveld, T. J., Guérin, U. and Egger, B., eds. (2013). *Manual for Activities directed at Underwate Cultural Heritage. Guidelines to the Annex of the UNESCO 2001 Convention*. Paris: United Nations Educational, Scientific and Cultural Organization.

Makriyianni, C., Argyrou, E., Blondeau, B., Izzet, V., Ertac, G., Ktori, M., Rogers, R., Counsell, C. (2011a). *Learning to investigate the history of Cyprus through artefacts – A Teacher's Guide*. Nicosia: Association for Historical Dialogue and Research.

Makriyianni, C., Argyrou, E., Blondeau, B., Izzet, V., Ertac, G., Ktori, M., Rogers, R., Counsell, C. (2011b). *Learning to investigate the history of Cyprus through artefacts; Student's Booklet*. Nicosia: Association for Historical Dialogue and Research.

Péchoux, J.-Y. (1996). La situation géographique. In: Aupert, P. ed., *Guide d'Amathonte* (Sites et monuments XV). Paris: De Boccard, pp. 9-12.

Petit, Th. (2007). The Hellenization of Amathus in the 4th century B.C. In: Flourentzos, P. ed., *From Evagoras I to the Ptolemies: the transition from the Classical to the Hellenistic period in Cyprus. Proceedings of the International Archaeological Conference, Nicosia, 29-30 November 2002 / Από τον Ευαγόρα Α' στους Πτολεμαίους: Η Μετάβαση από τους Κλασικούς στους Ελληνιστικούς Χρόνους στην Κύπρο. Πρακτικά του Διεθνούς Αρχαιολογικού Συνεδρίου, Λευκωσία, 29-30 Νοεμβρίου 2002*. Nicosia: Department of Antiquities, pp. 93-114.

Prête, J.-P. (2007). Topographie du centre monumental d'Amathonte à l'époque Héllenistique. In: Flourentzos, P. ed., *From Evagoras I to the Ptolemies: the transition from the Classical to the Hellenistic period in Cyprus. Proceedings of the International Archaeological Conference, Nicosia, 29-30 November 2002 / Από τον Ευαγόρα Α' στους Πτολεμαίους: Η Μετάβαση από τους Κλασικούς στους Ελληνιστικούς Χρόνους στην Κύπρο. Πρακτικά του Διεθνούς Αρχαιολογικού Συνεδρίου, Λευκωσία, 29-30 Νοεμβρίου 2002*. Nicosia: Department of Antiquities, pp. 115-130.

Prokopiou, E. (1996). La grande basilique sud-est. In: Aupert, P. ed., *Guide d'Amathonte* (Sites et monuments XV). Paris: De Boccard, pp. 162-164.

Prokopiou, E. (2006). Τα μνημεία της πόλης και επαρχίας Λεμεσού κατά την παλαιοχριστιανική, πρωτοβυζαντινή και μεσοβυζαντινή περίοδο 324-1191. In: Maragkou, A. and Kolotas, T. eds., *Λεμεσός: Ταξίδι στους Χρόνους μιας Πόλης*. Limassol: Limassol Municipality, pp. 113-126.

Raban, A. (1992). Archaeological park for divers at Sebastos and other submerged remnants in Caesaria Maritima, Israel. *The International Journal of Nautical Archaeology*, 21.1, pp. 27-35.

Raban, A. (1995). The heritage of ancient harbour engineering in Cyprus and the Levant. In: Karageorghis, V. and Michaelides, D. eds., *Cyprus and the Sea. Proceedings of the International Symposium organized by the Archaeological Research Unit of the University of Cyprus and the Cyprus Ports Authority, Nicosia 25-26 September, 1993*. Nicosia: University of Cyprus and Cyprus Ports Authority, pp. 139-189.

Ramos-Esplá, A. A. (2005). *Artificial Reefs in the Amathus Bay (Limassol, Cyprus)* (Technical Assistance Contract N° 06/2005). [Retrieved from: https://www.yumpu.com/en/document/view/16720475/artificial-reefs-in-the-amathus-bay-limassol-cyprus-file-size-, access 16 January 2016].

Robertson, E. C., Fernandez, D. and Zender, M. U. eds. (2006). *Space and Spatial Analysis in Archaeology*. Calgary: Calgary University Press & University of New Mexico Press.

Satraki, A. (2012). *Κύπριοι Βασιλείς από τον Κόσμασο μέχρι τον Νικοκρέοντα. Η Πολιτειακή Οργάνωση της Αρχαίας Κύπρου από την Ύστερη Εποχή του Χαλκού μέχρι το Τέλος της Κυπροκλασικής Περιόδου με*

Βάση τα Αρχαιολογικά Δεδομένα (Αρχαιογνωσία 9). Athens: University of Athens.

Schmidt, M. and Hadjisavva, I. (n.d.). *Γενικό Σχέδιο Διαμόρφωσης Αμαθούντας.* Cyprus.

Seibert, J. (2006). Introduction. In: Robertson, E. C., Fernandez, D. and Zender, M. U. eds., *Space and Spatial Analysis in Archaeology.* Calgary: Calgary University Press & University of New Mexico Press, pp. xiii-xxiv.

Stylianou, P. J. (1989). The age of the kingdoms. A political history of Cyprus in the Archaic and Classical Periods. In: Papadopoullos, Th. Ed., *Μελέται και Υπομνήματα II.* Nicosia: Archbishop Makarios III Foundation, pp.373-530.

Theodoulou, T. (2006). *Ναυτική Δραστηριότητα στην Κλασική Κύπρο. Το λιμενικό δίκτυο στα τέλη του 4ου αι. π.Χ.* (Unpublished doctoral dissertation). University of Cyprus.

Tuğberk, A., Pachoulides, K. and Makriyianni, C., eds. (2009). *Nicosia is calling... Teacher's Book.* Nicosia: Association of Historical Dialogue and Research.

Westerdahl, C. (1992). The maritime cultural landscape. *International Journal of Nautical Archaeology,* 21.1, pp. 5-14.

Westerdahl, C. (2011). The maritime cultural landscape. In: Catsambis, A., Ford, B. and Hamilton, D. L. eds., *Oxford Handbook of Maritime Archaeology.* Oxford: Oxford University Press, pp. 733-762.

APPROACH TO PRESERVAION OF HISTORIC PARKS IN 20'TH CENTURY

Iga Solecka
Department of Urban Planning, Environmental University in Wrocław

ABSTRACT

This paper talks about shaping the notion of preservation, legislative documents about preservation and describes different approaches to preservation of historic parks in 20'th century. Enumerates main characters who took part in the process of preservation of historical parks. In Poland after 2nd World War the pioneer in this field was Gerard Ciołek, and his followers Longin Majdecki and Janusz Bogdanowski. Janusz Bogdanowski presented holistic approach to landscape preservation, which is very similar to the approach of European Landscape Convention. This paper presents main resolutions of Florence Charter, which is an international document about protection, preservation and exploitation of historical gardens in a complex way. Publication shortly describes functions of historical parks before and after 2'nd World War to explain what kind of difficulties can appear in preservation of those areas, shows present tendencies related to preservation of historical parks and opens discussion about protection possibilities.

Keywords
Landscape preservation, historical park, historical garden

1. INTRODUCTION

In the eighteenth century, before shaping the concepts of conservation protection, owners of historic gardens conserved them through respect for their predecessors. Examples of such activities is the garden Wilanów, which since the seventeenth century stayed preserved with slight modifications of the system, expanding it only with new functions. At the end of the eighteenth century Ignacy Krasicki began to create one of the first collections of garden plans. In the same period, inventories of drawing and painting gardens created, among others, Zygmunt Vogel, Joseph Richter. In the second half of the nineteenth century we observed trends planning aimed at the rehabilitation of the garden regularly, although these were not actions that we can qualify for the group restoration work, but they expressed a strong need to refer to the earlier style garden eg. the work carried out in the years 1855-1856 by Boleslaw Podczaszyński that on the upper terrace of the garden Wilanów designed lawn fields in the place of old baroque partners (Sikora 2008: 156-182). The end of the nineteenth century formed the concept of protection and maintenance of the garden as a work of art, with rel. its historical significance and cognitive science, one of the most active researchers garden art at that time in Poland was J. Drege (1866-1908), who was the author of the first studies showing the Polish gardens over the centuries entitled "Gardens in Poland" (in pol. „Ogrody w Polsce") (Wildner-Nurek 2007: 87-105).

2. CONCEPTS OF CONSERVATION

2.1. 1st half of the 20th century

In the 1st half of the 20th century, the scale and scope of maintenance work gradually increase. In 1928 it formed the law on protection of monuments. This law envisages the protection of all the elements of the landscape in the vicinity of monuments, if they had an impact on the issue of views and perspectives. This initiates a discussion on reconstruct or maintain. Ministry of Arts and Culture in this discussion committed reconstruction of buildings in justified cases, while stressing that restaurant is aimed at strengthening and consolidation of the building without compromising the historical features. The then planners working in historic gardens, felt not only conservators, but also artists. They indulged in visions of how the object could look like in the past. Although known they are also more aware designers from this period, when the restorer introduced decorative elements associated with the Baroque French, because of the baroque tradition of this place (Franciszek Szanior in Kozłówka) (Sikora 2008: 156-182).

2.2. Gerard Ciołek

A leading figure in the field of restoration of historic gardens from the 40s to the early 60s of the twentieth century was Gerard Ciołek. Author of the first systematic attempts to approach the topic of native gardens entitled "Gardens of Polish" (in pol. "Ogrody Polskie") represented the point of view that the historic assumptions garden are monuments combining elements of architectural, urban and natural heritage (Wildner-Nurek 2007: 87-105).

Ciołek felt that issues concerning the restoration of historic gardens are different from the activities in the field of architecture and urban planning, as the main material of the garden is the vegetation, living material, it is variable in size and shape. Of the view that the elements of destructive historical spatial arrangement of the garden should be removed, both those arising as a result of natural succession, as well as those made artificially by humans (Sikora 2008: 156-182). Contemporary sources subject questioned the authenticity of the sources that were the basis of the restoration work and accuse the lack of criticism in this regard, without prejudice to it as to the merits (Campitelli 2008: 34-43).

Fig.1. The painting of Canaletto depicting palace and garden in Wilanów (www.zamek-krolewski.pl).

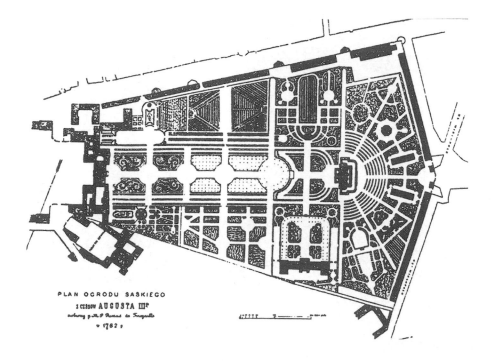

Fig.2. Plan of Saski Garden from the collection of J.Drege.

2.3. Longin Majdecki

Scientific activities of Longin Majdecki took place in Warsaw from the 70s to the end of the twentieth century. He emphasized that the garden monuments are associated with the space environment, and as a basic feature of the historic garden assumptions considered the dynamics of the composition of plant and its durability. He believed that spatial form of the garden can be extended by complementing plantings. For conservation activities considered those that contribute to the preservation of the garden in its distinctive, authentic form. He insisted on taking into account the dynamic nature of the garden in all activities of conservation (Sikora 2008: 156-182).

2.4. Janusz Bogdanowski

At a similar time in Krakow acted prof. Janusz Bogdanowski. Professor as a major cause of damage to the historic gardens named mistakes in the process of maintenance e.g. underestimation of the importance and necessity of research, incidental felling and uncontrolled planting blur compositional, excess creativity of the designer, the introduction of new forms of cubic capacity, overinvestment, ignorance as to the specific strengths of the historic garden. He defined maintenance as active measures aimed to maintain the monument in a specific and unchanging as possible, taking into account all the layers, up to our times. Allowed in special cases, the removal of some elements (e.g. self-seeding), as well as any additions (Sikora 2008: 156-182). He assumed that there are three possible courses of action for the park, gardens and historic landscape: protection, conservation, aiming to maintain the existing state; restoration including integration, which aims to merge by supplementing missing elements or stylistically earlier; reconstruction and recomposition in order to restore the old assumptions retained in the state far-reaching devastation (Bogdanowski 2000: 199-232).

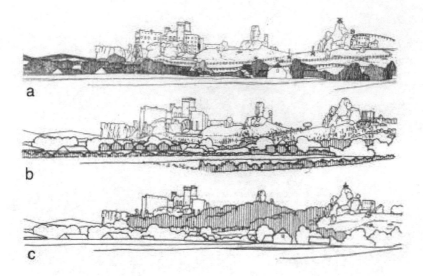

Fig.3. Study panorama of the castle Ogrodzieniec. A - current, B - wrongly planned plantings,
C - conservation guidelines for new plantings in the panorama of the castle Ogrodziniec (after: J. Bogdanowski).

2.5. Florence Charter

The turning point in shaping the thoughts of conservation was the adoption of 21 May 1981, the International Committee of ICOMOS-IFLA and the International Committee of Historic Gardens, the Florence Charter, which is the earliest document of international importance which deals historic garden and the issues of its protection, maintenance and use in a comprehensive manner. Historic garden is defined by it as an architectural composition whose main components are susceptible to damage and renewable plants. The appearance of the garden reflects the age-old balance between the cycle of the seasons, the growth and decay of nature and the desire of the artist and craftsman maintain it permanently unchanged. The historic garden includes: 1. Plan and topography; 2. Vegetation (species, proportions, habits trees, colors at different times of the year, the amount of individual copies); 3. The structural and decorative elements; 4. Water, fixed and current, reflecting the sky. Garden such can not be isolated from its own particular environment: urban, rural, artificial or natural. Charter points out that any change in the environment that can endanger the ecological equilibrium must be prohibited. Protection of historic gardens depends on their identification, and therefore emphasizes the authenticity of sources and their importance. Charter allows them the following courses of action: 1. Upkeeping; 2. Maintenance; 3. Restaurant; 4. In some cases it may be advisable reconstruction (Florence Charter 1981; Zachariasz 2008: 150-161).

3. FUNCTIONS OF HISTORIC PARKS

In Central Europe until 1945 historic gardens and parks were private and a measure of social status and prestige component. After World War II, most of the historical gardens changed its functions. Gerard Ciolek classify new features of historic gardens as: gardens which are mounted architectural plant palaces converted into museums and centers of art and culture (Wilanów, Nieborów, Rogalin); accompanying gardens for schools, universities folk, establishments of scientific research and experimental (Skierniewice, Otwock Wielki, Bialystok, Wolbórz); gardens associated with hospitals, sanatoriums and recreation houses (Choroszcz, Little Village). The socialization of historic gardens entailed organizing their protection,

conservation and adaptation to new goals and needs. Ciołek was aware of the consequences that suc
an approach was carrying. Conservator were covered only those objects that served as a new feature.
By Gerard Ciołek major causes of degradation gardens heritage in Poland: the changing socio-economic
place in the post-war period in Poland, no general concept of land use and buildings manor, inappropriate
use, accidental breaking up minority stakes and centers of court, as a result of the defective structure
of agrarian village (Sikora 2008: 156-182). No emotional relation of users to the park often led to the
operation of the park as an area of wild, isolated and neglect.

4. CONTEMPORARY TRENDS

Bogdanowski in its publication honored 4 contemporary trends shaping the landscape: utilitarian, "natural"
- protective, architectural-landscape regionalism and restoration, conservation direction. The direction of
conservation explained as devoted to the problems the care of historic gardens and parks that belong
to the group of monuments that combine elements of architectural, urban and natural. Stresses that the
first step is to protect the historical composition, but his way of seeing goes beyond the object itself and
treats the entire surroundings of the monument and urban systems, rural and landscape as a subject
of protection and the development of a new relationship marks the development of risk for the system
history. It emphasizes the role of landscape architecture in the maintenance, restoration and continuation
of the tradition. He sees the forms of cultural landscape as buildings and assumptions green, but also
urban systems (urban, rural), economy (farmlands, factories), social relations and political system (castles,
manors, tower of City Hall) and religious (church tower) (Bogdanowski 2000: 199-232). Such seeing the
landscape in a close contemporary, because it includes the whole spectrum of his wealth, which is also a
source of conflict.

A holistic approach to landscape marked the beginning of the ratification by Poland in 2005 European
Landscape Convention of 2000. The Convention defines the landscape as an area perceived by

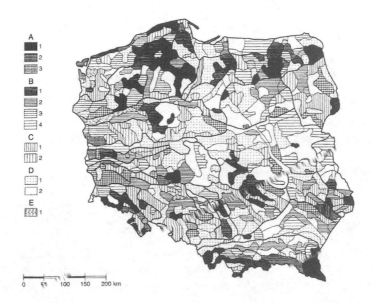

Fig.4. Contemporary desire should be that the whole country could be in some time one big park.
Polish division into regions according to landscape (after: J. Bogdanowski).

eople, whose character is the result of the action and interaction of natural and / or human factors, and management of the landscape as the action from the perspective of sustainable development, to ensure the regular upkeep of a landscape, so as to guide and harmonize changes resulting from the process of social, economic and environmental (European Landscape Convention 2000). This view of the landscape must also affect the maintenance of cultural landscapes, including historic gardens and parks, which were henceforth seen in a broader context. It began a process of cultural parks as comprehensively protected areas with unique cultural, natural and landscape (Myczkowski 2007: 105-116).

5. CONCLUSIONS

At the end of the nineteenth century it was shaped term protection and maintenance of the garden as a work of art. In 1928 law on protection of monuments was established, which qualifies as a historic garden as a monument and assumes the protection of all the elements of the landscape in the vicinity of monuments, if they had an impact on the issue of views and perspectives. Garden protection was therefore extended to all components connected to it in the landscape. In the 50s of the twentieth century Poland began to rise from the devastation of war. The pioneer of the restoration of historic parks in this period was Gerard Ciolek. But it was not yet time conscious use of historical sources. Unfortunately, the then system approach generates very selective and self-serving. Preserved were only parks that were to serve new functions for public institutions. His activity in the coming years to continue feeding Longin Majdecki and Janusz Bogdanowski. The approach of the latter distinguished by a holistic treatment to protect the historic park. He points out that in the first place should be protected historical composition assumptions and its landscape context. The European Landscape Convention defines the landscape very broadly, because as an area perceived by people, whose character is the result of the action and interaction of natural and / or human. This should begin discussions about what is the context of landscape and how to protect historic parks in the landscape.

BIBLIOGRAPHY

Bogdanowski, J. (2000). *Polskie ogrody ozdobne*. Warszawa: Arkady.

Campitelli, A., Goodchild P., Kaczyńska M., Rylke J. and Sikora D. (2008). *Przepisy prawa i zielone światy*. In: Zielone światy. Pod red. Rylke J., Kaczyńskiej M., Sikory D. Wyd. SGGW, Warszawa. pp.34-43.

European Landscape Convention (2000)

Florence Charter (1981)

Myczkowski J., *Park kulturowy jako forma obszarowej ochrony zabytków*. In: Ochrona Zabytków 2 (2007): 105-116.

Sikora, D. (2008). *Ochrona i konserwacja ogrodów zabytkowych w Polsce. Historia i tendencje współczesne*. In: Zielone światy, Pod red. Rylke J., Kaczyńskiej M., Sikory D., Wyd. SGGW, Warszawa, pp.156-182.

Wildner-Nurek I., *Z dziejów ewidencjonowania zabytkowych parków i ogrodów w Polsce*. In: Ochrona Zabytków 3 (2007): 87-105.

Zachariasz A. (2008) *Zabytkowe ogrody – problemy rewaloryzacji, utrzymania i zarządzania w świetle zaleceń Karty Florenckiej*. In: Prace Komisji Krajobrazu Kulturowego PTG Nr 10: 150-161

Official Website of The Royal Castel in Warsaw – Museum (www.zamek-krolewski.pl, Access 17.05.2016).

SUSTAINABLE LANDSCAPE DESIGN VS. THE NEW DUTCH WATERLINE 1-1

Łukasz Pardela
Wrocław University of Environmental and Life Sciences, Institute of Landscape Architecture

ABSTRACT

The inspiration for initiating this study was the restoration and investment of over 200 million euro into the New Dutch Waterline (Nieuwe Hollandse Waterlinie), which is now included in the Dutch tentative list of the UNESCO World Heritage sites. It is a well-known European example of a large-scale (85 kilometers long) military defence system (water hazards – irrigated land, vegetation and fortifications), originally designed in the central Netherlands in 1815 and systematically upgraded until 1963. The New Dutch Waterline was erected to protect the heart of the country against invaders and in the past was not accessible to the general public. It is also known as the 'best kept secret of the Netherlands'. Now the landscape has become a valuable public space supporting sustainable territorial development within one, common vision, which integrates cultural, economic and natural values in order to transform the New Dutch Waterline into a recognizable spatial entity for day functions such as agriculture, commerce, leisure, nature, and water management, mentioned in the application for the Landscape award of the Council of Europe.
Preservation through development was a goal for the restoration, enhancing visibility and accessibility of the cultural landscape along with the cities and rural areas.

Keywords
New Dutch Waterline, sustainable design, sustainable landscape, military landscape

1. INTRODUCTION – POST-MILITARY HERITAGE

Landscapes are memory
We need to allow for constant change while working with the historic layers and the identity they provide (IFLA, 2015)

Industrial landscape in the Netherlands developed from the mid-18th to the mid-20th centuries, and can still be seen in many places. This stage of industrialization was characterized by planning production landscapes (e.g. monocultures of fields and production forests). For decades, much of the land was excluded from use by or for the good of a majority of the public. The landscape became a 'landscape at a distance' and was subordinated to external markets and subject to governmental planning procedures (Vos, Meeks 1999: 6). Land was kept, managed, controlled and shaped by the armed forces, which had a negative impact on the environment, and today's post-military landscape is a type of industrial landscape. The same kind of exclusion applied to most of the areas controlled and maintained by the army. Military presence in the area of the New Dutch Waterline was etched on the landscape not only by fortifications in the form of complexes of buildings and earthen works but also – maybe primarily so – by zones called 'verboden kringen' ('forbiden circles', i.e. no-access areas around permanent fortifications). Land was left open (a field of fire), which was crucial for defending forts in case of short range fighting with invaders near the fortifications (Velden 2015: 12).

Many of the historically-shaped military landscape have become post-military 'large-scale models' or commemorative places rich in diversified terrain configurations, camouflage plantings, masonry and concrete works covered with green roofs. The meaning of the term 'military landscape' may still be open for discussion, but, traditionally, the term 'historical landscape' is understood as an interplay between military strategy and landscapes or 'terrain and tactics'. However, landscape established by the army can be experienced from various perspectives, starting with a personal-human scale. Sociologists consider military landscape from the position of a single soldier (Woodward 2014: 43).

On the one hand, treating post-military landscapes as museum-type, 'frozen' sites (Jelier *et al.* 2005: 163), only perceived as battlefields, could be restrictive for future development. On the other hand, easily recognizable, previously inaccessible landscapes with extraordinary landmarks and a huge potential for many modern activities are most welcome by the public. Very often (Środulska-Wielgus, Wielgus 2013: 172-173), they are transformed into sustainable leisure industry landscapes.

2. THE NEW DUTCH WATERLINE

The New Dutch Waterline is the youngest of the waterlines defending the Netherlands against invaders with an extraordinary mix of water obstacles (inundations) and fortifications. As is the case with many other Dutch waterlines, the predominant factor in its creation was the ability to bring about a large-scale inundation in the event of war. It was constructed between 1815 and 1963, is 81.5 km long and up to 5 km wide, and comprises more than 2,500 (1) structures (Meijer, Žuljević 2014: 191). The strategy of using an effective and fast military inundation in case of a threat was based on the Defensive Flooding Operations Act of 1896. There was also legislation providing for compensation to be paid to private landowners and farmers for any damage caused by military flooding. In 1868, the DWL defensive system was excessively dependent on water. Following some improvements (the construction of new canals, sluice gates, etc.), the time period of 26 days needed to prepare a good defensive flooding was radically shortened to 4-12 days. The inundation polders had been protected by fortresses, forts, defence posts.

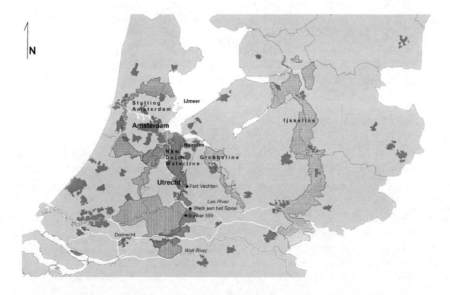

Fig.1. The New Dutch Waterline (construction by the author on the basis of the Atlas of the NDW).

Underwater obstacles, tripwires, barbed wire, barriers (palisades), and artillery batteries were placed along the embankments (Will 2009: 97-101). Everything was covered with camouflage vegetation. Each fort was surrounded by three rings of land, each with different housing restrictions, based on the *Kriegenwet* (Art. 3) of 1853 (repealed in 1951). The inner, small circle, with a 300-metre radius, was intended for the construction of wooden structures, easy to demolish during mobilization to prepare the land for a fight with an enemy. Milder restrictions applied to the middle ring, at 300-600 meters from the centre, and the outer ring, at 600-1,000 meters from the centre – here, buildings might have been partly or fully from brick or stone; however, they might have been demolished by the government during the mobilization of the fortress. This is why areas near the forts had limitations on housing until 1963 (Velden 2015: 68). The New Dutch Waterline has been mobilized a total of three times. First in 1870, during the Franco-Prussian War, then during World War I (1914-1918), when the water was held in 'preparation', and, subsequently, at the beginning of World War II (Will 2009). During the mobilizations related to WW1 and WW2, a large number of field fortifications for artillery units, infantry and ammunition dumps were built. Wide trenches, barbed wire, combat vehicle barriers and tank ditches determined the appearance of the New Dutch Waterline – the youngest of the Dutch waterlines. A number of infantry and machine gun bunkers as well as modern Quonset huts (a lightweight prefabricated hut structure made of steel, having a semicircular cross-section) and similar Nissen huts were erected along the line on both fort plots and in the areas in between (connecting sections with dikes and polders). (Aanwijzingsprogramma 2009: 48).

3. SUSTAINABILE LANDSCAPE PLANNING AND DESIGN

The Preamble to the European Landscape Convention states that it is concerned with achieving sustainable development, which is based on a balanced and harmonious relationship of social needs, economic activity and the environment. The term 'sustainable' refers to development. Landscapes are also considered a component (an essential one) of *people's surroundings,* which have become '*an expression of the diversity of their shared cultural and natural heritage, and a foundation of their identity*' (The Council of Europe, 2000). According to the Guiding Principles for Sustainable Spatial Development of the European Continent (The Council of Europe, 2000), redundant military land should be put into use again by being made accessible to users and attractive to investors thanks to the revitalization of such areas and their surroundings, including the natural environment. Furthermore, there are five aspects of sustainable landscapes: the environment, economy, society, governance, aesthetics. However, 'much of the justification for landscape's importance has been its visual appeal, coupled with intuitive (and perhaps demonstrable) associations between visual harmony, ecological integrity, human well being, and place identity' (Selman 2008: 24).

Following the European Landscape Convention (2000) and the UNESCO Universal Declaration on Cultural Diversity (2001), new sustainable development rules were proposed; these guiding principles encompassed four main themes: social, ecological, economic and cultural improvement ones (Hełdak, Raszka 2013: 396). Sustainability is related to long-term programs that minimize threats resulting from development.

Antrop (2006) describes cultural landscape design in a broader context as an interaction between nature, cultural history and people. Originality and quality are two most important characteristics, which can be visualized in landscape as a contribution of humankind and heritage considered as a kind of an intellectual capital. Usually sustainable preservation of cultural landscapes is considered from the perspective of their new functions, driven by tourism and monuments, and such new functions may have a destructive impact on the original qualities of the landscape. The *genius loci* is necessary to maintain its inherent qualities and values, including natural resources and cultural heritage; water, habitats, biodiversity, and landscape context with intangible values. Also the type of landscape, the scale and time horizon are crucial to sustainability. Sustainable landscape design needs to be supported by an integrated and holistic perspective of the landscape by integration of economy and ecological, and historical values (Antrop 2006: 190).

The presence of material heritage in cultural landscapes offers many opportunities for a so-called socio-economic 'boom', including tourism, recreation, leisure and other cultural activities. There is a growing concern for sustainable development and an increasing awareness of the regenerative potential of historic environments. This leads to the creation of socially inclusive but also economically vibrant landscapes, and heritage is now becoming a key resource to be used in redevelopment and regeneration schemes (Jannsen et al. 2014: 2).

The sustainable landscape shaping approach should not be applied only to landscapes that are outstanding in terms of natural beauty, but to all of them. It may involve creation, reinforcement, and restoration just as much as protection (Selman 2008).

Sustainable landscape design also means moving away from a 'set of pieces' towards systemic integrity. Integrity based on a human scale is usefulness (Iverson Nassauer 1995: 225), because landscape is culturally sustainable if people pay attention to its quality (Iverson Nassauer 1997: 68).

4. THE BELVEDERE MEMORANDUM AND THE PANORAMA KRAYENHOFF

On 11 June 1999, the Dutch government, after consultation with various ministries, adopted a ten-year policy document called *The Belvedere Memorandum* (nota Belvedere), in which heritage became the central point of interest. This means sustainable maintenance and development for patterns and elements that determine identity at the national level (landscapes of special national importance). The New Dutch Waterline is one of such places. The Memorandum also constituted a reaction to the prevailing fragmented and defensive heritage management practice in the Netherlands by involving architects, landscape architects and other planners interested in history and heritage as sources of inspiration and quality (Janssen et al. 2014: 3). The Memorandum is also concerned with sustainable development. The main objective of the Memorandum was to promote cultural and historical values in spatial development by ensuring effective future development of 'the undivided landscape of the past' ('*conservation through development*'), and by increasing the quality of its newly created surroundings. It can be recognized by the following subsidiary aims:

-    to recognize and to maintain the recognition of cultural-historic identity in both rural and urban areas, as a quality and basic starting point for further development
-    to strengthen and exploit cultural-historic identity and the qualities which go to define such
-    identity, in those areas of the Netherlands which are most valuable in terms of cultural history, the so-called Belvedere areas;
-    to create appropriate condition for the initiatives of third parties aimed at a thematic strengthening of cultural history;
-    to disseminate knowledge concerning cultural history and to promote opportunities whereby cultural history can be used as a source of inspiration in spatial planning and design;
-    to promote cooperation between citizens, organizations, local and regional authorities and government; and
-    to improve the practicality and use of existing instruments (Belvedere 1999).

When the *Belvedere Memorandum* was published, the Dutch society was dissatisfied with an increasing uniformity of towns and landscapes, manifested by growing urban sprawl and an overwhelming landscape identity crisis, as it were. So the Memorandum explored, in a general way, the theme of identity (*genius loci*), without determining whether it belonged to a rural or urban area, which was assumed to be significant, by projecting and strengthening local identities through discovering, protecting and enhancing existing landscapes (Janssen et al. 2014: 7). The Belvedere Memorandum constituted a turning point as regards landscape and heritage planning; with a holistic and regional approach to planning, space management, and balanced esthetics, ecology, economy and identity interests (Gonzales 2013: 17-18).

In 2004, the New Dutch Waterline was designated as a national landscape, and so new sources of finance became available for its protection and revitalisation. In 2011, when the heritage preservation system was changed (as a result of decentralisation, the relevant rights were transferred to the provinces), the status of the monuments became unclear (Self Analysis Report, 2012). After 2009 and the evaluation of the Belvedere Memorandum we know that better co-operation and dialog between architects and historians, public participation, valuation and estimation of the cultural research (Berg 2009: 23-24), using of the preservation of the heritage beneficially to other large scale historic structures including the estate landscape (real estate) in its broadest sense (Verschuure-Stuip 2014b), and better law regulations regarding to habitats protection (EU) (Kistenkas 2008: 91) are necessary.

Another document important to the development and protection of the New Dutch Waterline was announced in March 2004. The Panorama Krayenhoff Line Perspective was a vision of a common policy on spatial planning for the entire line at the provincial level (NDW 2004). The idea was to create a recognizable brand (ultimately: *Hollandse Waterlinie*) – one, common vision of the Waterline development, the heritage and the contemporary components in the process of 'conservation through development'. According to the rules of sustainable landscape design, the Panorama can be described as a document that emphasized the Waterline as a military facility, advocated further opening of the Prohibited Areas in the eastern section of the line as well as developing and expanding areas to the west of the line. In September 2009, the New Dutch Waterline was announced by the Minister of Culture as a protected heritage site. The protection also extends to the environment (e.g. ecological clusters), the surrounding water-connected landscapes. Simplified procedures were introduced so that private and government owners can work more effectively. Today a 'wide scope of issues to technological and restoration questions, procedural and social questions demands a wide variety of people and groups able to provide answers (Ros 2012: 67).

Today the New Dutch Water is on the tentative list of the UNESCO World Heritage Sites as an extension to an existing world heritage site – the Defence Line of Amsterdam, the combination of inundation fields, verdant landscape and the fortifications themselves (Project group 2014). Discussions about outstanding universal values and protection zones are nearing completion (Report 2015).

5. LINKING THE PAST WITH A FUTURE – EXAMPLES OF THE NEW DUTCH WATERLINE ON VARIOUS SCALES

Considering the above, sustainable adaptation is understood as a long-term, holistic process that takes into account social, cultural, historical, ecological, technical and financial aspects, as well as the process stakeholders when a new function for a facility or land is being introduced. As a result of the adopted planning assumptions, adaptation is often made by small steps, which allows one to verify – following an assessment – the assumptions and the applied solutions, in accordance with the principle 'smart to start small' (Meijer, Žuljević 2014: 199). This is due to the fact that there exists a danger that big projects – often over-financed (characterised by a short period of intensive financing) and aimed at a spectacular media effect (related to politics or a person's term of office) – may be inconsistent with the tourist capacity of a fortification and unprofitable (Pardela, Pałubska 2015: 221-222). In recent times, of special interest to designers and the public has been the revitalisation of Fort Vechten (1867-1870), located near Bunnik. An island with an area of 17 ha, where five out of a total of 26 bunkers (nearly 11,000 m^2 of usable area) have been exclusively adapted as winter habitats for bats (2). Terrace Battery H, designed to house 200 people, was selected as the first testing facility for further development of the complex. The existing conditions, i.e. the facts that the structure is partially embedded in the ground, that it has a green roof and massive, brick walls, were used to increase energy efficiency, to improve ventilation and the climate inside the structure. This was possible thanks to the use of equipment to be found in indoor swimming pools, which was hidden in the fort escarpments. Thanks to this, the original shape of the fort was not changed, contributing to the acceptance of the micro scale of the landscape interior (Meijer, Žuljevič 2014). In the years 2013-2015, Fort Vechten acquired a new form. This was due to the implementation of a land development project and the erection of a museum of Dutch waterlines – the National Waterline Museum (Waterliniemuseum) (3). A viewing opening in the form of an 80-metre strip was made to show the original shape of the earthen forms, while the rest of the fort was left overgrown, together with all the plants and endangered species. In order to improve the fort's accessibility from the outside, two bridges were constructed and the breastwork embankment was cut through at a height of eight metres. One of the new paths leads to an 'invisible parking lot' with an area of 3 ha, which was built using ground brick aggregate and profiles made from recycled concrete. The parking lot lighting system complies with the relevant environmental protection requirements and was designed not to interfere with the bats that live at the fort (Parklaan.nl 2015).

Fig.2. The entrance path leading from the parking lot to Fort Vechten, 2013. Photograph by author.

The new museum pavilion is hidden and not visible from the former foreground. It was constructed from concrete and covered with earth, like the shelters located within the fort. It is entered through a barracks bunker, which was erected in 1880. The pavilion is an isolated building, which uses energy-saving technologies, by recovering heat and controlling CO_2 from the ventilation system. Only very small amounts of energy are needed to heat the building. It is also provided, just like the parking lot, with a bat-friendly lighting system. In the central part of the patio there is a 50-metre long concrete model of the New Dutch Waterline, where visitors can themselves effect an inundation, using almost 19 m^3 of water. Unfortunately, as part of greenery management, many historical trees were removed, including a row that had constituted the back screen for the barracks bunker and some fruit trees. However, most of them have been replaced with new plantings.

A much smaller project was implemented in the years 2009-2012, when the historic work Werk aan het Spoel (a former military outpost with an area of 4,8 ha), located near the town of Culemborg, was revitalised – as part of the project, the earthen works and brick military buildings were recreated and substandard structures were removed. The work was given the form of a 'green sculpture' embedded in landscape, by making use of the surrounding meadows and floodplains of the Lek River. A viewpoint

Fig.3. The model of the New Dutch Waterline in the Museum patio. Photograph by author.

Fig.4. Werk aan het Spoels as a 'green sculpture' in landscape, 2013. Photograph by author.

Fig.5. The cut-through Bunker 599 with a long boardwalk leading to an inundation polder, 2013. Photograph by author.

tower for watching birds, with a small restaurant with a cookhouse on the ground level, was also erected. Planned landscape openings were made by cutting through the earth embankments of the breastwork and eliminating greenery along selected axes, to show a far view of the breastwork. The work is home to meeting places, where art, culture (a sculpture workshop and an amphitheatre for 300 people), nature and history coexist.

A characteristic, widely known symbol of the New Dutch Waterline is now a cut-in-half bunker called 'Bunker 599'. It is located near the Amsterdam-Maastricht motorway near a weir (Diefdijk). The bunker was built in 1940 and it acquired its present form thanks to a brave design in 2010 (The Dutch Design Award 2011 and The Architectural Review Award 2013). The area around the facility was put in order and a path was built through its middle – it forms a 'historical section' along a new viewing axis, at the end of which there is a pier and a small pond that illustrates a military inundation (Verschuure-Stuip 2014a). Not only was access to the bunker from the causeway improved, but visitors are also now able to experience the massive structure better, because they can walk through it.

Apart from examining big, commercial adaptations of former military structures, such as forts, artillery platforms, bunkers, huts, military buildings, one can gain a fuller understanding of the landscape context of a fortification by analysing landscaping components created for didactic purposes. This is possible thanks to three-dimensional land models that are not necessarily to be found within fort limits. For instance, models of selected New Dutch Waterline forts have been placed on concrete bases of former containers for sand spread on roads between the forts in winter. Because the containers do not perform their intended function anymore, and their original covers became rusted, they were replaced with models of the nearby forts. The models (including ones for the forts of Asperen, Everdingen and Vuren) are made from cast iron and can be seen when one travels between the forts (Pardela, Pałubska 2015: 225).

3. CONCLUSIONS

Sustainable landscape design in the case of the New Dutch Waterline is reflected in environmentally-friendly actions of various scales and taken at various levels. 'Preservation through development' is a true goal of restoration, which enhances visibility and accessibility of cultural landscape in cities and rural areas alike. Sustainability means that development becomes a 'self-propelled machine' within one, clear vision – steam to the wheel. Sustainable landscape design is not limited to turning the former fortifications into dozens of museums and putting soldier-playing actors wherever possible. It is implemented mostly by respecting the existing habitats and by meeting the needs of the local communities. In the case of the revitalisation of the New Dutch Waterline, 'sustainable' means 'with attention to detail', 'on a human scale', 'making a historical contribution to a present-day landscape', a 'story-telling, multi-layered landscape' with a clear historical context. Furthermore, the recent years have shown that the sustainable development of the New Dutch Waterline fortifications has become predominated by issues related to water and energy conservation, harmful waste limitation, habitats protections, and reduction of maintenance costs. Nature-based solutions have become an ally again. However, the new development calls for effective law regulations, public participation, maintenance and management to ensure fully successful revitalisation.

NOTES

[1] All are catalogued and marked in accordance with the code used for the Waterline.

[2] Bat protection attracts much attention and so many of the facilities along the New Dutch Waterline are used as habitats by the mammals. See: Boer, F.,D., Koppel, S., Knegt, H.,J., Dekker, J. (2013). Hibernation site requirements of bats in man-made hibernacula in a spatial context. *Ecological Applications*, 23(2), pp. 502–514.

[3] The Museum was opened on 8 October 2015.

BIBLIOGRAPHY

Antrop, M. (2006). Sustainable landscapes: contradiction, fiction or utopia?. *Landscape and Urban Planning* 75, pp.187–197.

Bandarin, F., Oers, R. (2012). The Historic Urban Landscape: Managing Heritage in an Urban Century, Chichester, John Wiley & Sons, p.60-61.

The Belvedere Memorandum (*Nota Belvedere*) (1999*). Beleidsnota over de relatie cultuurhistorie en ruimtelijke inrichtin.* Available at: https://www.rijksoverheid.nl [Access 10 Jan. 2015].

Berg, W. (2009). Biedt de Nota Belvedere een mooi (voor) uitzicht?. Master Thesis. Faculty of Humanities. Utrecht University. Available at: http://dspace.library.uu.nl [Access 20 Jan. 2015].

The Council of Europe, (2000). *The European Landscape Convention.* Florence. Available at: http://www.coe.int [Access 15 Jan. 2015].

The Council of Europe, (2000). *Guiding Principles for Sustainable Spatial Development of the European Continent. CEMAT,7,* Hanover.

Available at: http://www.coe.int [Access 15 Jan. 2015].

The Cultural Heritage Agency. Ministry of Culture, Education, and Science, (2009) *Aanwijzingsprogramma Nieuwe Hollandse Waterlinie.* Amersfoort, p. 48.

Available at: http://culturalheritageagency.nl [Access 20 Jan. 2015].

Gonzales, P., A. (2013). Cultural Parks and National Heritage Areas: Assembling Cultural Heritage, Development and Spatial Planning; Cambridge Scholar Publishing, Newcastle upon Tyne: pp. 17-18.

Hełdak, M., Raszka, B. (2013). Evaluation of the Local Spatial Policy in Poland with Regard to Sustainable Development. *Polish Journal of Environmental Studies*, Vol. 22, No. 2 pp. 395-402. Available at: http://www.pjoes.com [Access 28 Jan. 2015].

The International Federation of Landscape Architects, (2015). *Learning from Landscape Resolution*, Lisbon. Available at: iflaeurope.eu [Access 19 Jan. 2015].

Iverson Nassauer, J. (1995), Culture and changing landscape structure. *Landscape Ecology*, Vol. 10 no. 4 SPB Academic Publishing bv, Amsterdam, pp.229-237.

Available at http://deepblue.lib.umich.edu [Access 28 Jan. 2015].

Iverson Nassauer, J. (1997). Cultural Sustainability: Aligning Aesthetics and Ecology. *Placing Nature. culture and Landscape Ecology.* Washington: Island Press, pp.67-83. Available at http://static1.squarespace.com [Access 28 Jan. 2015].

Janssen, J.,Luiten, E., Renesc, H., Rouwendalc, J. (2014). Heritage planning and spatial development in the Netherlands: Changing policies and perspectives. *International Journal of Heritage Studies*, Vol. 20, No. 1, 1–21, http://dx.doi.org/10.1080/13527258.2012.710852.

Jelier, A.J., Nijman, J-H., Somsen, A., J.(2005). Planning for the future; towards a sustainable design and land use of an ancient flooded military defence line, *Landscape and Urban Planning*, 70, pp. 153-163.

Kistenkas, F.,H., Pleidooi voor meer afdwingbaarheid. *Landschap: tijdschrift voor Landschapsecologie en Milieukunde*, Vol. 25 (2), p.87-91.

Available at: www.landschap.nl [Access 10 Jan. 2015].

Meijer, G., Žuljevič, I. (2014). *Heritage development: what is heritage development and why do we need it?* Proceedings of the International Conference on Fortified Heritage: Management and Sustainable Development, pp.191-201.

The New Dutch Waterline. (2012). AT FORT Self Analysis Report New Dutch Waterline, Utrecht. Available at: http://www.atfort.eu [Access 20 Jan. 2015].

Pardela, Ł., Pałubska, K. (2015). Krajobraz zrównoważonej adaptacji zabytkowych fortyfikacji Nowej Holenderskiej Linii Wodnej na wybranych przykładach. *Ochrona wartości w procesie adaptacji zabytków,* Polski Komitet Narodowy Międzynarodowej Rady Ochrony Zabytków ICOMOS, Muzeum Pałacu Króla Jana III w Wilanowie, Politechnika Lubelska, Warszawa, p.221-228.

Parklaan.nl, (2015). *Parklaan Landschapsarchitekten Official Website*. [online] Available at: http://www. parklaan.nl [Access 25 Jan. 2015].

The Waterline UNESCO Nomination Bid. (2014). *Aanloop naar het nominatiedossier Stelling van Amsterdam en Nieuwe Hollandse Waterlinie samen sterker!*, Utrecht, p. 36

The Waterline UNESCO Nomination Bid. (2015). Report International Expert Meeting on World Heritage Nominations New Dutch Waterline &Defence Line of Amsterdam, Utrecht, 49 p.

Ros, P.(2012). New Dutch Waterline. Implementation leads to new questions. The Reuse of Ancient fortified settlement from middle ages to early time, *Europa Nostra Scientific Bulletin*, 65, p. 55-67. Available at: http://issuu.com/europanostra/ [Access 20 Jan. 2015].

Selman, P. (2008). What do we mean by sustainable landscape?. Sustainability: science, practice, & policy 4(2): pp.23-28 . Available at: http://sspp.proquest.com [Access 28 Jan. 2015].

Środulska-Wielgus, J, Wielgus, K. (2007). Krajobrazy "przemysłu czasu wolnego", *Czasopismo Techniczne*, 10. *Architektura, Vol.* 5-A, pp.172-173.

Working group National Project New Dutch Waterline (2004). *Panorama Krayenhoff Linieperspectief Samenvatting*, Utrecht. Available at: http://hollandsewaterlinie.erfgoedsuite.nl [Access 15 Jan. 2015].

Will, Ch. (2009). *Water resistance: How the water defence line works*, Atlas of the New Dutch Water Line, 010 Publishers, Rotterdam, p. 207.

Woodward, R. (2014). Military landscapes: Agendas and approaches for future research. Progress in Human Geography, Vol. 38(1) 40–61.

Vervloet, J., Nijman, J. H., Somsen, A. J. (2005). Planning for the future; towards a sustainable design and land use on an ancient flooded military defence line. *Landscape and Urban Planning*, 70, pp.153-163.

Velden, K. (2015) *Kernkwaliteiten Nieuwe Hollandse Waterlinie ten zuiden van de Lek DEEL I Nationaal Landschap handboek voor beschermen én ontwikkelen*: pp. 68. Available at: http://www.ruimtelijkeplannen. nl [Access 28 Jan. 2015].

Verschuure-Stuip, G. (2014a). The Story of the Place; Different types of stories of a place, the Netherlands. Proceedings AESOP 2014: Annual Conference "From control to co-evolution", Utrecht/Delft, Available at: http://repository.tudelft.nl [Access 22 Jan. 2015].

Verschuure-Stuip, G. (2014b). Project New Dutch Waterline and Project Arcadian Landscapes; Guidelines for new spatial development based on heritage. Proceedings AESOP 2014: Annual Conference "From control to co-evolution", Utrecht/Delft. Available at: http://repository.tudelft.nl [Access 22 Jan. 2015].

Vos, W., Meekes, H. (1999) Trends in European cultural landscape development: perspectives for a sustainable future. *Landscape and Urban Planning*, 46, pp.3-14.

MYSTERY AND VALUE OF PLACE. ON COEXISTENCE
OF LANDSCAPE AND SENSUAL NATURE OF SITE-SPECIFIC ART

Katarzyna Kołodziejczyk
Cracow University of Technology, Faculty of Architecture

ABSTRACT

In the article an issue of peculiar and odd space, found landscape, place at the same time however shaped by the works of art, getting essence was brought up and restoring his memory. That kind of art forms are aimed at emphasizing coexistence of the art with the space, interrelation, values complementing each other. Site-specific art is using peculiar code, literary language being means of communication in itself, unique composition of signs closed in the legible form. The landscape similarly to the works of art constitutes kept tracks of the memory, tender registers of senses: of colour, smell, sound, touch; symbols of both the financial presence and metaphysical meanings. The present article was devoted to analysis of work of chosen artists of the refined class i.e. Dani Karavan, Nancy Holt, Robert Smithson, James Turrell, Charles Ross, Walter Benjamin in terms of contents, the form and their function with reference to the context of the place. Shown works constitute the indissoluble part of the space, in which they came into existence and which belong to. The universal symbolism, intelligible to the wide circle of recipients and character of chosen spaces of the creative act are linking work of chosen artists. This art-devoted space is a place of experience of not only the author but also the experiencing spectator which through his participation is reviving the works of art and is granting the new quality him.

Keywords
art, contemporary art, land art, site-specific art, art in landscape

> In the mystery of each man there exists an inner landscape: with untouched plains, with valleys
> of silence, with inaccessible mountains, with hidden gardens. (de Saint-Exupéry 1948: 169)

1. INTRODUCTION

The article addresses the issues of the specific and peculiar space, the found landscape though at the same time shaped by a work of art, highlighting the essence of the place and restoring its memory. We are talking here about *site-specific* (Kołodziejczyk 2005: 101-102) art in the character of a multi-dimension reflection, deeply contextual i.e. dependent on place and time. Such artistic activity is aimed at emphasising the coexistence of art and space, mutual relations and complementary values. *Site-specific* art uses a specific code, an artistic language which was a means of communication in itself, a unique composition of signs enclosed in a legible form. Like a work of art, the landscape keeps the preserved traces of memory, tender registers of the senses: colour, smell, sound, touch; symbols of both material presence and metaphysical meanings. This article is devoted to the analysis of work of selected artists regarded as outstanding in the world of art, such as: Dani Karavan, Nancy Holt, Robert Smithson and James Turrell, viewing their art in terms of content, form and function in relation to the context of place. Indicated works constitute an inextricable element of the space in which they were created, and to which they belong. Works of the selected artists are connected by universal symbolism understandable for a wide audience, and the character of selected spaces of the creative act. The artists I have indicated emphasise the significance and specificity of the place, because their works create a consistent whole with the landscape. It is a kind of conceptual art, highly intellectual, constituting a manifestation of the mystery of existence and humanity, a celebration of human spirit and its coexistence with the nature, environment and space. In all the realisations of the chosen artists it is space that plays the key part in the creative process. Space has become the greatest fascination, passion and even obsession of modern artists. They redefined it, putting special stress on values essential for a given venue by highlighting its meaning, restoring its forgotten history, returning to the source. Authors of those semantic experiments make the place unique. Owing to them, it becomes the whole world or, as Martin Heidegger called it *world-picture* (Heidegger 1977: 128-167). In this approach the *picture* is a specific notion, determining the space of a symbolic transformation. It is a word, a place and a symbol maintaining the continuity of the creative process. The manner of forming the picture expresses the man's attitude to the world, to his being within the matter, and is of an intentional character. Therefore, a visual image of the artist reflects the primary cultural form of a concrete social group. Both the man's individuality, and the experience of space which becomes a part of the artwork through interactions of its recipients, are of much significance here. This space is the place of experiments not only for the creator, but also for the viewer experiencing it whose participation enlivens the work of art and gives it a new quality.

2. INFLUENCE OF ROMANTIC PAINTING ON SITE-SPECIFIC ART. OWN OBSERVATIONS

Land art is a romantic tendency in modern art, using frame and the matter of nature. Analysing works of selected artists one can pose a thesis that this kind of creative discourse betrays a fascination with the art of an English painter known mostly for his romantic landscapes, a precursor of Impressionism – Joseph Mallord William Turner. Looking at Turner's paintings we are witnessing a breakthrough in art bursting with symbolic enthusiasm. According to John Gage (in: *Colour and meaning*), there rises from them *a wonderful scene, an enchanted landscape* (Gage 2010: 162-165), with colour visibly treated in a way contemporary with us. It is not abstract emphasis yet, but it radically departs from the then prevailing rules and principles of "realism" or "naturalism". Turner was fascinated with science experiencing of which allowed him to treat the matter of the painting freely, almost wilfully. The discovery of non-reducible number of elements in nature and art enhanced the artist's interest in the simplicity of geometrical forms and primary colours inscribed in them. Turner based on the conviction that colour and light were substances, thus adding a symbolic layer to the *spectrum*[1] (ed. Cacha 2001: 32, 386-387) occurring in nature. (Gage 2010: 162-165) Joris-Karl Huysmans (cor. Charles-Marie-Georges Huysmans), a scandalising French writer most frequently associated with decadent movement, but also an eminent art critic, wrote about Turner's painting: […] *all is balanced. Before your eye of a non-believer there rises a wonderful scene, an enchanted landscape with an illuminated river which flows in sparkling sun rays. Pale sky, vanishing in the distance where it is swallowed by pearly horizon, reflects and shifts in the foaming water of rainbow colours like a soap bubble. What land, what Eldorado, what Eden is burning with such demented brightness, when streaming light refracts in milky-white clouds dotted with fiery red and slashed with violet as in the precious depths of an opal? After all they are real places,* […] (Huysmans 1889 after Gage 2010: 162).

3. DEFINITION, REDEFINITION, BEYOND DEFINITION

The connections of romanticism and land art find their meeting point in the meaning of the notion *site-specific*. Land art is a modern-day expression of longing for nature, a call for freedom, for space, for breaking away from the overwhelming force of commercialism, progress and civilisation. Remaining in a close relation to the conceptual art and art of installation, the land art absorbs the former in a natural way, creating a perfect whole (though the conceptual art was the first and laid the foundations for the construction of the activities created as a consequence). Their coexistence involves their mutual interpenetration and supplementation.

The notion of conceptual art refers to the artistic activity started in the mid-1960s. Artists began to depart from their attachment to form, recognising the primacy and supreme value of the idea of the creative act. The previous way of thinking about art was rejected, and any - even the smallest - stress on the form, the appearance of the work of art started to be reduced, or even radically eliminated. That opposition was caused by a profound conviction that it was the concept of art that was the most important and should be predominant over its realisation. The accepted artistic attitude was the consequence of the increasing criticism of traditional art at the time, as well as of political and economic systems that supported it. (ed. Renshaw 2013: 365) A similar situation took place in the case of artistic installations where the key part was played by the conveyed message and not the form of its expression. Therefore, we can see that the idea was based on conceptual art. Since the 1970s, it was a more and more popular phenomenon in the world of art which for its visual activity used a wide range of materials, techniques and connections with other disciplines. The privileged position was always given to the relation between diverse media, understood as their personal combination, adding autonomy to the whole work of art. Simultaneously, a *biomorphic* form of art developed (in the philosophical context, i.e. philosophy of nature), which used inborn, natural elements occurring in nature. It appeared in the late 1960s in reaction to the growing commercialisation of art and industrialisation of the traditional museum context, at the same time being an answer to the increasing environmental fears. Artists created monumental work, initially transferring nature into gallery space, creating delicate, intricate and frequently impermanent works of art, documented merely by means of photographs. (ed. Renshaw 2013: 365) Art and nature are close to each other, and exist in harmony. The art of nature, or rather the nature of art provokes to invest into nature and landscape. It is land art that addresses the issues of the modern world, tells about the man, his position in the world, and promotes life in harmony with the environment. Such a convention of art was accepted by representatives of the following artistic movements: land art, art in situ, art environmental and earthworks. They used nature as a workplace and exhibition space. They were united by the same idea of moving art outside the museum space. Alluding to my own observations, I would like to stress that:

Visual arts falling outside the traditional image of presentation, by entering the public sphere address the issue of social activation of various milieus, interaction in a massive dimension. Through unconventional means of expression, modern technologies and the range of used media beyond the limits of a traditional artistic language, artists engage and sharpen all the viewer's senses. Verification of the approach to the matter, shaping a new creative awareness are probably the consequences of civilisational and cultural changes which generated a completely new way of expression. The change in thinking about art led to its redefinition, re-evaluation of relations between the idea, the matter and the viewer. A work of art became an announcement, a record of a creative process, a register of signs, symbols and images in the space filled with meaning and sensual elements favouring the viewer's interaction. The medium is fluid, open and independent, gives a completely new value to the work of art. The artwork becomes a multi-level creation endowed with a mass striking power, a great, autonomous formula of our times. (Kołodziejczyk 2005: 103-104)

4. PRESENTATION OF SELECTED WORKS OF THE ARTISTS REFERRED TO IN THIS ESSAY

4.1. Nancy Holt, *Sun Tunnels*

Nancy Holt was an American artist, who even after her death is still regarded as one of the most talented in the world of modern art. She was primarily connected to the land art movement, though she also practised photography and film, which techniques often constituted a starting point for further work on a selected subject continued by the author in a new form i.e. a sculpture or installation. She was interested in various natural phenomena to which a human eye reacted. However, she was most fascinated by the phenomenon of light, its intensity and angular distribution, dispersion of light by means of a prism or diffraction grating. She was interested in physics as a source of individual sensations, personal experience, and dependence of man on the most powerful force that of nature. The acquired knowledge gave rise to artistic experiments. The possibility of obtaining coloured light e.g. red, green or violet, wave properties of the light revealed in such phenomena as: diffraction or interference (ed. Cacha 2001: 152-153) became the subject of the artist's creative research. The phenomenon of light whose strongest sources are stars, especially those closest to the Earth like the Sun, added a characteristic and unique rhythm to the work entitled *Sun Tunnels,* created in 1938. The installation was situated in the Great Basin Desert – one of four deserts in the USA, located between the Rocky Mountains and the Sierra Nevada in east California. (ed. Renshaw 2013: 365)

This fascination with nature had a greatest impact on artwork created with the landscape. The work of Nancy Holt perfectly fits into the principles of land art which, around 1960, under the influence of the ecological movement then rapidly developing in the United States, promoted protection of natural environment and the accompanying awareness of the *eco-live-style*. Land art transformed that life style (not only in the philosophical context) onto the plane of creating the existence of the artwork itself within the natural space, leading the artwork –its form with the conceptual foundation – out of the gallery and museum spaces.

Like many art pieces from the American land art of the 1970s, the artist's work entitled *Sun Tunnels* requires the viewer to literally set off on a journey, a pilgrimage, and to make the intellectual effort in order to experience and understand the work of art. That majestic object was situated app. 8 km southwards from the abandoned town of Lucin dating back to the end of the 19th century, in Utah (also known as Umbria Junction, and colloquially referred to as a "ghost town"), and 48 km from the nearest living town.

Fig.1. Sun Tunnels viewing with Nancy Holt, organized by the Utah Museum of Fine Arts (UMFA) as part of Nancy Holt: Sightlines, a traveling exhibition organized by the Miriam and Ira D. Wallach Art Gallery, Columbia University, on view October 19, 2012 – January 20, 2013 at the UMFA. UMFA photo; http://umfa.utah.edu/suntunnels_selfguide.

The symbolic installation comprises four large cylinders lying on the ground forming an open letter X (the unknown quantity, sought and found via experimenting), in the middle of a large deserted area with rarely occurring scarce and scattered vegetation burnt out by the sun. In the distance one can discern the mountains topped with snow, hardly visible on the horizon, which appear tiny, almost miniature in comparison with the vast area of the empty desert and the canopy of the sky stretched (opened) above it. Four tubes specially designed for this place, were made in the same shape and from the concrete of the same strength and endurance. The work makes up a whole through interaction with the sun and stars. In the upper section of each tunnel holes were drilled to create the constellations of the Dragon, Perseus, Dove and Capricorn. The cylindrical forma was thought out in such a way that, depending on the weather, time of day, rising or setting sun, light angle, as well as the direction of the stream of light, our perception of time and space, perspective and experiencing the landscape changed. The artist experiments with perception, carries out an artistic analysis of our imagination and intelligence on which depends our organization and interpretation of sensory impressions in order to understand our surroundings. She is interested in our sensory perceptions which are frequently deformed by our expectations, needs, emotions, which are initiated by our subconscious. Each of us differently registers the external environment which is connected to individual verbal identification and reaction to stimuli. (ed. Renshaw 2013: 55)

4.2. Robert Smithson, *Spiral Jetty*

Robert Smithson was an American artist who was a painter, a sculptor, a photographer and a performer. His creative activity involved all those art forms. He died tragically in 1973 in airplane crash, but had made a name in the history of modern art as an art pioneer and the creator of *land art*.

The majority of works derived from land art (such as *art in situ*, *environmental art*, *earthworks*) conveys an ecological message and promotes *eco-live-style*. One example of such artistic realisations is the work by Robert Smithson, entitled *Spiral Jetty* from 1970, which drew the attention of contemporary art critics and cased heated discussions concerning its reliability towards the ecological sphere. The spiral causeway created by Smithson from natural materials i.e. mud, salt crystals, basalt rocks, earth and water, was situated on the north-east shore of the Great Salt Lake, located in Utah (west part of the United States). Starting on the lake shore, the installation stretched further along the lake surface, covering the area of app. 450 m long and 4.5 m wide. The artists formed the installation in the shape of a left-hand spiral, symbolising concentration, introversion, regress, destruction, death and shrinking. The spiral is a universal symbol associated with cyclical transformations in in nature. (Kopaliński 1990: 399-400) This fundamental form in nature, known since the ancient times, was used by the artist in order to contrast various states of matter (solid, liquid, gas) by means of art. The process of salt crystallisation occurring on rocks was to point out the context of time and place since crystallisation is the process of continuous creation. That unique and monumental composition was equipped with a profound ideological message. Undoubtedly, it has a contemplative and meditative character which encourages to reflection, to internal rebirth, to transformation. It constitutes an extremely moving reflection on the world, its ceaseless change, entropy, fragility of existence. It is a symbol of the mystery of life and death, the powerful force of nature against the weakness of man. (ed. Renshaw 2013: 56)

Technically speaking, construction of this artwork required loosening, removing and shifting the earth, profiling the land using a bulldozer, as well as blowing up rocks with dynamite; hence the doubts concerning the care for the natural environment in realisations of this type, expressed by art critics and ecologists. Such criticism forced Smithson and his wife, Nancy Holt, to redefine their views yet not enough to transform them completely, because the artists did not agree to create art renovating the landscape which, in their opinion, would have been camouflaging abuse and an intention to hide the truth. (Wilkoszewska 1993: 269-270)

Fig.2. Robert Smithson, *Spiral Jetty* (1970). Photograph by Gianfranco Gorgoni.
Art © Estate of Robert Smithson/Licensed by VAGA, New York; http://umfa.utah.edu/land_art_spiraljetty.

4.3. James Turell, *Roden Crater*

My desire is to set up a situation to which I take you and let you see. It becomes your experience.
(Turell: http://rodencrater.com/about/)

James Turell is an American conceptual artist. He was born in Los Angeles, California. He lives and works in Flagstaff, Arizona, and Inishkeame West in Ireland. (Renshaw 2013: 36, 68-69) His works belong to the *site-specific* art. They are objects in the form of installations which consist of three fundamental aspects: light, space and man. They are created not only in the natural landscape, but often are constructions built into the already existing architecture. It is the mutual relation between the light, space and the viewer that seems to be a source of the artist's creative process. In his works, he pays attention primarily to the physical nature of light. And though his artworks are of meditative or contemplative character, those issues refer rather to the research and analyses of the human perception, then of the spiritual context of light. The human mind, the centre of all the conscious and subconscious psyche of man, which decides about his perception, thinking, remembering or feeling of emotions, plays the greatest part in Turell's works. Turell is fascinated not only by the nature of light, but also the nature of man, which are linked by the mystery of being, unfathomable, undefinable, like the inner space of man. Although the spiritual aspect of light is not the key one in the artist's work, his aspirations to closeness to the truth, to experiencing it through cognition is still visible. Turell is interested in the light as a factor shaping the reality, the way in which a man perceives light, and how the light influences the behaviour of man by revealing his personality, individual preferences and interpretative abilities. The light for an artist is the fundamental creative material, the image, the language for expressing the world, a medium which determines the viewer. The artist puts the latter in the situation of co-creating the artwork. The experiment involves engaging all the senses of the viewer as a result leading to reflection. Turell uses the possibilities of light in order to create a three-dimensional illusion, levitating spaces, and moving objects. Not only does he use natural light whose colour depends on weather conditions, but knowing its properties he mixes the inside and outside light, opening spaces towards the sky. (Renshaw 2013: 36, 68-69)

Since 1976, the artist has been working on his greatest and most complicated project, entitled *Roden Crater*. The object is a transformation and adaptation of the meteorite crater of an extinct volcano, located on the *Painted Desert*. It is a semi-desert in the American state of Arizona, on the Colorado Plateau. It stretches from the Grand Canyon National Park to the Petrified Forest National Park on the north bank of the Little Colorado River. The object was designed in the form of a structure of tunnels, linking the crater with exhibit rooms in various places of the volcano. It is not a random layout because the location of each room was precisely calculated with regard to the position of the Sun, Moon and stars. The coefficient of sunlight energy transmittance depends on the sunrays gradient. Each room reveals a different aspect of the light, the sunrise, the sunset etc., because the surface reflectivity coefficient also depends on the type of surface. Turell converts the existing landscape into a magical space serving to observe the sky and stars. *Roden Crater* is a kind of artistic astronomical observatory. (Renshaw 2013: 36, 68-69)

Fig.3-4. Roden Crater, 2016 Skystone Foundation; all images James Turrell; http://rodencrater.com/spaces/crater-bowl/.

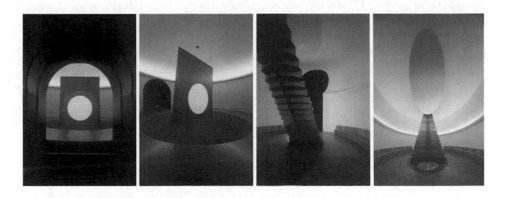

Fig.5-6. *Sun-Moon Chamber,* 2016 Skystone Foundation; all images James Turrell; http://rodencrater.com/space/ sun-moon-chamber/; Il. 7, 8. East Portal, 2016 Skystone Foundation; all images James Turrell; http://rodencrater.com/ spaces/east-portal/.

4.4. Dani Karavan, *Essence of the Place*

Dani Karavan is an Israeli sculptor, born in Tel Aviv. He is known for his original monuments constituting an integral part of the landscape. To a large extent, his artistic work was subordinate to the impact of the international style architecture (Bauhaus). White, geometrised, simple forms in the open space are

Fig.7-8. Alpha East Tunnel, 2016 Skystone Foundation; all images James Turrell; http://rodencrater.com/spaces/alpha-east-tunnel/.

characteristic for him. Karavan's open-air sculptures reflect his view of the world, respect and understanding of the surrounding environment. He possesses the unique ability or the outstanding talent to create sculpted compositions, spectacular images, visual activity within natural space, giving his objects a historical and social context. The artist employs universal symbols relating them to human experience. Karavan's works possess both a philosophical and emotional element. (ed. Chrabąszcz 2015: 244-245)

In 2015, the International Centre for Culture in Krakow hosted an exhibition of Dani Karavan's artwork, entitled *Makom. Essence of place.* The Hebrew word *makom* has many meanings. The basic meaning of the word *makom* is place, space, area occupied by man. In the more universal meaning it is one of the names of God and Nature. According to the Jewish religion, God is present in every place of the universe, and therefore He is referred to by the word Makom. (ed. Chrabąszcz 2015: 132)

For an artist, each place is unique, has a specific atmosphere and is an inspiration for creative activity. Karavan's works are placed within the *site-specific* art because of the artist's strong attachment to the place, its context and used material. The artist uses such materials as e.g. stone, wood, water, sand, sun, plants, trees, wind or bird song. He uses nature and landscape, and combines it with permanent elements i.e. concrete, steel or glass, looking for their mutual relations. His works can be seen both within natural, urban or gallery-museum space.

4.4.1. *Kikar Lewana (White Square)*

The artwork entitled *Kikar Levana* (White Square) was created in the years 1977-1988, and was located on top of a hill above Tel Aviv. Perfectly incorporated into the landscape of the blue Mediterranean Sea, this sculpted complex pays homage to the symbolic town, one of the largest centres of modernist architecture built in 1909. To realise his work the artist used the following media: wind, sunlight, water, grass, an olive tree, glass, and white concrete. Its concrete, simple, geometric form with its pristine white colour symbolises the international style represented by the Bauhaus School in the architecture of the 1930s.

The roots of this artwork can be found in the antique places of cult, yet it touches upon the issues of the modern, free and democratic world. The work comprises several symbolic elements:
a rectangular tower, a dual dome, two pyramids, stairs and a split wall. Each of those forms is a metaphor of universal principles ruling the world, recorded in the history of human civilisation, culture and art. (ed. Chrabąszcz 2015:135)

The strongest relations between the artist and nature are revealed in his realisations from Japan. In the sculpture entitled *Murou Art Forest* the artist alludes to the Japanese way of understanding space. The greatest inspiration here was the notion of *ma* (emptiness, a spatial and temporal interval). That artistic creation is an abstract geometric form, perfectly harmonised with natural elements. The majestic object was included into its cyclical and smooth rhythm. The artist himself spoke about his work in this way: "*All things that people know come from nature. All forms, hidden or open, can be found in nature. Even those things that exist merely in our imagination, or the subconscious, come from nature.*" (ed. Chrabąszcz 2015: 224)

The harmony mentioned by Karavan is visible in many of his works and both reveals the artist's attachment to the European understanding of shape and space, and is close to the Japanese aesthetics characterized by its transience, evanescence and being underspecified.

Fig.9-10. *Kikar Lewana* (White Square), 1977-1988, Edith Wolfson Park, Tel Aviv, Israel; http://mck.krakow.pl/wystawy/ makom-dani-karavan-esencja-miejsca; https://www.tygodnikpowszechny.pl/kikar-lewana-bialy-plac-28822.

4.4.2. *Murou Art Forest*

Murou Art Forest (1998-2006) is a unique sculpture-architectural complex, the layout of which was created in order to revitalise the Murou area (Uda, Nara Prefecture, Japan) within a government campaign. It is the region in which the oldest Buddhist temples are located. The Nara Prefecture is the cradle of Japan, therefore the artist emphasised the uniqueness of this site through his work. He drew attention to the inseparable ties of man and nature. Karavan introduced elements in keeping with the topography of the land, which besides their artistic overtone were to fulfil a structural role i.e. prevent landslides. The whole work maintains the character of a spatial ritual, in the manner of crossing subsequent zones, stages, orders, arranged rhythmically and preserving their cyclical nature. A narrow water channel, a waving tree-lined avenue, an underground tunnel from which a staircase leads straight into a round concrete platform with water meandering towards wooden piers, they all indicate the motion of the Sun and lead to the astronomical Tower from which one can admire a view of the park, and the cedar-cypress wood enclosed from the south by a water amphitheatre and a scene from the island. (ed. Chrabąszcz 2015: 227)

Fig.11-12. Murou Art Forest, 1998-2006, Murou, Uda, Nara Prefecture, Japan, http://archirama.muratorplus.pl/architek-tura/wspolczesna-architektura-rzezba-pomniki-daniego-karavana,67_4017.html.

5. CONCLUSION

The basic assumption of this work was showing that *site-specific* art is not a visual activity devoid of its roots, but through its ambiguous and multi-dimensional character reaches back to the oldest cultural traditions, and draws on not only related avant-garde trends preceding it, but it is rooted in the history of art and of the environment. There exists a visible connection and relation, both ideological and physical, between changes that occurred throughout centuries in the environment of artistic forms and images. According to the research on the aesthetics of art conducted by Krystyna Wilkoszewska (Prof. dr hab., Institute of Philosophy UJ, Unit of Aesthetics), one can talk about a whole group of significant trends in art emerging in particular periods, which were linked by the so-called "environmental stress". During the 1960s, Rachel Carson wrote a book entitled pt. *Silent Spring* (1962). The author described in it the death of wild nature and its inhabitants as a result of using pesticides in agriculture. The book gained popularity and caused the reassessment and redefinition of opinions concerning environment protection. It contributed to shaping new public awareness and determined the opinion of the world of politics. Traditional values began to be questioned; other relations and connections between art and society were sought after and discovered. A new approach to nature, interpreted as the force generating life, led to the appearance of yet another trend in modern art, namely *environmental art*. That kind of art encompasses works from the borderline of *earth art* or *artworks*, created in landscape. Fauna and flora became a material, a way of naturally combining art with earth. Next tendencies, related to that kind of artistic activity are *minimal art* and *process art,* also created in the 1960s. They expanded previous limits of the artistic language. It was nature itself that was to determine the form and content of a work of art. The idea was to visualise the forces of nature, the processes and phenomena occurring in it. It was art that crossed the boundaries of gallery and museum walls. Entering the space of nature and becoming its part, the *site-specific* art broke the outdated conventions and became entirely free and independent (Wilkoszewska 1993: 226).

NOTES

[1] Spectrum is the visible part of electromagnetic radiation. It involves visible light (and frequently ultraviolet and sometimes infrared). It refers to colour vision in which signals concerning colour are received i.e. the human eye responds to light of varying wavelength. There are primary colours i.e. red, green and blue. Other colours are obtained by mixing them in appropriate proportions.

BIBLIOGRAPHY

Renshaw, A., (2013). *Art & Place. Site-Specific Art. Of the Americas.* New York.

Huysmans, J.-K. (1889). *Certains.* G. Moreau-Degas-Chéret-Wisthler-Rops-Le Monstre-LeFer, ect., Paris.

de Saint-Exupéry, A. (1999). *The Wisdom of the Sands* (Twierdza), Warsaw.

Chrabąszcz, M. ed. (2015). *Dani Karavan. Essence of place*, International Centre of Culture in Kraków. Kraków.

Gage, J. (2010). *Colour and meaning. Art, science and symbolism*, Kraków.

Heidegger, M. (1977). The Age of World Picture In: *Build, Live, Think. Selected essays*, Warsaw.

Kołodziejczyk, K. (2005). Site-specific art and its avant-garde solutions in the cultural space of a historic city, *Czasopismo Techniczne* 6A, pp. 97-107.

Cacha, R. ed. (2001). *Encyclopaedic Dictionary. Physics,* Wrocław.

Wilkoszewska, K. (1993). Ecological Art, *Art and Philosophy* 7, pp. 265-276.

INFLUENCE OF URBANISATION ON HERITAGE REGISTER SITES. RZESZÓW MANOR-GARDEN ENSEMBLES CHANGES OVER TIME

Agnieszka Wójcik
Uniwersytet Rzeszowski, Zakład Architektury Krajobrazu

ABSTRACT

Landscape of Rzeszów dramatically changed within last century. At the beginning of XXth century the city was still small, living in the shadow of other regional centres. Particularly quick urban and territorial development took place after WWII. Within the area of Rzeszów commune remain 7 manor-garden complexes set in XVIIIth and XIXth century. Four of them are recorded in heritage register. Apparently it were not the war acts that brought the greatest damages to the manors and its surroundings. Actually it were extensive investments in 1970's and 1980's. Historical ensembles in Staromieście, Załęże, Zalesie and Słocina after WWII were nationalized and there were allocated different public functions. This investments entailed most often far changes in land use of former manor-park ensembles.
The article depicts changes in landscape of the city in XXth century, especially public investments in planned economy system. Spreading urbanization, particularly location of public services buildings in second half of XXth century changed former spatial structure of manor ensembles.

Keywords
manor park, influence of urban development on heritage sites, heritage protection

1. INTRODUCTION

Rzeszów settlement existing in the valley of Wisłok on the route leading from Kraków to Russia received city rights in 1354. In the initial phase the city developed very slowly, creating a new spatial composition around the main square at a small distance from the original settlement in today's Staromieście. Faster development of the city came under the Austrian annexation, especially after the train connection linking up the biggest centers of northern Galicia - Cracow and Lviv. In the early XXth century, Rzeszów was still a local center, with an area of 7 km², inhabited by about 23,000 people. Until the mid- twentieth century, the city was used as a small service center for the inhabitants of the surrounding villages. The villages belonged to landowners and there were elected attractive places for manors and surrounding gardens. Changing the country's borders after World War II and the establishment of the province of Rzeszow increased the importance of the city, which has become a regional center. At that time, there has been intensive industry development and a large inflow of people. In the 1950s, the city expanded its territory by more than 30 km² and for a decade the population has more than doubled, exceeding 60,000 people (Marcinkowski 2003:9-11). Expropriated after World War II manors were adapted to public functions. The parks surrounding residences were gradually depleted and adajusted to new functions.

2. MANOR PARKS IN HERITAGE REGISTER OVER TIME

2.1. Manor park in Staromieście

Staromieście in XIXth century still called the Old Town, was the actual cradle of Rzeszów, the prelocation settlement (Mamulski 1979:1). In XVth century already existed there a wooden fortified manor house. It was situated along the historical Rus' trade route (Kus 2008) on the high banks of Przyrwa Stream the mouth to Wisłok rive (Mamulski 1979:1). It was created by Rzeszowski family coat of arms Półkozic, derived from the first owner of the town Jan Pakosławic from Stróżyska. At the end of XVIth century along with other Rzeszowski's estates Rzeszow passed into the hands of Mikołaj Spytek Ligęza. After moving city to the north and the construction of the castle mansion became the center of the Old Town folwark farm. From the mid-seventeenth to the late eighteenth century these estates belonged to Lubomirski family. Brick mansion at the site of the present palace was built probably in the second half of XVIIIth century. A one storey building had two corner avant-corps from the front and one in the southern facade. Indebted property (Staromieście, Miłocin and Ruska Village) was sold in 1792 to Ignacy Skrzyński. As a result of affinity and purchases the property eventually went into the hands of Adam Jędrzejowicz, owner of few villages north from Rzeszów (Zaczernie, Trzebownisko, Nowa Wieś) in 1880. Jędrzejowicz family involved Tadeusz Stryjeński, well-known galician architect to rebuild the manor. As a result of this extension there was created spacious 2 storey palace with 17 rooms on the ground floor (Czarnota 2001:80) and an attractive, sculptured facade. Investments covered the surrounding park, which has been enlarged (Mamulski 1979:5) in relation to the area shown on the cadastral map from 1849. The farm and agricultural part was transferred to the territory of the former Obozisko and in the composition there was dragged the northern courtyard. At this time it was also created regular four-piece utility garden (Mamulski 1979:5). On the cadastral map the composition of the park it is not applied. The area of the park was similar to current one (approx. 3 ha). During interwar period park area was expanded again to 4,3 ha. At that time, park layout was separated by a fence from the folwark part, greenhouse and palm house were created.

Landscape park composition was shaped with the major axis defined by the entrance to the palace. Before the front façade there was a lawn, followed by the central clearing with exotic plants. In the western part of the clearing was a tennis court. The eastern part opened up to low flower bed and vast landscape of meadows and pastures spreading towards river Wisłok (Mamulski 1979:6-7). In the eastern part there was linded grove with shrine (Mamulski 1979:21). After land subdivision w 1944 the folwark was divided between locals. Park was used by cooperative 'Jedność' ('Unity'). In the manor there were offices and flats for employees. In the park and cold frames there were grown vegetables. There were also cut trees to make room for new pitch (Czarnota 2001:80, Mamulski 1979:3). In 1947, in the south-east corner of the park stood Monument to the Victims of Terror, commemorating ten people working for railway murdered by the Nazis (Kwiatkowski 2010). When Staromieście was incorporated to Rzeszów, part of the park with the manor was handed over to the Regional Hospital. In 1957, the palace was adjusted to anti-tuberculosis hospital, folwark area was used by the Miejskie Przedsiębiorstwo Motorowe (Municipal Motor Enterprise - currently parking lot) and the Miejskie Przedsiębiorstwo Oczyszczenia (Municipal Cleaning Enterprise - currently Labour Office). Plans for new hospital buildings were prepared in 1955 (1.).

All manor buildings, apart from the palace were demolished over the years. Within approx. 50 years the park-manor complex area was reduced by approx. 2.2 hectares. In the north-eastern part, where there was a gardener's house and greenhouses, Miejskie Biuro Projektowe was build (Municipal Project Office). The old stables were adapted to the offices of the Municipal Cleaning Enterprise, cowshed and piggery served as garages and workshops. In the north-western part of the estate Zakłady Naprawcze Sprzętu Medycznego (Medical Equipment Repair Center) was located. Inventory map (Mamulski 1979: Map No. 8) from this period shows hospital buildings created in the eastern and north-eastern part of the manor-park complex. Location of new hospital buildings destroyed one of the oldest parts of the composition - avenue planted with trees visible on the cadastral map from the mid-nineteenth century. It is possible that its

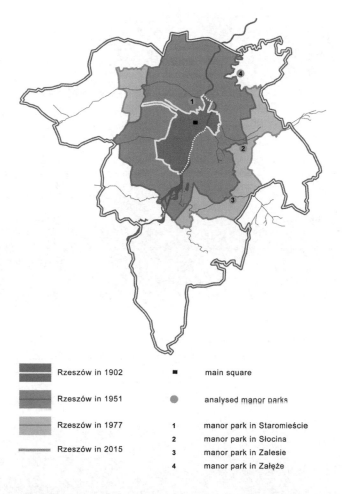

Rzeszów in 1902	■		main square
Rzeszów in 1951	●		analysed manor parks
Rzeszów in 1977	1		manor park in Staromieście
	2		manor park in Słocina
Rzeszów in 2015	3		manor park in Zalesie
	4		manor park in Załęże

Fig.1. Location of analysed manor parks over spatial development of Rzeszów. Prepared by author, according to grafic annex B17 to City Council act No.XXXVII/113/2000 as amended and study of spatial development (http://www.rzeszow. pl/miasto-rzeszow/rozszerzenie-granic-miasta/jak-roslo-nasze-miasto, access 10.01.2016).

history goes back to the days when Staromieście manor was the main residence of the owners of Rzeszów (Mamulski. 1979: 4). At the site of the barn and the granary the first hospital building was establish. In the area of the former vegetable garden there were built boiler-house, dissecting-room and outhouses (Mamulski 1979:11). Gatehouse was demolished. Fenced driveway was introduced from Rycerska Street to the hospital, perpendicular to the main axis. This resulted in a clear division of park into two unequal parts and the complete loss of the integrity of the object. The park manager introduced many changes in the composition, particularly in the immediate vicinity of the palace. Access roads were built both from the front and from the east of the palace, eliminating the flower beds. In the central part of the clearing circular fire tank enclosed by a high net was located, which clearly does not fit to the park composition (Mamulski 1979:12). The health condition of trees at the time was assesed as neglected. In the central clearing dense conifer plantings plantings, as if concealing a new frontier park (Mamulski 1979:20-21). Along the Rycerska Street in the 1970s 10-storey blocks were built, creating a new neighbourhood for the park. After 1979 one more hospital wing was created.

Fig.2. Jędrzejowicz family palace in Staromieście. Picture taken by Edward Janusz between 1896 and 1918.
Courtesy of Krzysztof Szela, director of Regional Museum in Rzeszów.

Fig.3. Former Jędrzejowicz palace, currently regional centre of pulmonary diseases.
Current state. Photo by author.

In 2007 the wall surrounding the park from the south and the east was demolished (Kuś 2008). From that moment the inhabitants can freely enter the area where lately benches and litter bins where introduces. Unfortunately, the devastation of the palace is progressing and today it is hard to see traces of its former glory. Monuments conservator recommends capital restoration and cutting down spruce trees planted in the 1970s too close to walls. It is also hard to imagine the full restoration of the park composition.

2.2. Manor park in Zalesie

The first documentation of restoration of the manor in Zalesie was carried out in 1976, and entry for register of monuments took place two years later. The study preceeded a handover of the estate to the branch of the Agricultural University in Krakow. At that time manor complex covered the area of about 2.6 ha. In 1850 the manor buildings together with the folwark and a small ornamental garden was entirely on left side of the Matysówka Stream. Manor facing south had a view on the river and on the right bank with some greenery, possibly a small forest. It was probably demolished during the construction of the current manor which is one of the administrative buildings of the University of Rzeszów. The new mansion was built probably as a result of remodelling of the brick outbuilding from the end of the nineteenth century. It is situated perpendicular to the road, opposite the former Orthodox church, nowadays the catolic church of Assumption of the Blessed Virgin Mary. Around this time, park was expanded with the part on the other side of Matysówka Stream. It is the only part of the park, where old trees survived. Both parts of the park were connected by a wooden bridge with stairs, which was destroyed during the flood in the 1930s (Peret 1976:3). By the manor there was round bed, alleys were gravel. Orchard was located in the east part of the park. The park was enclosed partially with the brick wall, partially with interwoven picket fence (Peret 1976:3). Behind the palace there was a manor kitchen building. The buildings included also smithy, stables, barns, piggeries, barns, granary and a treadmill. *'Gumiński's folwark was considered as one of the best managed'* (Marcinowski 2003:26). In 1944 parcelation of private properties took place. After 2nd World War it housed primary school, library and post office. In the 1970s the area belonged to the Tyczyn municipality. The mansion was used for residential purposes, among others, as house for teachers. On the east side of the house it was planned to build a school, but the work was halted. This led to significant changes in the spatial arrangement of the older part of the park - stand preserved only on the eastern side (Peret. 1976:8). The whole park was run down with no-maintained paths. Right-bank part of the park was used for arranging festivals and playing football matches. There were also here playing equipment for children (Peret 1976: 5).

Zalesie likewise Słocina in the XVth century belonged to the tyczyński estate (Zachariasz, Hoszowski, Uruska-Suszek 1990). In the 1970s the area belonged to the municipality Tyczyn. The manor was used for residential purposes, among others, as housing for teachers. On the east side of the house it was planned to build a school, but works were halted. However this decision led to significant changes in the spatial arrangement of the older part of the park. It is well preserved only on the eastern side (Peret 1976:8). The whole park was run down, without paved paths. Right-bank part of the park was used for arranging festivals and football matches. There were also playing equipment for children. (Peret 1976:5). According to dendrological cataloguing carried out in 1976 in park there were circa 200 trees. Age of trees was estimated for 70-120 years. In late 1970's park area was similar to the state from 1930's (Peret 1976: 7-8). In 1982-84 during general renovation of the building it was adapted for the needs of Rzeszów branch of the Agricultural University in Kraków. It became administrative building (Wajdowicz 1994). The northern part of the park is a flat area around 1,7 ha (Nowosiad-Sobańska 1997). The oldest trees are preserved in the north part along the Wieniawski street and the east side. Condition of trees was determined as neglected. Remains of the park are in fairly good condition. In the vicinity of the manor there are new university buildings. Manor is available from inside, it belongs to the University of Rzeszów Department of Biology and Agriculture (Libicki 2012: 401).

2.3. Manor park in Słocina

The history of Słocina village is dated for the early XVth century. The village belonged to Zalesko-Tyczyński estate and was owned by the Pileck family. Elżbieta Granowska - third wife of the king Władysław Jagiełło inherited this village after her parents (Zachariasz, Hoszowski, Uruska-Suszek 1990). The village remained in the hands of Pilecki family to the end of the XVIth century, then it was in the possession of the family Kostka, Branicki, Poniatowski and Potocki. The establishment of the manor and the park in the mid-nineteenth century should be associated with Countess Marianna Mostowska and Maurycy Szymanowski. However, it is thought that earlier in this place was well functioning folwark estate. On the cadastral map from 1849 is presented fully formed object - garden in the English style in a picturesque type. The last owners of the property were Anna and Maurycy Chłapowski. After the expropriation of landowners in 1945, Gminna Spółdzielnia Samopomoc Chłopska (Communal Peasant Self-Help Cooperative) took over the manor-park and adjacent farm (Bosak 2007). Initially the manor was used as a dwelling. In the 1950s, in the building functioned postal office, Register Office, and the Gromadzka Rada Narodowa (National Community Council). General renovation conducted in 1961 resulted in numerous modifications of the interior and the loss of equipment. Change of user for the years 1976 - 1978 resulted in another renovation. Almost 20 years it was the headquarters of the orphanage. Former farm was used by Gminna Spółdzielnia Samopomoc Chłopska. Steward house functioned as Teacher's House and then was converted to flats. In area of orchards and vegetable gardens new buildings emerged since 1980's. After the transfer of the orphanage to another place residence was gradually devastated. Since 2008 the southern part of the park along with the manor building belongs to the Diocese of Rzeszów. Unused for almost 20 years building requires general restoration and dense afforestation needs maintenance and clearances. Undertaken works are only aimed at temporary protection. Manor building is very important in park composition. It plays role of a keystone of composition. Originally, the building was typical modest manor in classical style. In the mid-nineteenth century tower annex was added, which gives the building romantic character (Bosak 2007).

Unlike the other analyzed objects, park in Słocina has not changed significantly. The area is very similar to that registered in the cadastral map. Despite the neglection, it is still possible to find in the area many characteristic features for the picturesque style (according to Mitkowska, Siewniak. 1998:187-188). These are mainly freely sketched paths, border merging into the landscape and exposition of the plants with special visual qualities, mainly exotic. Park uses "natural landscape and values of the place," including openings (Zachariasz, Hoszowski, Uruska-Suszek 1990). The main axis was directed at ponds located in the northern part of the complex (Zachariasz, Hoszowski, Uruska-Suszek 1990). The interior of the park was composed by freely growing group of trees. Worth-mentioning is the relationship between the residentional garden and dike limiting the north side and the watercourse Młynówka (Pyrkosz 2001). The landscape surrounding the manor had rural character. In the closest neighbourhood were few houses, mostly wooden. Farm was located to the west part, it was separated by the road of similar line to today's Powstańców Śląskich street. In term of the composition type manor park complex should be considered as mixed in the western part very natural park, in south-eastern part geometric vegetable garden and orchard (Zachariasz 1996). To the folwark buildings were stables, granaries and barns. In the northern part of the park ponds were supplied with water from Młynówka Stream. The hornbeam alley created the western boundary of the complex. In the southern part there were also other buildings such as: so called kitchen or hunting lodge and steward house (Bosak 2007). In the mid-nineteenth century in the north-eastern part of the manor were wooden houses for servants. According to tradition of the villagers in the park there was also an icehouse (Inglot. 1998). In the first half of the XXth century in front of the manor grew hydrangeas and roses (Zachariasz, Hoszowski, Uruska-Suszek 1990). In the interwar period the park was fenced partially with brick wall, partially with wooden fence. On the island there was a chapel, closing the axis (Inglot 1998). At the manor about 30 people were employed, including gardener, cook, blacksmith, driver

(Niemaszek 2010: 32). As a result of the land reform the manor building was severely devastated and needed repair. Stables became empty (Niemaszek 2010: 107).

The object was entered in the register of historic monuments in 1968. Currently, the former composition is slightly illegible. The main road, the entrance gate and the hornbeam avenue are still preserved. Park has been reduced by the construction of roads, creation of new building in folwark, orchard and vegetable gardens area (Piórecki 2008). Park is considered to be in relatively good condition, while manor stay in poor condition (Libicki 2012: 400).

2.4. Manor park in Załęże

Originally existed here one story manor dated back probably to the late XVIIIth century (Polakowski 2012: 423). Załęże and Pobitno folwarks were bought together with Jasionka and Zaczernie by Jan Jędrzejowicz. Cadastral map from 1849 shows how it looked like when Jan Jędrzejowicz was the owner. The whole complex is divided by routes into 3 parts: the eastern part - with manor house probably surrounded by a small decorative garden (lack of documentation), the western part - typically agricultural, with wooden buildings forming a courtyard, the south part - most likely with orchard and home of the gardener. To the east of the whole complex, on the road from the village Załęże was a foresters's lodge. From the west side the folwark was limited by the road (today's Załęska Street). In 1865 the estate was inherited by Władysław Jędrzejowicz from his father. Eclectic manor in Załęże was built or expanded by Tadeusz Stryjeński in 1880-1889 (Kuźniar-Błotko 1994) by a small stream on the north side (Kogut 1983: 6-7). There were added tower and porch with terrace on the first floor. In 1890 Adam Jędrzejowicz, the owner of Staromieście, inherited the estate after his childless brother. In 1903 the property was bought by Potocki family from Łańcut. In the 1930s' the property was passed to Tarnowski family, owners of Dukla and Rudnik. In the interwar period the property was surrounded by a wall (manor house, rządcówka, stables and backyard piggeries in the west, granary and wooden houses for servants). In front of elevation there was a law with rosebed and a small swimming pool. From the west side grew a hawthorn hedge, and the eastern part was framed by hornbeam avenue. Some researchers believe that Stryjeński built the palace in a different place, that the former manor was in different place (Kogut 1983:2-4). The park covering the area of 4.8 ha was created in the late XIXth century.

By 1944, Countess Wanda Tarnowska lived in the palace with her son (Kogut 1983:1). After the agrarian reform the assets were expropriated and manor functioned as hotel for UB (Department of Security) officers. Summer camps for their children were organized here. Piggeries in the northern part of the property continued to perform their function (Kuźniar-Błotko 1994; Kogut 1983: 1). In the years 1949-1956 there was school for UB officers. In 1970 the mansion was adapted for flats for employed in nearby prison. Outbuilding dated probably for the late eighteenth century (perhaps the original mansion) was demolished in 2007. Construction of the prison destroyed the historical spatial arrangement. Remained the brick entrance gate, fence wall fragments and some old trees (Polakowski 2012: 423-424). The palace was renovated in 1971-73. (Kogut 1983). The eastern part was reduced. It is limited by the prison wall. It's northern part (including the granary from the first half of the nineteenth century) has been absorbed by the penitentiary facility. The palace served as living quarters. From the west the area was also reduced. The area for the Zakład Budowlano-Remontowy (Company of Building and Restoration) was separated. There were built administrative building, workshops, sheds used to store building materials and a transformer station. Access road to the house was asphalted and the paths in the park had only curbs, without filler. (Kogut 1983:6-7). Garden elevation has retained its original character, with a two-storey tower and a wide porch supporting the terrace on the first floor. Avant-corps corners are decorated with bossage. The village to the mid-nineteenth century belonged to Łętowski family, then to Jędrzejowicz family. Park is described as neglected. Currently manor is inhabited by many families (Libicki 2012:401). It was entered in register of monuments in 2009.

3. CONCLUSIONS

Analyzed objects are associated with mighty families that had great significance for the development of Rzeszów, region and even whole country. Villages Zalesie and Słocina belonged to wealthy Tyczyński estate, which was ruled by Pilecki family, affinal to the king Władysław Jagiełło. Staromieście called Antiqua Reschow was a place of pre-location settlement. The manor remained an important property for the city owners for few centuries. Manor in Załęże was made as the last and there is not much information about its history. There are a lot of things connecting those objects. Starting with manor complex type - residentional-park complex - with an extensive edible part. All the parks were created in the English style in XIXth century. Like all estates in the country they have been expropriated because of the 1944 agrarian reform. With the territorial development of Rzeszów, after the WWII the parks underwent significant spatial transformations. Firstly, the farm area and edible gardens were parceled. New buildings were created there. Then there were many new investments in the manor parks. The only the manor park in Słocina resisted from vast investments. However it park could not resist the influence of time and the lack of constant care.

Manor Parks in Słocina, Zalesie and Załęże have a common provenance - formerly, all of them were farms. Later, appreciating the proximity to the city center (no more than 4 km), the opportunity to establish a park with representative-leisure functions in an attractive landscape and ease of managing the whole property, the owners started to build manors and surrounding gardens. Palace and park in Staromieście derived from defense court, however folwark part also played a major role there. Worth-mentioning is fact that all the mansions were built nearby streams. Most likely, both from the practical and esthetic reasons. External facades of residential buildings did not change significantly, but the layout and interior design were adapted to the new functions. Currently condition of palaces in Staromieście and Załęże is defined as average. Different kinds of conservation works are required. In the worst condition is Chłapowski manor in Slocina abandoned for almost 20 years. The best preserved building is manor in Zalesie. After the agrarial reform, the authorities had used the expropriated objects for public purposes. This helped meeting the needs of the population in the early postwar years. Along with economic and territorial development of the city and the inclusion of rural areas manors became an attractive area for public investments.

These investments are difficult to assess in terms of monuments conservation. On the one hand, it should be criticized as a programmatic destruction of heritage of 'kulaks', without paying any attention to the timeless values represented by manors. However, analyzing the problem more deeply, the Polish economic realities after World War II should be taken into account. Because of the necessity of providing citizens with the opportunity to live and develop in a country affected by the ravages of war, spatial economy has become very pragmatic. In the empty buildings were located public services, which to this day are considered as an adequate succession of functions for historic monuments. It should also be noted the simple fact that, despite the obvious problems with the management of these objects, they were still in use. This is extremely important because unused objects quickly fall apart. Great example of this is the devastation of the mansion and park in Słocina. In other words, if the objects were abandoned for 70 years, until today probably nothing would have survived.

NOTES

[1] Technical blueprint of regional anti-tuberculosis station in Rzeszów, Krasicki Street. 1955. National Archive. Branch in Rzeszów.

BIBLIOGRAPHY

Bosak, B. (2007). *Karta ewidencyjna zabytków, dwór Rzeszów – Słocina.* Regional Heritage Monuments Protection Office Archive in Rzeszów.

Czarnota, M. (2001). *Rzeszowskie ulice i okolice: gawędy telewizyjno-gazetowe.* Rzeszów: Mittel.

Inglot, T. (1998). *Szkice z dziejów Słociny.* Słocina: Poligrafia Wyższego Seminarium Duchownego w Rzeszowie.

Kogut, S. (1983). *Katalog parków województwa rzeszowskiego. Załęże.* Urząd Wojewódzki w Rzeszowie. Regional Heritage Monuments Protection Office Archive in Rzeszów.

Kuś, M. (2008). *Karta ewidencyjna zabytków. Pałac Jędrzejowiczów w Staromieściu, ob. szpital przeciwgruźliczy.* Regional Heritage Monuments Protection Office Archive in Rzeszów.

Kuźniar-Błotko V. (1994). *Karta ewidencyjna zabytków. Pałac. Rzeszów-Załęże.* Regional Heritage Monuments Protection Office Archive in Rzeszów.

Libicki, P. (2012). *Dwory i pałace wiejskie w Małopolsce i na Podkarpaciu.* Poznań: Rebis.

Mamulski, A. (1978). *Ewidencja zabytkowego parku dworskiego w Staromieściu, Rzeszów-Staromieście, ul. Rycerska 2.* Regional Heritage Monuments Protection Office Archive in Rzeszów.

Cadastral map of Słocina, Staromieście, Zalesie, Załęże. Rzeszów Kreis, Galicja. 1849. National archive. Branch in Rzeszów.

Marcinkowski, M. (2003). *To wszystko działo się w Zalesiu. Cz. I Moje rodzinne Zalesie.* Rzeszów.

Mitkowska A., Siewniak M. (1998). *Tezaurus sztuki ogrodowej.* Warszawa: Oficyna Wydawnicza Rytm.

Niemaszek, R. (2010.) *Żegnaj dawna Słocino.* Warszawa-Rzeszów: Ad Oculos.

Nowosiad-Sobańska, K. (1997). *Aktualizacja inwentaryzacji zieleni i gospodarka drzewostanem w parku podworskim przy ulicy Wieniawskiego.* Rzeszów-Zalesie. Regional Heritage Monuments Protection Office Archive in Rzeszów.

Peret, S. (1976). *Katalog parków województwa rzeszowskiego, gm. Tyczyn, Zalesie.* Regional Heritage Monuments Protection Office Archive in Rzeszów.

Piórecki, J. (2008). *Ogrody i parki dworskie województwa podkarpackiego.* Rzeszów: Procarpathia.

Polakowski, S. (2012) *Pozostałości założeń dworskich województwa podkarpackiego.* Krosno: Lygian.

Pyrkosz, B. (2001). *Słocińskie korzenie.* t. II. praca zbiorowa, Słocina: SP 27 w Słocinie.

Wajdowicz M. (1994). *Karta ewidencyjna zabytków, dwór Rzeszów – Zalesie.* Regional Heritage Monuments Protection Office Archive in Rzeszów.

Zachariasz A., Hoszowski M., Uruska–Suszek D. (1990). *Park dworski im. Władysława Szafera w Słocinie.* Kraków. Regional Heritage Monuments Protection Office Archive in Rzeszów.

Zachariasz, A. (1996). *Plany katastralne ogrodów jako świadectwo rozwoju idei ogrodu angielskiego" (na przykładzie Beskidu Niskiego i Pogórza), t.II Aneksy.* Praca doktorska, promotor: Bogdanowski J. Kraków.

CULTURAL LANDSCAPE OF NOWY KORCZYN.
RELICS OF THE OLD HERITAGE

Dominika Kuśnierz-Krupa
Cracow University of Technology, Faculty of Architecture

ABSTRACT

The former town of Nowy Korczyn is situated in the Ponidzie region, in the Świętokrzyskie Voivodeship, at the border of the Lesser Poland Voivodeship. Since the time of its foundation which took place in the mid-13th century, until the 17th century Nowy Korczyn was among the most important towns in Lesser Poland, which is confirmed by monuments preserved till today in the form of two churches: the post-Franciscan of St. Stanisław from 1257 and the Holy Trinity from the 16th century; the 18th-century synagogue, the medieval market square and relics of historic buildings round the market. Nowadays, it is a forgotten and neglected town with partially preserved relics of its eventful past. The progress of civilisation and not fully controlled development negatively influence the cultural landscape of this exceptional town, as indicated by the article's author. There seems to be no idea here for the revalorisation of historic space and simultaneous tourist-oriented activation of the town. Paradoxically, it is the cultural landscape and eventful past of Nowy Korczyn that offer the town a chance for development.

Keywords

Nowy Korczyn, cultural landscape, heritage, historic buildings, medieval market square

1. INTRODUCTION

The aim of this article is to address the issue of protecting the cultural landscape of a historic town on the example of Nowy Korczyn in the Świętokrzyskie Voivodeship, a centre with eventful past and valuable monuments, which has been badly neglected and in consequence has fallen into oblivion.

At the beginning of this article it is worth considering what a cultural landscape really is and why it requires protection and care. The Heritage Protection and Care of Monuments Act says that cultural landscape is cultural landscape is "a space perceived by people, including natural elements and products of civilisation, historically formed by natural factors and human activity" (ACT from 23 July 2003 concerning heritage protection and care of monuments with later amendments.). Therefore, it can be claimed that cultural landscape is a landscape transformed by man as a result of civilisational development. A cultural landscape consists e.g. of objects and spaces created (built) or formed in the past. They are historic public utility objects (including e.g. religious buildings, town halls), castles, palace-and-garden complexes, residential buildings, as well as market places and town squares. All the mentioned elements of cultural landscape bear evidence of history of a given settlement, the level of its o civilisational development, wealth, and the part it played in the past. Therefore, those objects and spaces should be protected, properly revalorised, as well as taken care of so that they could play a concrete part in the current life and functioning of a settlement.

2. CULTURAL LANDSCAPE OF NOWY KORCZYN – STATE OF RESEARCH

The issues of history of architecture and spatial development in Nowy Korczyn, and subsequently transformations in its cultural landscape still pose a challenge for scientists researching the past of Polish towns. So far, the history of the town was described in a complex way in just one publication entitled: *Nowy Korczyn Throughout Centuries. Sketches from the History of Nowy Korczyn and its Surroundings* (*„Nowy Korczyn przez stulecia. Szkice z dziejów Nowy Korczyn i okolicy"*), published in Kielce in 2001 (Przybyszewski 2001). Besides that there are joint compilations in which the issue of the town history was also addressed. First of all, two studies written by F. Kiryk ought to be mentioned here, namely: *Lesser Poland Towns of the Middle Ages in Modern Times* ("*Miasta małopolskie w Średniowieczu w czasach nowożytnych*") with its chapter entitled "*Town Foundations on the Vistula in the 13th-14th century*" (Kiryk 2013), and *Urbanisation of Lesser Poland: Sandomierz Voivodeship: 13th-14th century* ("Urbanizacja Małopolski: województwo sandomierskie: XIII-XVI wiek") (Kiryk 1994), in which the author presented the history of the town in the Middle Ages i.e. its heyday. Nowy Korczyn is also mentioned in such publications as *Polish Towns in the Millenium* ("*Miasta polskie w Tysiącleciu*") (Siuchniński 1965) and *the Geographical Dictionary of the Polish Kingdom and Other Slavic Countries* ("*Słownik geograficzny Królestwa Polskiego i innych krajów słowiańskich*") (Sulimierski 1883). An analysis of the urban layout of the town was attempted by B. Krasnowolski in his work *Foundation-Town Layouts within the Krakow Region in the 13th and 14th century ("Lokacyjne układy urbanistyczne na obszarze ziemi krakowskiej w XIII i XIV wieku*") (Krasnowolski 2004) . The historic architecture of the town was depicted in a few publications (e.g. Wróblewski 2006, Sypkowie 2003, Ginalska 1999, Lawera 2006), but the most important is undoubtedly the *Catalogue of Art Monuments in Poland*, in which such objects as the church of the Holy Trinity and St. Lawrence and Elizabeth, the church of St. Stanisław the Bishop and the Franciscan monastery, the synagogue, houses on the market square and roadside shrines were characterised in detail (Łoziński 1957).

3. TOWN HISTORY

The beginnings of organised settlement in the area of the later town date back to the 11th century. A that time, a trade settlement of Stary Korczyn had already existed on the right bank of the Nida river, situated along the trade route leading from Krakow to Ruthenia. In 1226, in Stary Korczyn Duke Bolesław Wstydliwy (the Chaste) was born, which proves that the ducal court must have existed here already in the 13th century. Before 1258, that ruler issued the town charter for Nowy Korczyn (Kiryk 2013: 157) which was founded according to the German law on the other side of the river Nida. Supposedly, the locator of the town and its first alderman was Henryk, mentioned in the document bestowing hereditary aldermanship on Hynek (Kiryk 1994: 78).

The town developed rapidly to which, besides numerous privileges, contributed its advantageous location at the crossroads of trade routes and close proximity of the ducal court. In the 14th century, King Kazimierz Wielki erected a masonry castle in Nowy Korczyn which, during the next centuries, hosted almost all Polish monarchs (Zaniewski 2012: 47). The first information about the existence of the castle comes from app. 1370, from Cracow Cathedral Chronicle (Kronika Katedralna Krakowska). Jan Długosz (who lived in Nowy Korczyn in 1421 and attended a school here) wrote in his Liber beneficiorum that the castle in Korczyn was built from fired brick, and had a chapel dedicated to the Holy Trinity and St. Stanisław (Długosz: 438). The castle was situated on an artificial hill measuring app. 100 x 100m, on the right bank of the Nida River, about 100 m south of the chartered town (Wróblewski 2006: 83). The object must have been built on the quadrangular plan. The building was protected by its location on the hill, brick walls on stone foundations and moats. Originally, in the times of Kazimierz Wielki the castle was small. It was extended by Władysław Jagiełło, who also modernised its defensive perimeter. In the 16th century, the complex was repeatedly altered to form a Renaissance residence (Olszacki 2011: 272-273). Since the 17th century, the castle began to lose its importance. The object was badly damaged during the Swedish Deluge (like many other castles in southern Poland e.g. the castle in Skawina (Kuśnierz-Krupa 2012: 43). In the following years it gradually fell into ruin, which ultimately resulted in its demolition in the year 1776 (Wróblewski 2006: 84). Currently there is no trace left of it. As a result of conducted archaeological research only relics of castle walls and moats were discovered (Górska 1963: 215-258).

During the medieval and Renaissance period Nowy Korczyn, thanks to being located in the heart of the then Lesser Poland, was a site of political conventions and noblemen's meetings (Sulimierski 1883: 395). The town developed owing to the favour of subsequent rulers. Besides being involved in erecting a masonry castle, Kazimierz Wielki also founded other masonry buildings in the town and initiated the process of tidying its layout (Sulimierski 1883: 395). In the 15th century, Nowy Korczyn had a town hall, hospital, baths and a water supply system, which undoubtedly confirmed the affluence of its inhabitants (Zaniewski 2012: 47). The dynamic development of Nowy Korczyn was interrupted in 1473, when a fire broke out in the town almost razing it to the ground (Kiryk 1994: 80). Thanks to numerous reductions, e.g. exemption from rent, labour cost and duties, the centre was quickly rebuilt. King Zygmunt August contributed much to the new prosperity of Nowy Korczyn, since he allowed the town to charge bridge and causeway tolls, extended to hospital and gave permission for a new town hall to be built in 1566 (Sulimierski 1883: 395 and Kiryk 2013: 162).

A slow decline of Nowy Korczyn began in the 17th century and was caused e.g. by moving the capital from Krakow to Warszawa, which weakened the political significance of Lesser Poland nobility (Przybyszewski 2001: 55). The town did not rise up during the following centuries. It was harassed by continuous enemy raids (e.g. the Swedish Deluge, the Rakoczy army invasion), numerous fires and plagues. As a result of the Partitions, Nowy Korczyn found itself within the territory under Russian occupation. The downfall of the town was ultimately sealed by the loss of its town rights in 1869.

Fig.1. Town of Korczyn (New town in Korczyn) on a fragment of Heldensfeld map
(Map of Western Galicia) from 1808, Map after: Łódz University Library, sign. K 11627.

4. CULTURAL LANDSCAPE OF THE TOWN – OBJECTS AND SPACES

Religious objects such as the church of the Holy Trinity and St. Lawrence and Elizabeth, the Franciscan church-and-monastery complex, the synagogue, as well as relics of traditional buildings are important elements of the cultural landscape of the town (Fig. 2).

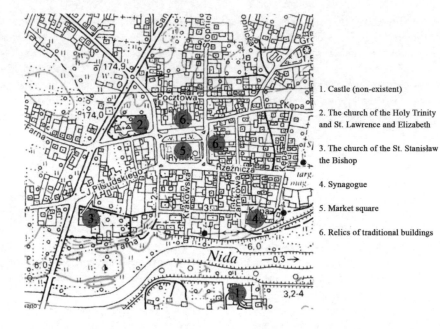

1. Castle (non-existent)

2. The church of the Holy Trinity
and St. Lawrence and Elizabeth

3. The church of the St. Stanisław
the Bishop

4. Synagogue

5. Market square

6. Relics of traditional buildings

Fig.2. Contemporary plan of Nowy Korczyn with significant elements of cultural landscape marked on it.
Prep. by D. Kuśnierz-Krupa.

Fig.3. Church of the Holy Trinity and St. Lawrence and
Elizabeth on a 19th-century sketch.
Photo after:
Archive of the Chair of HAUiSzP WA CUT, s.v.

Fig.4. Church of the Holy Trinity and St. Lawrence and
Elizabeth at the beginning of the 20th century.
Photo after:
Archive of the Chair of HAUiSzP WA CUT, s.v.

Fig.5. Church of the Holy Trinity and St. Lawrence and Elizabeth nowadays.
View across the market square. Photo: D. Kuśnierz-Krupa 2015.

Fig.6. Church of the Holy Trinity and St. Lawrence and Elizabeth nowadays.
View of the front elevation from the west. Photo: D. Kuśnierz-Krupa 2015.

The church of the Holy Trinity and St. Lawrence and Elizabeth is the parish church for Nowy Korczyn. It is located to the north-west of the market square. The earliest mention of its existence came from 1326. It is also known that in the 15th century the church was made of wood, but was completely refurbished in 1608 (Ginalska 1999: 68).

Since 1585 the church belonged to the Jesuits. In its present form the temple includes Gothic, Renaissance and Baroque elements. It is oriented, built from brick and plastered. From the south and east it is surrounded by an old wall. Moreover, the church is encircled with buttresses and has a profiled base course. The presbytery is elongated, three-span, enclosed with a polygon. The main nave has a rectangular shape. The body of the church is encircled with early-Baroque chapels of Our Lady of the Rosary, St. John Cantius and Jesus Christ (Ginalska 1999: 70). The temple is covered with a soaring, gabled roof, while the chapel of St. John Cantius which adjoins the church on the north side – with a pulpit roof. A particularly valuable element of the church is the Baroque main altar with paintings representing the Crucifixion and the Descent from the Cross (Łoziński 1957: 37-38). The object is undoubtedly a very valuable example of religious architecture. Currently it is in good condition, though requires renovation, particularly its external bulk.

The church dedicated to St. Stanisław the Bishop was created as a part of the church-monastery complex. It was erected in the mid-13th century by Bolesław Wstydliwy and his wife Kinga. The church itself was repeatedly extended and modernised. It owes its first transformation to King Kazimierz Wielki; next took place in: the 2nd half of the 15th c., the 17th, 18th and 19th century (Ginalska 1999: 77). The object is oriented and was built from brick in the Gothic style. The oldest part of the church is an early-Gothic presbytery with narrow, ogival windows, to which the monastery wing is attached on the south side. The main nave of the church, originally Gothic, was lowered and altered during the Baroque period. On the south side the nave is adjoined by a rectangular tower. The temple is covered with a soaring, gabled roof. The interior of the church is dominated by Baroque and late-Baroque decoration (e.g. altars, sculptures and paintings). Additionally, in the 18th century the walls were decorated with polychrome painting. Only in few places (mainly in upper sections of the chancel arch wall from the side of the nave) fragments of early-Gothic paintings have been preserved. Currently the church is in a fairly good technical condition, yet it requires constant care, especially as far as the oldest preserved interior elements are concerned.

By the church there is the bell tower, added to it on the north-west side in the mid-18th century. It was built on the plan of a square and was covered with a tent roof. It has two storeys and pilaster divisions. In the basement there is a vestibule with a barrel vault (Łoziński 1957: 41-42).

The Franciscan monastery, adjoining the described church, was built in the mid-13th century. It fell into disrepair in the mid-15th century. It was only after an intervention of Jan Olbracht that the church regained its former glory. Unfortunately, numerous fires which consumed the town in the following centuries resulted in the fact that only the east wing of the Gothic monastery, which adjoins the church on the south side, has been preserved. Currently it serves as a vicarage (Łoziński 1957: 44).

The historic synagogue in New Korczyn is one of the most interesting objects of that type which have been preserved in southern Poland. It was erected in the 2nd half of the 18th century in the classicist style, though some sources claim that on the same site there had been an earlier temple erected in 1659 by the

Fig.7. Franciscan church and monastery complex at the beginning of the 20th century.
Photo after: Archive of the Chair of HAUiSzP WA CUT, s.v.

Fig.8. Church of the St. Stanisław the Bishop nowadays. View of the front elevation from the south-west. Photo: D. Kuśnierz-Krupa 2015.

Fig.9. Synagogue at the beginning of the 20th century. Photo after: Archive of the Chair of HAUiSzP WA CUT, s.v.

Fig.10. Synagogue nowadays. View of the front elevation from the north-east. Photo: D. Kuśnierz-Krupa 2015.

privilege of King Jan II Kazimierz (Kiryk 2013: 157). The synagogue is a two-storey masonry object, built on the rectangular plan, and covered with a gabled roof. On the west side it has a ground-floor porch. In the two-storey section, on the first floor there is a men's room, a matroneum for women, and a room. The altar, also built in the classical style like the whole object, was framed by two columns which supported the tables with commandments. Porches were located in the west elevation on the ground floor (slightly protruding from the face). In the middle there is the entrance opening with two niches on the sides. All these together serve as a pedestal for the eight-column portico of the first floor which is topped with a pediment. Side elevations are divided by pilasters which support a cornice with corbels. After World War II, the object gradually fell into ruin. Its technical condition in 2012 was so critical that local authorities, fearing a construction disaster, undertook short-term protective work in the object. In connection with the above, authorities should be requested to provide funds for carrying out a complete revalorisation of the temple which constitutes a valuable element of the town cultural landscape.

Several examples of traditional buildings characteristic for a small town have been preserved in Nowy Korczyn until today. Relics of those buildings can be mostly admired in the centre, on the market square

Fig.11. Relics of traditional buildings in Nowy Korczyn nowadays. View of the fragment of the north market frontage.
Photo: D. Kuśnierz-Krupa 2015.

Fig.12. Relics of traditional buildings in Nowy Korczyn nowadays.
View of the fragment of the east market frontage. Photo: D. Kuśnierz-Krupa 2015.

(in the north and east frontage). They are one-storey masonry houses, with their broader sides facing the street. In the past, the predominant part of the town buildings were one-storey houses, originally with their gable walls facing the street. Most houses were wooden, though there were few masonry buildings founded by the king or noblemen (Kiryk 2013: 157). Those individual examples of buildings in Nowy Korczyn, which have been preserved till today, ought to be given conservation protection and their owners should be assisted in the process of obtaining funds for renovation.

Besides the already mentioned historic object, the cultural landscape of the town is also, or primarily, created by the market square laid out during the medieval period. Even the initial analysis of the layout allowed for stating that the town was measured out in two stages. First, the market square measuring probably 3 x 2.5 large Krakow 'sznur' and covering the area of app. 1.4 ha was established, and then a single strip of building blocks around the market square. The urban layout of Nowy Korczyn resembles the plan of Skawina which also developed in two stages (Kuśnierz-Krupa 2012: 34). A minor inaccuracy in the assumed regular planning of the market square is visible in the north frontage, which can be associated with its additional measuring after the fire that consumed the town in 1473. However, it is only a hypothesis requiring further research.

Fig.13. Fragment of the market square in the 2nd half of the 20th century. View from the east onto a fragment of the north frontage and the north-west corner. Photo after: Archive of the Chair of HAUiSzP WA CUT, s.v.

Fig.14. Fragment of the market square nowadays. View from the west onto fragments of the north and east frontages. Photo: D. Kuśnierz-Krupa 2015.

5. SUMMARY

Since the time of its foundation, Nowy Korczyn was among the most important towns in the then Lesser Poland, which is confirmed by the historic objects and the medieval market square preserved until today. Currently it is a forgotten and neglected centre with relics of its eventful past. What seems to be lacking is an idea for revalorisation of the historic space with simultaneous tourist activation of the town. Despite the recently conducted revitalisation work of the market square (Złowodzki 2011: 287-307) the town has not risen from stagnation, and its cultural landscape, which has so far been created by e.g. its small-town buildings, is slowly dying. This process of deterioration ought to be stopped as soon as possible; otherwise the town will share the fate of other settlements - nondescript, anonymous, falling into oblivion. In the author's opinion, making appropriate use of the eventful history of the town and its cultural landscape could offer a real chance for the development of Nowy Korczyn. For this purpose, continuation of revalorisation and revitalisation work in the town is called for. One should prepare a conservation project for a complete refurbishment of the synagogue, and think how to include the object in the calendar of cultural events in the town and region. A panorama of the town is also a part of its cultural landscape. The one in Nowy Korczyn is relatively well preserved. Besides houses, it currently consists of two churches and (in the view from the east) the synagogue. The silhouette differs from the medieval one because it lacks the two predominant features which no longer exist: the castle and the town hall.

Among conservation demands referring to the preservation of the cultural landscape of Nowy Korczyn one should add the need to take particular care of relics of the market square buildings, since those objects require revalorisation. Town authorities also ought to consider the possibility of involving the town in the system of educational routes functioning in the region. The first step towards revalorisation of Nowy Korczyn has already been taken: the surface of the market square has been modernised. Now it's time for further action, in order to preserve the cultural landscape of this unusual town for next generations.

BIBLIOGRAPHY

Długosz, J. (1863-1864). Liber beneficiorum dioecesis Cracoviensis. V.2. In: Joannis Dlugossii senioris canonici Cracoviensis Opera omnia, cura Alexandri Przezdziacki edita. Kraków: Ex typographia Kirchmajeriana.

Ginalska, T. (1999). Nowy Korczyn - gmina u zbiegu Wisły i Nidy. Krosno: Apla.

Górska, I. (1963). Archeologiczne badania na terenie średniowiecznego zamku w Nowym Korczynie, powiat Busko. In: W. Antoniewicz, P. Biegański, ed., Archaeological research in the Wiślica area. Warszawa: PWN, pp. 213-259.

Łoziński, J. and Wolff, B. (1957). Katalog Zabytków Sztuki w Polsce. Vol. III. Kieleckie Voivodeship. P.1. Busko District. Warszawa: Państwowy Instytut Wydawniczy.

Kiryk, F. (1994). Urbanizacja Małopolski: województwo sandomierskie: XIII-XVI wiek. Kielce: Regional Centre for Cultural Environment Studies and Protection.

Kiryk, F. (2013). Miasta małopolskie w Średniowieczu w czasach nowożytnych. Kraków: Avalon.

Krasnowolski, B. (2004). Lokacyjne układy urbanistyczne na obszarze ziemi krakowskiej w XIII i XIV wieku, P. II. Catalogue of foundation-town layouts. Kraków: AP.

Kronika Katedralna Krakowska. (1874-1883). In: Monumenta Poloniae Historica. Vol.2. Kraków: Publ. F. Piekosiński.

Kuśnierz-Krupa, D. (2012). Skawina w średniowieczu. Zagadnienia urbanistyczno-architektoniczne. Kraków: CUT.

Lawera, H. and Bata, A. (2006). Gmina Nowy Korczyn. Krosno: Apla.

Olszacki, T. (2011). Rezydencje królewskie prowincji małopolskiej w XIV wieku - możliwości interpretacji.

Czasopismo Techniczne - Technical Transactions. Architecture series, V. 7-A/2011, pp. 251-297.

Przybyszewski, S. M. and Bienias, A. (2001). Nowy Korczyn przez stulecia. Szkice z dziejów Nowego Korczyna i okolicy. Kielce: AW Gens.

Siuchniński. M. ed., (1965). Miasta polskie w Tysiącleciu. Wrocław, Warszawa, Kraków: Zakład Narodowy im. Ossolińskich.

Sulimierski F., Chlebowski B. and Walewski W. ed., (1883). Słownik geograficzny Królestwa Polskiego i innych krajów słowiańskich. V. IV. Warszawa: Publ. W. Walewski.

Sypkowie. A. R. (2003). Zamki i warownie ziemi sandomierskiej. Warszawa: Trio.

Wróblewski. S. (2006). Zamki i dwory obronne województwa sandomierskiego w Średniowieczu. Nowy Sącz: Gold Druk.

Zaniewski. P. A. (2012). Zamki Kazimierza Wielkiego. Kraków: Arco.

Złowodzki M., Wiszowany A. and Zawada-Pegiel K. (2011). Koncepcja rewitalizacji Nowego Korczyna. *Czasopismo Techniczne - Technical Transactions. Architecture series,* V. 5A/2011, pp. 287-307.

RANKING OF THE PROJECTED CULTURAL PARKS OF THE LUBELSKIE VOIVODESHIP IN TERMS OF PROVIDING CULTURAL ECOSYSTEM SERVICES

Barbara Sowińska-Świerkosz

Department of Landscape Ecology and Nature Conservation, University of Life Sciences in Lublin

ABSTRACT

The aim of the manuscript is to assess cultural ecosystem services (CES) for the selected projected cultural parks (CP) of the Lubelskie voivodeship. The implementation of this goal adopted a four-stage procedure: (1) typological analysis of a set of projected CP; (2) selection of representative areas; (3) analysis of aesthetic, recreational, cultural heritage, cultural diversity and educational services; (4) comparison of parks and determination of their ranking in terms of services provision. The assessment involves ascribing grading points to each of the subcategories of CES, and then summing them to determine the overall benefits generated by a given site. The result showed that 7 typological groups were distinguished in the analysed set of cultural parks, and that 5 parks are of unique features and cannot be included in any of the groups. The highest rank in terms of generating benefits was attributed to the Nadwiślański CP and the Renaissance City Complex of Zamość CP, and the lowest to the Hrubieszowski CP. The novelty of the adopted approach is to reflect the intangible character of CES in an objective manner.

Keywords
cultural ecosystem services, cultural parks, lubelskie voivodeship, numerical values

1. INTRODUCTION

The term ecosystem services means a set of products and functions that are useful to human society, satisfying their fundamental needs and have a direct impact on human health and material well-being (Solon 2008: 26). In other words, these are the elements of nature which are directly consumed, felt or used to enhance human well-being (Boyd and Banzhaf 2007: 617). According to the classification of the Millennium Ecosystem Assessment (MEA 2005:7) ecosystem services are divided into four basic categories: provisioning, regulating, supporting and cultural services. This document stresses that the first three categories are of tangible character, while the cultural services (CES) refer to non-material values and / or benefits. They are defined as 'the non-material benefits people obtain from ecosystems through spiritual enrichment, cognitive development, reflection, recreation and aesthetic experiences'. There is a large number of CES categorization. The most frequently analysed are services such as: aesthetic, recreational, spiritual and religious, educational, inspirational, relating to cultural heritage, and those which refers to social relations and the spirit of the place (Costanza et al. 1997; Darvill and Lindo 2015, Hein et al. 2006; Millennium Ecosystem Assessment 2005). Some researchers also define more detailed classifications covering services such as: therapeutic values (Alessa et al. 2008), the possibility of choice (Chan et al. 2012) or the calm (Norton et al. 2012). However, despite of the extensive categorization of

CES and many theoretical discussions concerning their essence, in practice they are rarely identified and so far have been assessed only marginally (Schaich et al. 2010: 270). This is due to the fact that there are many problems in their identification. They concern in particular: the intangible nature of this category of services - some values cannot be appreciated without their direct experience (Chan et al. 2012: 11-12), the difficulty of monetary their evaluation (Schaich et al. 2010: 270), the problem of determination of the scale of research or identification of the appropriate landscape unit (Martín-López et al. 2009: 1057-1058), the replacement used and blending of the concepts of "services", "benefits" and "values" (Boyd and Banzhaf 2007: 2200-222; Chan et al. 2012: 12-13), and the difficulty in recognition of the importance of different cultural services categories (Gilipin, 2000).

Despite of the numerous methodological difficulties, however, there are still ongoing work aimed to identify the CES and to integrate them into the overall scheme of ES assessment. Simultaneously with sociological analysis (Wilson and Howarth 2002), economic valuation (Kumar and Kumar 2008) and determination of the spatial location of services (Brown and Raymond 2007), there is an approach originating from cultural landscape research (Schaich et al. 2010). For both areas (ecosystems services and cultural landscape research) mutual is the determination of social expectations regarding landscape and the assessment of benefits which people may receive from environment. Commonly accepted definition of landscape which based on the European Landscape Convention (ELC 2000) emphasizes that the social dimension of the landscape is not limited to the negative human impact on the ecosystem and to benefits he gained, but primarily includes people emotions and feelings and human intellectual and socio-economic contribution, which in many cases enriches the diversity of the landscape and creates its specificity. Hence, the cultural landscape research offering a methodology to evaluate cultural services at regional and local level (Schaich et al. 2010).

At the local level, cultural parks (CP) are areas which undoubtedly should be an important CES provider. This form of protection was introduced by the Protection of Monuments Law (2003), defining it as 'a specific area established to protect cultural landscape and preserve the outstanding areas with monuments typical for the local tradition of building and settlement'. Such areas should be characterized by the space historically shaped by human activities, containing products of civilization and the elements of nature. As areas with a high share of monuments they are important areas for scientific research. The presence of harmonious natural-cultural landscape usually makes them popular tourism destinations. Besides, as defined in the Law they feature high aesthetic values and high degree of landscape diversity. According to the data from the National Heritage Board of Poland (http://www.nid.pl/en/), so far 30 cultural parks have been established in Poland (state 31 December 2015). However, despite of the number of methodological studies (Kałamucka 2008) and the development of a list of proposed cultural parks (Spatial Development Plan of the Lublin voivodship, 2002) to the end of the 2015 any of such type of area has been created in Lublin province.

The aim of the study was to establish the ranking of the projected in Lublin province cultural parks in terms of CES providing. In order to simplify the work, the analysis were concentrated on objects (parks) which are representative for groups defined as a result of typological analysis. As a result, areas which should be first of all taken under protection have been identified.

2. METHODOLOGY

2.1. Typological analysis

In the first stage of the research was executed a typological analysis of projected cultural parks of the lubelskie voivodeship. In order to define mutual similarity between parks, a hierarchical clustering method with squared Euclidean distance was applied. The analysis employed software called Dendrite specifically designed for this purpose. The list of areas was based on the proposal of cultural parks according to the Spatial Development Plan of the lubelskie voivodeship (2002) containing 47 objects. Ten variables were selected to reflect the diversity of resources, values and state of maintenance of cultural objects. There were: (1) type of park; (2) park' spatial extent; (3) the period of creation of key cultural objects; (4) dominant type of buildings; (5) type of cultural landmarks; (6) share of historical monuments; (7) state of maintenance of cultural heritage; (8) the significance of natural elements; (9) type of natural landmarks; (10) rank of an area as cultural centre (Table 1). Those criterion also affect the level of CES provided by given area. This approach permits grouping parks located in various parts of the study area into so-called "clusters" (typological groups) with a maximum possible similarity of the selected variables (Sowińska and Chmielewski 2012: 279; Sowińska-Świerkosz and Soszyński 2014: 145). As a result, a dendrite graph was obtained illustrating distance between objects – the measure of their similarity. The mutual spatial relation between these objects allowed for classifying them into typological groups. This operation allowed in the next stage of the research selecting from a parks' set areas with common high cultural heritage heterogeneity constituting the detailed study areas for the further stages of the study.

2.2. Assessment of cultural ecosystem services

Due to the specificity of study areas services assessment was focus on following subcategories deriving from Millennium Ecosystem Assessment (2005): aesthetic, recreational, cultural heritage values, cultural diversity and educational values. The assessment was executed based on a standard model used in landscape valorisation. It involves ascribing grading points to each of the subcategories of CES, and then summing them to determine the overall benefits generated by a given site. The 5-point grading scale was adopted to reflect the diversity of resources of analysed areas. In the case of recreational benefits the overall assessment was based on a mean score obtained for all 3 sub-indices. The ranking criterions referring to each analysed subcategory are presented below.

2.2.1. Aesthetic values

According to MEA (2005: 40), many people find beauty or aesthetic value in various aspects of ecosystems. It is difficult, however, to predict which element of environment would contribute to perceived beauty as each person ascribe different values to different landscape components (Kumar and Kumar 2008: 815-818). But as suggested Jagt et al. (2014) the majority of people perceive landscape harmony in the same way (to a certain extent). Thus, aesthetic values may be assess as the level of landscape harmony.

Level of harmony (LH) – based on the presence of disharmonious building and other man-made elements such as wind power plants, high-voltage network etc.: (1) Very low; (2) Low; (3) Medium; (4) High; (5) Very high.

2.2.2. Cultural heritage values

MEA (2005: 40) states that 'many societies place high value on the maintenance of either historically important landscapes ("cultural landscapes") or culturally significant species'. The rang of those values inter alia reflects by a form of the legal protection of a cultural site resulting from public debate (Turner et al. 2014: 91). Thus cultural heritage values of parks may be reflects by the number of historical objects under legal protection.

Number of protected objects (NPO) (relatively to the area of projected park) – based on the list of historical monuments of the lubelskie voivodship, status 31 December 2014 (Decree No. 1/2015): (1) Very low; (2) Low; (3) Medium; (4) High; (5) Very high.

Table 1. The description of selected vectors of differentiation of units (table by author)

	Variables		Vectors of internal diversity
I	Type of park	1	Archaeological
		2	Fortress
		3	The historic centers of cities and smaller towns with preserved historic urban structure
		4	Residential
		5	The harmonious landscape with historical monuments of different types
II	Park' spatial extent	1	Single space complex
		2	Village or town
		3	City or part of the city
		4	Complex of villages
		5	Rural areas
III	Period of creation of key cultural objects	1	To the half of X century
		2	Since the end of the first half of X century to XV century (Middle Ages)
		3	Since the beginning of XVI century to the first half of XVII century (Renaissance)
		4	Since the half of XVII century to the first half of XVIII century (Baroque)
		5	Since the half of XVIII century to the first half of the XX century (1939) (classicism, eclecticism, art nouveau, modernism)
IV	Dominant type of buildings	1	Defense constructions
		2	Sacral buildings
		3	Palaces or manor buildings
		4	Residential buildings (houses, cottages)
		5	Other type
V	Type of cultural landmarks	1	Temple
		2	Palace or manor house
		3	Castle, fort, fortifications
		4	Mound, slavic burgwall
		5	Other type
VI	Share of historical monuments	1	Insignificant
		2	Slight
		3	Moderate
		4	High
		5	Very high
VII	State of maintenance of cultural heritage	1	Very good
		2	Good
		3	Average
		4	Bad
		5	Residual
VIII	Significance of natural elements (in relation to cultural elements)	1	Key
		2	Equivalent
		3	Complementary
		4	Slight
		5	Lack
IX	Type of natural landmarks	1	Landforms
		2	Water (river, lake, ponds)
		3	Forests
		4	Open green spaces
		5	Lack
X	Rank of an area as cultural centre	1	International or national
		2	Transregional
		3	Regional or sub-regional
		4	Supralocal
		5	Local

2.2.3. Cultural diversity

According to MEA (2005: 40) 'the diversity of ecosystems is one factor influencing the diversity of cultures'. However, in the case of designation of cultural parks more importance is put on the diversity of cultural objects, than of ecosystems. Thus, the rank of park in terms of providing this subcategory of CES may be reflecting as a number of different types of landscape elements, such as fortifications, castles, palaces, temples,

Number of different type of cultural objects (NTO) – based on the list of historical monuments of the lubelskie voivodeship: (1) Very small; (2) Small; (3) Medium; (4) High; (5) Very high.

2.2.4. Recreational benefits

The assessment of recreational benefits was based on MEA (2005: 40) which states that 'people often choose where to spend their leisure time partly based on the characteristics of natural or cultivated landscapes in a particular area'. Thus, the diversity and wildness of natural landscape and the state of traditional landscape preservation may be treated as a predictors of area attractiveness as a tourist resort. Thus, the assessment to this subcategory was based on 3 below criterions:

Diversity of natural landscape (D) – based on the variety of land forms and number of different, natural land cover forms: (1) Very low; (2) Low; (3) Medium; (4) High; (5) Very high.

Level of wildness of natural landscape (LW) – based on the presence of not-transformed water, peat-bog and forest ecosystems: (1) Very low; (2) Low; (3) Medium; (4) High; (5) Very high.

State of preservation of traditional cultural landscape (SP) – based on the share of traditional rural buildings: cottages, farm building, windmills, chapels etc. and/or historical tenement houses: (1) Very low; (2) Low; (3) Medium; (4) High; (5) Very high.

2.2.5. Educational values

MEA (2005: 40) states that 'ecosystems and their components and processes provide the basis for both formal and informal education in many societies'. However, the specificity of study area indicates that educational values mainly served man-made objects. The key role in this field play: museums, open-air museums, and regional memorial hall.

Number of museums (NM): (1) Very small; (2) Small; (3) Medium; (4) High; (5) Very high.

3. CONTENTS

3.1. Results

3.1.1. Results of typological analysis

As a result of the typological analysis 7 groups were distinguished in the analysed set of cultural parks (A-G). The additional 8th group (H) included parks with exceptional features which due to their unique character cannot be classified to any of the selected groups. There are units Nos. 9, 25, 28, 29, 41) (Table 2).

The most numerous is typological group A which composed of ten cultural parks (Nos. 15, 17, 26, 27, 31, 36, 39, 41, 46, 47). They represent harmonious rural landscape with many historic buildings of different state of preservation originating from the turn of the XIX/XX century (two objects located peripherally in relation to the center of group originating from the Middle Ages). Characteristic is the dominance of residential buildings and an existence of a specific type of cultural landmarks.

Table 2. The list of projected cultural park belonging to each typological group and vectors of internal differentiation assigned to each variable

No.	Projected cultural park	Assigned vectors of internal differentiation									
		I	II	III	IV	V	VI	VII	VIII	IX	X
	Group A										
15	Okrzejski Cultural Park	5	5	5	4	5	1	3	3	4	5
17	Cultural Park Florianka	5	2	5	4	5	1	1	1	3	5
26	Cultural Park Siedliszcze	5	4	5	4	2	3	4	3	4	5
27	Cultural Park Stołpie	5	5	2	1	3	2	4	3	1	4
31	Podlaski Cultural Park	5	5	5	4	5	4	2	2	4	4
36	**Roztoczański Cultural Park**	5	5	5	4	5	2	3	1	2	3
39	Studziański Cultural Park	5	5	5	1	5	1	4	3	1	4
42	Urzędowski Cultural Park	5	4	2	4	5	3	3	3	5	4
46	Wyrycki Cultural Park	5	5	5	4	5	2	4	3	3	5
47	Żółkiewski Cultural Park	5	5	5	4	5	1	3	2	1	5
	Group B										
1	Archeological Cultural Park (Łubcze–Hubinek–Posadów)	1	5	1	1	4	2	5	2	1	4
5	Horodyski Cultural Park	1	5	1	5	4	2	5	4	3	3
6	**Hrubieszowski Cultural Park**	1	5	1	5	4	2	5	4	4	1
	Group C										
19	Cultural Park Horostyta	5	5	4	2	1	2	2	3	3	5
30	Pawłowski Cultural Park	5	5	5	4	1	2	2	3	3	5
37	Sawiński Cultural Park	5	5	5	4	1	2	3	3	3	5
40	Suchowolski Cultural Park	5	5	5	4	1	2	2	3	4	5
45	**Wojsławicki Cultural Park**	5	5	5	4	1	2	3	3	4	5
	Group D										
7	**Jabłoński Cultural Park**	4	1	5	3	2	2	3	3	5	5
18	Cultural Park Hola	5	2	5	4	1	2	2	4	4	5
24	Cultural Park Rejowiec	5	3	5	2	2	3	3	4	5	5
34	Romanowski Cultural Park	3	1	5	3	2	1	2	3	4	5
44	Wohyński Cultural Park	5	2	5	4	1	1	2	5	4	5
	Group E										
10	Łukowski Cultural Park	3	2	5	4	1	4	2	5	5	4
11	**Międzyrzecki Cultural Park**	3	3	5	4	1	4	2	4	5	4
16	Parczewski Cultural Park	3	2	2	4	1	3	2	4	5	4
21	Cultural Park Kocka	3	3	5	4	2	3	2	5	5	4
	Group F										
2	Bialskopodlaski Cultural Park	5	5	4	4	2	4	2	3	3	3
12	Mysłowski Cultural Park	5	4	5	4	2	4	3	4	4	4
13	**Nadwiślański Cultural Park**	5	5	3	4	3	5	1	1	2	1
14	Nałęczowski Cultural Park	5	4	5	4	5	5	2	1	1	2
22	Cultural Park Leśna Podlaska	5	4	4	4	1	4	2	2	3	5
23	Cultural Park Łabunie	4	4	4	4	2	5	2	3	4	5
	Group G										
3	Chełmski Cultural Park	3	3	4	2	1	4	2	3	1	3
4	Czemiernicki Cultural Park	3	5	4	2	2	3	2	2	2	5
8	Kodeński Cultural Park	3	2	4	2	1	3	2	4	2	4
20	Cultural Park Jabłeczna	3	2	5	2	1	4	5	2	2	5
32	South Roztocze Cultural Park	3	2	5	2	1	2	3	2	1	5
33	Radzyński Cultural Park	4	3	4	3	2	4	2	1	2	4
35	Różański Cultural Park	4	1	5	3	2	4	4	3	2	5
38	**Sosnowicki Cultural Park**	3	2	5	2	2	3	1	2	2	4
43	Włodawski Cultural Park	3	3	5	2	1	4	2	4	2	4

(cont.)

	Group H										
9	Kryłowski Cultural Park	2	1	3	1	3	2	5	2	1	4
25	**Renaissance City Complex of Zamość Cultural Park**	3	3	3	4	5	5	1	5	5	1
28	**Cultural Park Świerże**	4	1	5	3	5	2	4	3	2	5
29	**Cultural Park of Brześć Fortification**	2	4	5	1	3	4	4	1	1	2
41	Tyszowiecki Cultural Park	1	5	2	1	3	2	5	1	1	1

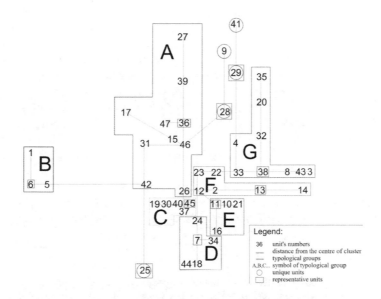

Fig.1. Dendrite of the typological diversity of projected cultural parks of the lubelskie voivodship presenting typological groups and representative objects.

The least numerous is typological group B which composed of 3 objects (Nos. 1, 5, 6). They are archaeological parks covering a vast rural areas, with a slight contribution of remains of defense constructions originating from Before Christ. This group is very homogeneous as to 6 variables were assigned the same vectors of internal differentiation. Besides, it significantly differs from other groups, which illustrates its peripherals location on dendrite diagram (Fig. 1).

High internal homogeneity also characterized group C (Nos. 19, 30, 37, 40, 45) composing of areas featuring the harmonious rural landscape with a slight share of historical objects of good or average state of preservation originating from the turn of the XIX/XX century. Typical is the dominance of residential buildings and temples constituting cultural landmarks. Besides, characteristic is the existence of natural landmarks in the form of forests or open green spaces being of complementary significance in the relation to the cultural heritage. The rank of all areas belonging to this cluster is local.

Characteristic for group D (Nos. 7, 18, 24, 34, 44) is the insignificant or slight share of historic buildings, originating since the half of XVIII century to the first half of the XX century, which are in good or average state of preservation. Cultural landmarks constituting temples or palaces/manor houses and natural ones open green areas. The rank of all areas belonging to this cluster is local.

Cultural parks belonging to group E (Nos. 10, 11, 16, 21) constituting historic centers of cities and smaller towns with preserved historic urban structure mainly dating from XIX century. There are characterized by the high or moderate share of historical buildings preserved in good condition, a temple as a cultural landmark and the lack of natural landmarks. The rank of all areas belonging to this cluster is supra-local.

The complex of towns with high or very high share of historic buildings preserved in good or very good condition belong to group F (Nos. 2, 12, 13, 14, 22, 23). Those areas differ in the type of landmarks, but common for them is the dominance of residential buildings.

Group G (Nos. 3, 4, 8, 20, 32, 33, 35, 38, 43) composed of the historic centers of cities and smaller towns or residential complexes buildings from the Baroque of later periods. The share of historic buildings is high or moderate. Characteristic for this group is the presence of cultural landmarks in a form of a temple or a palace/minor house and existence of natural landmarks such as peculiar forms of land relief or surface waters. This cluster features the highest internal diversity as there is a lack of variable with same vector assigned to all objects.

The most significant variables in the grouping process occurred to be: type of the park, period of creation of key cultural objects and dominant type of buildings. For example, harmonious rural landscape characterized 3 typological groups, and the high contribution of residential buildings 4 groups. On the other hand, share of historical monuments, significance of natural elements and type of natural landmarks proved to be of the lowest significance. Type and importance of natural objects were only crucial in the case of distinguishing groups C and E.

At the next stage of the works, constituting the essence of typological analysis 10 cultural parks representative for selected groups were selected, including one object from each typological group, and three objects from the group of parks possessing exceptional features (H). The selection criterion was the park representativeness of each group reflecting by its location on the dendrite graph (marked by the red square). As a results was selected parks Nos. 6, 7, 11, 13, 25, 28, 29, 36, 38, 45 (in bold in Table 2).

3.1.2. Results of cultural ecosystem services assessment

In the next stage of the study was defined the rank of representative cultural parks in terms of providing services. The highest rank was attributed to the Nadwiślański CP (21.33 points). Similar high rank was also given to the Renaissance City Complex of Zamość CP (21.00 points) (Table 3).

This position derives from the fact that both parks provided plenty of cultural diversity and educational services. Moreover, Nadwiślański CP features unique recreational values of Vistula river, loess ravines, and multispecies forests. Whereas, the Renaissance City Complex of Zamość CP obtained the highest rank in the term of aesthetic and cultural services due to the presence of well-preserve historical urban structure. Rest of the analysed areas provided much lower cultural benefits. For example, the third position with 15 point was given to the Cultural Park of Brześć Fortification possessing high rank in terms of aesthetic and cultural heritage subcategories, but low of educational and moderate of recreational. Other projected parks are of similar significance as regards CES – between 11 and 14 points. This resulted from the fact that they provided either high aesthetic and/or cultural or recreational services. The lowest rank from the analysed set of objects was attributed to the Hrubieszowski CP (11.00 points) covering the archeological site. In adopted criterions it provides no educational benefits (lack of museum and similar institutions) and very low cultural diversity services (presence of one type of cultural object – archeological structures).

4. CONCLUSIONS

4.1. The new approach of CES assessment

The proposed concept presents a new approach of the assessment of ecosystem services. It attempts to propose an objective way of CES presentation, including the categories of intangible nature such as

Table 3. The ranking of representative cultural parks in terms of providing cultural services

Projected cultural park representative for each typological group			Rank of CES subcategories							Total	Rank
			Aesthetic	Cultural heritage	Cultural diversity	Recreational			Educational		
Typological group	No	Name	LH	NPO	NTO	D	LW	SP	NM		
A	36	Roztoczański CP	5	2	2	3	4 3.67	4	1	13.67	4
B	6	Hrubieszowski CP	5	2	1	4	4 3.00	1	0	11.00	9
C	45	Wojsławicki CP	4	2	4	2	1 2.33	4	0	12.33	6
D	7	Jabłoński Cultural Park	4	2	3	2	1 1.67	2	1	11.67	8
E	11	Międzyrzecki CP	4	4	3	1	1 2.00	4	1	14.00	4
F	13	Nadwiślański CP	3	5	5	5	4 4.33	4	4	21.33	1
G	38	Sosnowicki CP	4	3	3	2	2 2.33	3	1	13.33	5
H	25	Renaissance City Complex of Zamość CP	5	5	5	1	0 2.00	5	4	21.00	2
H	28	Cultural Park Świerże	5	2	3	2	2 2.00	2	0	12.00	7
H	29	Cultural Park of Brześć Fortification	4	4	3	3	3 3.00	3	1	15.00	3

aesthetic values. It enable the use of a numerical value reflecting the rank of a given cultural park in terms of generating benefits. The approach may be further developed and ranking scheme may be adopted to other CES subcategories, such as religious or social relation values. It would simplify the assessment of services not only in relation to cultural parks, but if modified and extended, of more subcategories of other types of areas.

Clearly, the approach does not resolve the problem of monetary evaluation of CES, which is emphasized by many authors (Chan et al. 2012: 11-12; Satz et al. 2013: 676-680). However, many authors stated that due to their intangible character cultural services cannot be treated as other ES categories and cannot be fully reflected as a certain amount of money (Baron and Spranca 1997; Brosius 2010; Hernández-Morcillo et al. 2013; Tetlock 2003). It is also proved by review of literature as, apart from recreation benefits, there is a lack of examples of monetary evaluation of other CES categories. Besides, such economic approach also implies that all values are for sale, even religious and spiritual (Spash 2008: 265-267). Besides, as stated Gilipin (2000) there are universal values (courage, honesty, happiness) as well as the relative value of a thing (monetary value). For economists only count the value of having a direct impact on material benefits, but research has shown that in the process of individual assessment a key role plays the quality of life (clean air, water, green) and sensory qualities, as well as emotions and moods associated with a place, and consequently determining the assessment (Kumar and Kumar 2008: 816).

The manuscript also takes a voice in the discussion of the need of distinction among services, benefits and values (Boyd and Banzhaf 2007; Chan et al. 2012; Fisher et al. 2009, Groot et al. 2005; Schaich et al. 2010). In the proposed approach CES are treated as values possessing by a certain area not as direct benefits that generate. Those values are understood in two different ways. The rank of cultural heritage and educational values reflects the opinion of general public resulted in an establishment of protected or educational object (Turner et al. 2014). Aesthetic, cultural diversity and recreational values are based on the visible landscape features and its state what can be assess via the observation in the field. Thus, it reflects the way in which the majority of the people percept the landscape and evaluate it. Such approach is mutual with Chan et al. (2012: 14) conception, which in reference to ES proposed to define values as preferences, principles and virtues which perceive a single people as well as the general public.

4.2. General conclusion based on the results

Firstly, discuss should be the validity of the typological analysis as a tool of clustering cultural parks into groups that generate similar level of CES. It may be suppose that the differences in the character of landscape of parks belonging to the same group may significantly affect the benefits generate by them. In order to verify the rightness of adopted criteria of typological analysis the level of services provided by parks located the farthest from the center of each group was estimated. These objects possess the considerably amount of features that distinguish them from the whole set, so it can be assumed that they provide greatly different level of CES than representative objects. Analysis revealed the following ranking points in relation to each group: Group A 13.00 (No. 27); Group B 12.00 (No. 1); Group C 12.00 (No. 19), Group D 11.67 (No. 44); Group E 13.00 (No. 16); Group F 20.00 (No. 14); Group G 13.33 (No. 35). Comparison of these results with those obtained for the representative objects shows that the difference is between 0 (Groups D and G) and 1.33 point (Group F) which corresponds to the maximum difference at the level of 6.2%. This justifies the accurate selection of criterions adopted in typological analysis and indicate the usefulness of the method in the terms of selection of representative cultural parks.

The results indicate that a key factors deciding on both the highest and lowest rating position are the richness and diversity of cultural heritage, as well as the number of educational institutions. Nadwiślański and Renaissance City Complex of Zamość CP possess the highest values of all those subcategories (4 or 5), whereas Hrubieszowski CP the lowest (0,1 or 2). In majority of the cases those sub-categories are correlated. In the case of parks with many historical monuments the diversity is more probable than incases of the areas where there are only a few objects important for cultural heritage. The less important revealed to be recreational subcategory, which value differs among the parks of the highest and the lower ranking position.

Besides, it is worthy to emphasize that in adopted scheme the highest weight possess aesthetic values, as the mean value of this category is 4.3. Whereas, the lowest educational benefits of the mean value 1.3. It derives from the fact that landscape physiognomy is one of the factors determining the establishment of cultural park according to law provision. Presence of museums, open-air museums, or regional memorial hall are generally not taken into account on the stage of park boarders' designation.

Finally, in the light of the results one should ask whether the parks of the highest rank should be established firstly? Do the level of services provision should be taken into account on the stage of protected areas designation? In the process of delineation of cultural parks as key factors are taken into account: values, state of preservation and threats to objects of cultural heritage (Kałamucka 2008: 314). Economic benefits, which parks generates or may generate, are generally not analyzed. Of course, financial issues are important, as for example a self-financing palace-museum provides opportunity to its maintenance in a good condition. However, they should not be of the primary importance because such approach would result in the loss of many valuable cultural objects, as well as harmonious cultural landscapes whose value cannot be directly measured (Spash 2008: 265-267). Such thinking is consistent with the approach adopted in the manuscript as services are understand as values rather than economic benefits. Besides, the need of creation in the first place parks which received the highest scores in the conducted ranking, was indicated by others. Inter alia prof. Andrzej Tomaszewski et al., (1996) mentioned Kazimierz Dolny and Nałęczów surrounding area and the Roztocze region and by The Regional Centre for Research and Documentation of Monuments in Lublin lists Nadwiślański, Zamość and Brześć Fortification CP (Kałamucka 2008.). Thus, the results are consistent with other researcher and the presented methods gives a new tool helpful in the process of cultural parks designation.

BIBLIOGRAPHY

Alessa, L., Kliskey, A. and Brown G. (2008). Social-ecological hotspots mapping: a spatial approach for identifying coupled social-ecological space. *Landscape and Urban Planning,* 85, pp. 27–39.

Baron, J. and Spranca, M. (1997). Protected values. *Organizational Behavior and Human Decision Processes,* 70, pp. 1-16.

Boyd, J. and Banzhaf, S. (2007). What are ecosystem services? The need for standardized environmental accounting units. *Ecological Economics* 63, pp. 616–626.

Brosius, J.P. (2010). Conservation trade-offs and the politics of knowledge. In: N. Leader-Williams, W.M. Adams, R.J. Smith, ed., *Trade-offs in Conservation: Deciding What to Save,* Wiley-Blackwell, Oxford, UK, pp. 311-328.

Chan, K.M.A., Satterfield, T. and Goldstein, J. (2012). Rethinking ecosystem services to better address and navigate cultural values. *Ecological Economics,*74, pp. 8–18.

Costanza, R., D'Arge, R., De Groot, R., Farberk, S., Grasso, M., Hannon, B., Limburg, K, Naeem, S., O'Neill, R.V., Paruelo, J., Raskin, R.G., Suttonk, P. and van den Belt, M. (1997). The value of the world's ecosystem services and natural capital. *Nature,* 387, pp. 253–260.

Brown, G. and Raymond, C. (2007). The relationship between place attachment and landscape values: towards mapping place attachment. *Applied Geography,* 27, pp. 89-111.

Darvill, R. and Lindo, Z. (2015). Quantifying and mapping ecosystem service use across stakeholder groups: Implications for conservation with priorities for cultural values. *Ecosystem Services,* 13, pp. 153–161.

Decree No. 1/2015 of Regional Conservator of Lublin voivodship on the list of monuments inscribed in the Register of immovable monuments of Lublin province and Register of archaeological sites of Lublin province

Delimitation of Cultural Parks. The evaluation of the Spatial Development Plan of the Lublin voivodship (2006). The Regional Centre for Research and Documentation of Monuments in Lublin on behalf of the Spatial planning office, Vol. 3. Lublin, materials reproduced

Fisher, B., Turner ,R.K. and Morling, P. (2009). Defining and classifying ecosystem services for decision making. *Ecological Economics,* 68, pp. 643–653.

Gilipin, A. (2000). *Environmental Economics: A critical Overview.* Wiley, Chiscester, UK.

Groot, R.S., Wilson, M.A. and Boumans, R.M.J. (2002). A typology for the classification, description and valuation of ecosystem functions, goods and services. *Ecological Economics,* 41, pp. 393–408.

Hein, L., van Koppen, K., de Groot ,R.S. and van Ierland, E.C. (2006). Spatial scales, stakeholders and the valuation of ecosystem services. *Ecological Economics,* 57, pp. 209–228.

Hernández-Morcillo, M., Plieninger, T. and Bieling C. (2013). An empirical review of cultural ecosystem service indicators. *Ecological Indicators,* 29, pp. 434-444.

Kałamucka, W. (2008). Cultural parks in Lublin province. Management of cultural landscape. *Dissertations of the Cultural Landscape Commission* 10, pp. 310-318.

Millennium Ecosystem Assessment (MEA), (2005). *Ecosystems and Human Well-being: Current State and Trends*, Volume 1. Findings of the Condition and Trends. Working Group of the Millennium Ecosystem Assessment. Island Press Washington, Covelo, London.

Jagt, A.P.N., Craig, T., Anable, J., Brewer, M.J. and Pearson, D.G. (2014). Unearthing the picturesque: The validity of the preference matrix as a measure of landscape aesthetics. *Landscape Urban Planning*, 124, pp. 1-13.

Kumar, M. and Kumar, P. (2008). Valuation of the ecosystem services: a psycho cultural perspective. *Ecological Economics* 64, pp. 808-819.

Martín-López, B., Gómez-Baggethun, E., Lomas, P.L. and Montes, C. (2009). Effects of spatial and temporal scales on cultural services valuation. *Journal of Environmental Management,* 90, pp. 1050–1059.

Norton, L.R., Inwood, H., Crowe, A. and Baker A. (2012). Trialling a method to quantify the 'cultural services' of the English landscape using Countryside Survey data. *Land Use Policy*, 29, pp. 449–455.

Protection of Monuments Law, (2003). Journal of laws 2003, No.162, item 1568.

Satz, D., Gould, R.K., Chan, K.M.A., Guerry, A., Norton, B., Satterfield, T., Halpern, B.S., Levine, J., Woodside, U., Hannahs, N., Basurto, X. and Klain, S. (2013). The Challenges of Incorporating Cultural Ecosystem Services into Environmental Assessment. *AMBIO,* 42, pp. 675-684.

Schaich, H., Bieling, C. and Plieninger T. (2010). Linking Ecosystem Services with Cultural Landscape Research. *GAIA,* 19, pp. 269–277.

Tomaszewski, A., Bogdanowski, J., Michałowski, A., Łuczyńska-Bruzda, M., and Malinowska, H. (1996). The fifth programme. Protection and conseravtion of the hitorical cultural landscape. Sketch of the concept of the National System for the protection of historic cultural landscapes in Poland (1996). *Studies and materials. Landscapes series*, 16 (28), Centre for the Protection of Historic Landscape, National Institution of Culture, Warsaw 1-40.

Solon J. (2008). The concept of "Ecosystem Services" and its application in the study of ecological and landscape. *Landscape Ecology Problems* 21, pp. 25-44.

Sowińska, B. and Chmielewski, T.J. (2012). Local landscapes of Roztocze: delineation, diagnosis, design guidelines. *Problems of landscape ecology,* 33, pp. 277-290.

Sowińska-Świerkosz, B. and Soszyński, D. (2014). Landscape structure versus the effectiveness of nature conservation: Roztocze region case study (Poland). *Ecological Indicators,* 43, pp.143-153.

Spash, C.L. (2008). How much is that ecosystem in the window? The one with the bio-diverse trail. *Environmental Values,* 17, pp. 259–284.

Spatial Development Plan of the Lublin voivodship, (2002). Spatial Planning Office. Lublin

Tetlock P.E. (2003). Thinking the unthinkable: sacred values and taboo cognitions. *Trends in Cognitive Sciences,* 7, pp. 320-324.

Turner, K.G., Vestergaard Odgaard, M., Bøcher, P.K., Dalgaarda,T. and Svenning, J.H. (2014). Bundling ecosystem services in Denmark: Trade-offs and synergies in a cultural landscape. *Landscape and Urban Planning,* 125, pp. 89-104.

Wilson, M.A. and Howarth R.B. (2002). Discourse based valuation of ecosystem services: establishing fair outcomes through group deliberation. *Ecological Economics,* 41, pp. 431–443.

online sources

http://www.nid.pl/pl/Informacje_ogolne/Zabytki_w_Polsce/rejestr-zabytkow/ - National Heritage Board of Poland web page [access 15.12.2015]

THE LANDSCAPE RECOMPOSITION OF THE FESTUNG KRAKAU – A NEW APPROACH BASED ON AIRBORNE LASER SCANNING POINT CLOUD PROCESSING AND GIS SPATIAL ANALYSES

Karolina Zięba, Piotr Wężyk

University of Agriculture in Krakow, Faculty of Forestry, Institute of Forest Resources Management,
Department of Forest Management, Geomatics and Forest Economics

ABSTRACT

The landscape is a key resource of a fortified area, with camouflage greenery being an important element. Understanding of a historic fortification system in its entirety and the associated cultural and environmental heritage is the main argument calling for the necessity of having an interdisciplinary approach to the research of historic fortification greenery and the landscapes of historic fortifications. The enormous area of the sites, the techniques that went into designing them based on an analysis of the topographical landscape and the scope of the changes made to the landscape demonstrate the advanced level of military engineering that went into creating this structured greenery, the remains of which have amazingly survived to the present.
The composed arrangements of fortress greenery are a valuable part of the natural environment, would guarantee that endangered species of flora and fauna are preserved in the environment. The contemporary role of fortress greenery is to serve as the foundation for consolidating or renovating areas on the outskirts of the city that were part of the former fortification landscape. This is also a guideline for the modern use of the imitative method in connection with undesirable areas in the landscape
With Airborne Laser Scanning data this study identifies forms of fortifications, visualizes data and analyzes visibility to project recomposition of landscape of III Fortified Sector of Festung Krakau.
ALS data are new form of geospatial data useful for landscape architects. These data gives new means to protect and revitalize cultural landscape. Study discusses possibilities of adaptation and modernization of fortification based on landscape conservation theory and project practice.Possibility of using III Fortified Sector of the Festung Krakau for recreational and didactic purposes is proposed. Project based on visibility analysis and historical materials show way to restore compositional values of landscape with fortifications.
Analysis 3D GIS showed high usefulness to identify fortification, visualization of these objects and performance analysis visibility. In contrast to traditional methods (inventories and historical documentation), data from laser scanning are the new generation of geospatial data. They offer an opportunity to develop a new, faster technology used in the restoration, preservation and inventory of military architecture.

Keywords
Spatial GIS analyses, Airborne Laser Scanning, fortified landscape, recomposition, fortress Krakow

1. INTRODUCTION

Krakow, because of its strategic situation is a city with the traces of fortifications originating from various historical periods. The stronghold of Krakow (Festung Krakau) is a historic complex of constructions and fortifications surrounding the city and specific management of the urban and suburban space from 18th till 19th century, which was the result of military functions of Krakow, which were fulfilled since the end of the First Republic of Poland, through the Partitions, until the Independence. The objects of fortification are not only interesting by themselves, but also due to their attractive situation, i. e. landscape context. From the beginning they were constructed in a strict linkage with natural relief and the complexes of vegetation. Nowadays they are in the city centre and on the outskirts of the city, often in the areas of particular landscape values (Bogdanowski, 1993). One of the methods, which can help in making decisions referring to the management of a valuable landscape of the stronghold, is airborne laser scanning, a technique allowing precise obtaining of information on the appearance and shape of the area with no need to contact the object directly (Wężyk, 2006).

The article presents the technology of airborne laser scanning, used in the inventory and modelling of 3D architectonic objects and landscape connections. To prove the usefulness of this tool, the inventory of selected fortifications of Festung Krakau. The studies were carried out to identify the form of fortification, visualise these objects and make the analyses of the visibility, which would be helpful at the landscape re-composition of the historic layout of Festung Krakau.

The carried out analyses are aimed at showing the potential of data obtained from airborne laser scanning, in the work of the landscape architect, as a new generation of geospatial data applied in the protection, inventory and revitalization of cultural landscape.

1.1. Material and Methods

1.1.1. Festung Krakau

In the area of the Commune of the Krakow City there are 35 forts (counting those beyond the administrative borders of the city the number grows to 49), 4 fortress gates, 15 ammunition bunkers, batteries, sangars and caverns. Only some of the still preserved Festung Krakau objects are in use. Others are not managed and not available to visitors.

The area of the this study is located in the western part of Krakow. The studies were carried out in the area of Defence Region III of Festung Krakau, located in Forest Wolski and on the borders of Forest Wolski (upper part of the Vistula River – the Rudawa Valley), regarding objects included in the Trail of Festung Krakau, i.e.: Fort 39 Olszanica, Fort 38 Skała, Fort „Bielany" („Krępak"), Fort „Gumańczy Dół", Ammunition Bunker „Kazamata", Machine Gun Stand at Sangar IS-III-2, adjacent batteries (Battery FB 36 „Ostra Góra", Field Battery FB 35 „Srebrna Góra") and objects not lying directly on the path of the historic Stronghold: the Camaldolese Monastery in Bielany and the Józef Piłsudski Mound of Independence (Fig.1). Objects of Festung Krakau were selected in such a way that fortifications are reasonably well preserved. Additional criterion of selection was the location of the constructions. On one hand the forts giving a good view to the surroundings, on the other hand more hidden forts were selected to do analyses if different visibility.

Forts and other military objects are usually building covering large areas, the combinations of buildings and earth objects, with difficult access to them. Moreover, these objects are often overgrown with abundant vegetation or even "hidden" in forests (Środulska-Wielgus, 2005). Forts of the Festung Krakau, after the Second World War became forgotten objects, around which secondary succession of trees and shrubs occurred, which definitely make the traditional inventory more difficult.

Nowadays traditional tools in the studies of the fortification are first of all geodetic measurements, historical documentation and project documentation as well as archival photographs, written texts and airborne photos (Molski, 2012). Contrary to these methods, laser scanning data make new generation of geospatial data. They create the possibility of new quick technology used in the protection and inventory of military architecture, as well as doing spatial analyses.

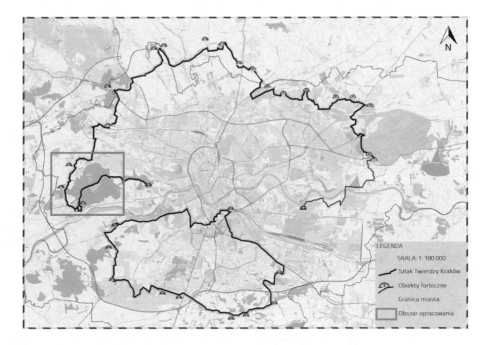

Fig.1. Objects of fortifications on the Trail Festung Krakau – north loop with the marked study area (by K. Zięba).

1.1.2. Airborne Laser Scanning

In the inventory and measurement of military objects, the technology of airborne laser scanning (ALS) is particularly useful. Laser beam has great ability to penetrate the vegetation covered areas and due to this, sufficiently dense cloud of points is made, containing information on the scanned objects, also those hidden under the vegetation (Wężyk, 2008). The cloud of points is a source of information on the state of scanned objects, especially on geometric parameters of the objects.

Applied in this paper altitude data come from the Centre of Geodetic and Cartographic Documentation (Centralny Ośrodek Dokumentacji Geodezyjnej i Kartograficznej – CODGiK) in Warsaw. The analyses were based on the cloud of points coming from the airborne laser scanning of Krakow, which was obtained during the flights from 07/07/2012 till 9/07/2012 within the project of ISOK (Informatyczny System Osłony Kraju) - Information System of the Protection of the Country against the extraordinary threat. Scanning covered the area of 492 km2. The flight was carried out on the Cessna T206H plane. The height of the flight was about 880 m, maximal speed of the aeroplane during scanning the rows was 41.2 m/s. The type and model of the applied laser scanner was LMS-Q680i RIEGL, type and model of system GPS/INS: AeroControl, airborne camera model is Hasselblad50 (CODGiK, 2012).

The majority of spatial data is put into archives in cartographic modules, called calculation sheets. The study area was covered by 56 sheets in the system of co-ordinates of flat perpendiculars PUWG-92 in scale 1:1250 (1/64 sheet 1:10 000, i.e. the area of about 0.5x0.5 km), and height (Z) refer to the system of normal heights „Kronsztadt 86". Files contain the cloud of ALS points, written according to standard 1.2 published in 2008 by ASPRS (American Society for Photogrammetry and Remote Sensing). The correctness of the classification of points is not lower than 95%. Mean density points is 12 pts/m2 (Standard II according to ISOK). Apart from coordinates (XYZ), these files contain the information the class of the point and the intensity of the reflection and three ranges of the visible part of electromagnetic radiation (RGB), obtained from airborne images.

1.1.3. Processing of the Cloud of LiDAR Points and 3D Modelling

Correct altitude classification of the cloud of ALS points is important for possibility of differentiation of such elements as: ground, buildings, or vegetation: low, medium and tall. It also allows later generation of the Digital Terrain Model (DTM), Digital Surface Model (DSM) and normalized Digital Surface Model (nDSM). In case of objects such as forts, a particular attention should be paid. According to the ISOK standard, objects such as fortifications should not belong to category „Building", just to class „Ground". This is often caused by the vegetation on the roofs growing on such objects, their partial covering of these constructions with soil, as well as often matching the relief. This situation, during the correction of classification requires reclassification of points lying on the ground and belonging to the class of buildings to detect fortification objects correctly.

Modelling 3D (DTM/DSM) is a stage, which gives great opportunities of further obtaining information about the analysed object. First of all, unlike the cloud of points, 3D models provide the image, which is more understandable for the user. The object is represented not by single points, but by a network of triangles of the mutually connected triangles – triangulated irregular network (TIN) making the surface. The obtained models give precise image of the scanned area.

DTM covers only data from class „ground" (Fig. 2). DSM is a model containing data from all the classes of the point cloud, while nDSM is made as a result of subtracting the values of the DTM data from DSM. The effect of such an action is a model considering vegetation, buildings and other elements not being the ground, of relative altitude from the ground. Generating normalized Digital Surface Model (zDSM), which contains information on the objects covering the area of relative altitudes from the ground level, which allows precise analyses of the spatial structure of vegetation (Wężyk, 2008). To compare the results analyses of GIS visibility, modified DSM was also made without vegetation class and DSM without buildings class.

Fig.2. ALS data (ISOK) for Fort no. 38 Skała - points cloud, 2,5D view. Colours in the cloud of points, according to ISOK classification (FugroViewer).

2. CONTENTS

Data from the laser scanning in the form of the cloud of ALS points, or as altitude models are not graphic information, which can be interpreted only visually. Due to the fact that every point obtained during the scanning process scanning has its situation in the local and global system of coordinates, it is possible that making many analyses and their processing to obtain subsequent data and statistics (Vatan, 2009). Similar works made with traditional methods, would make the inventory of the object very time consuming, thus impossible to be carried out.

The formed DTM were used in the identification of the forms of fortification and the assessment of their preservation state. The recognition of the instruments and elements of fortification objects was made based on historical notes and project documentation, as well as maps and archive maps. Based on the collected information the identification of elements, based on hillshade DTM, 3D views and cross-sections was made. In the majority of cases it was possible to identify in detail the elements of forts, sometimes not even marked in archival drawings and not visible in ortho-photomaps.

As an example Fort „Olszanica" can be taken, which is preserved in a satisfactory state or, if other objects of Festung Krakau are taken into account, the state can be regarded good. Model 2,5D (Fig. 5) gives an accurate image of the whole fort; many of the elements visible in the model cannot be seen or reached while moving on the object. The model of the area shows a well preserved shape of the object with the moat.

The infantry Fort IS-III "Gumańczy Dół" is earth fortification. The ramparts and the moat centrally surrounded a concrete shelter, which was not preserved until now. Being in the area of the object, its layout is totally illegible for the visitor, bushes and trees obliterate its shapes and the destruction as it suffered as a result of the collapse of the ramparts make the fort look like ordinary trenches. Model 3D shows the full view of the discussed object. An intact initial outside and inside layout is also visible.

Fortifications from the beginning were built in a strict linkage with natural relief or sets of vegetation, supplementing this way natural obstacles and

Fig.3. DTM, 2D view with the hillshade effect. Clearly visible characteristic element in the field: earth fortress objects: Fort: Olszanica, Skała, Gumańczy Dół, Krępak, Battery: „Srebrna Góra", „Ostra Góra" and the J. Piłsudski Independence Mound.

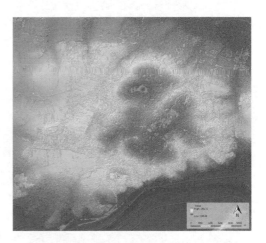

Fig.4. DSM (right), 2D view, colours: red –maximal altitudes, blue – minimal altitudes.

shields. Works in the area of landscape revitalization of Festung Krakau one should start marking the series of viewing points (localized on 3D model) on the old Bow Box Road (Droga Rokadowa joining all the forts (today: tourist Path of the Festung Krakau) and based on the information acquired to establish the directives to form this part of the city to make future management of this part of the city, so that future urban architectonic structure influenced the elevation of the quality, e.g., by opening the view and not to degrade the landscape.

The openings of the view from some objects to other objects in Festung Krakau, allow us to understand the character of the fortification and relationships between its elements, however, in many cases these views are not clear or even not existent, because of the high vegetation. The analyses of the view will help to answer the question how the visibility changed, and consequently, how fortification landscape changed over the years. Using traditional methods, such papers were written with the use of maps, and their verification was based on site inspections. The presented method applies DTM and DSM as data to analyse:

I.   Actual area of visibility, based on DSM;
II. Defining the potential visibility based on the relief - DTM;
III. Defining visibility based on the modified DSM without vegetation;
IV. Defining visibility based on the modified DSM without buildings.

The analyses of the area of view are based on the assumption that the light is penetrating the homogenous environment, that the light penetrates in homogenous environments in a straight lines. The applied in the visualizations digital models of light totally disregard phenomena of the overlapping and deflection of electromagnetic waves. It does not, however prevent the application the simulation of spatial phenomena proper for landscape rocks, because overlapping and deflection has a significance in the

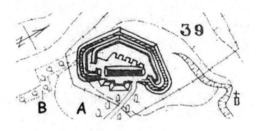

39 - A - droga dojazdowa, B - zadrzewienie maskujace

Fig.5. Archival drawing of Fort 39 Olszanica;
A - driveway, B - masking trees.

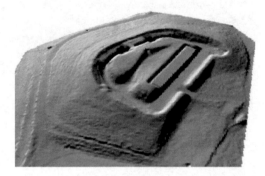

Fig.6. Visible elements of Fort Olszanica on the hilldhade
DTM, isometric 2,5D view.

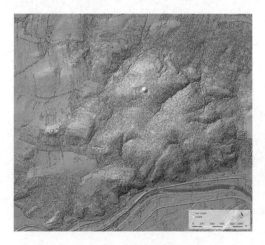

Fig.7. Actual range of visibility from Fort 38 Skała based
on DSM (ArcMap 10.1 Esri).

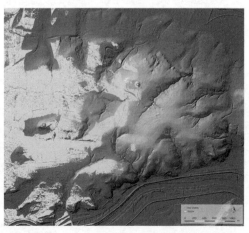

Fig.8. Range visibility from Fort 38 Skała based on DTM
(ArcMap 10.1 Esri).

distances comparable for the length of waves. Computer visibility analyses use digital models of light to determine visible elements. The light of these models is covered geometric objects as a result of algorithms determining visible areas (Ozimek, 2002). To mark the visibility areas the algorithm Observer Point (ArcMap 10.1, Esri) was applied. The observer was given the height corresponding the average height of a human, i.e. 1.70 m. The model of point light situated in the viewing point sent rays on the surface of 3D height model (DTM/DSM), exposing them and giving unambiguous information on visible and invisible elements (0;1) from a given place of observation.

Visibility maps clearly show the verges of the view shadow, occurring on the opposite side of the areas coloured towards the observer's point. They are the result of the relief features, or the occurrence of the curtain view in the form of trees.

To check the visibility line from point do point (between forts) algorithm Line Of Sight (3D Analyst) was applied. The order was applied both on DTM and DSM to observe the influence of the vegetation and buildings on visibility between forts. If the target object is visible from the observation point, a visible part of the vision line is green, and the line outside the point of covering is red.

Tabela 1. Visibility range from Fort 38 Skała in the framework of the paper based on DSM

Name	Visibility	Value [ha] / [%]	Study area [ha] / [%]
Fort 38 Skała DTM	0 – invisible	1387 / 78.2 %	1773 / 100%
	1 – visible (yellow)	386 / 21.8 %	

Tabela 2. Visibility range from Fort 38 Skała in the framework of the paper based on DTM

Name	Visibility	Value [ha] / [%]	Study area [ha] / [%]
Fort 38 Skała DSM	0 – invisible	1770 / 99.8 %	1773 / 100%
	1 – visible (yellow)	3 / 0.2 %	

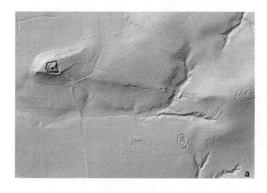 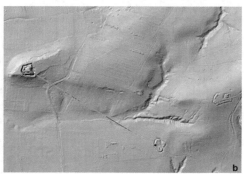

Fig.9 **a.** Visibility line on the DTM: I. From Fort Skała to Fort Gumańczy Dół; **b.** Visibility line on the DTM: II. From Fort Gumańczy Dół to Fort Skała (green line – visible part, red line- invisible part).

Fig.10 **a.** Visibility line on the Digital Surface Modelu: from Fort Skała to Fort Gumańczy Dół (green line - visible part, red line - invisible part); **b.** Visibility line on the Digital Surface Modelu: from Fort Gumańczy Dół to Fort Skała (green line - visible part, red line - invisible part).

Forts of the Festung Krakau were built in the distance of 3 km one from another, to provide protection and to be mutually visible. Based on the analyses it can be concluded that while constructing the Stronghold, when masking trees were not that visible, the visibility line was peserved (the example with DTM application).

3. CONCLUSIONS

In the paper the opportunities of the application of the cloud of ALS points from ISOK (Information System of the Protection of the Country) project in the methods of studying military architecture (complexes of newer fortification) and fortification landscape were analysed. The 3D GIS analyses showed great usefulness of the application of data from laser scanning in the identification of fortification forms, visualisation of these objects from the visibility analyses. Contrary to traditional methods of getting information (field inventories combined with historic documentation), data from laser scanning make new generation of geospatial data. They make possibility of making new faster technology used in revitalization, protection and inventory of military architecture in Poland.

The obtaned results of the carried out analyses allow the statement that the application of data from ISOK can be used to the analysis of the topography of fortification complexes in studying the landscape. Geospatial data can be used on many accuracy levels, at the same time preserving great legibility and high resolution, contrary to traditional geodetic materials (general maps and topographic maps). Analysing the cloud of ALS points, in the State Geodetic and Cartographic Resource, the errors in their classification were found. The errors referred both to badly classified fragments of fortifications and the whole objects. Thus, it is necessary to edit the classification, especially in more detail applications.

The formed terrain models allowed the analysis of the same architectonic objects are fortifications – examining the degree of their preservation, due to the opportunities of visualization in 2.5D view without the surrounding vegetation. The studies show that the results of the carried out analyses are useful in inventory works. The presented forms of the visualization of the relief are distinct and legible for persons with no professional preparation. They can be a valuable supplementation of the presentation of different problems connected with widely understood sustainable management of the living space surrounding us.

Comparing the obtained DTM wits old photographs and topographic maps, one can conclude about the state of the preservation of fortification and destruction that were inflicted over the time. The analysis of the course of the ground (DTM) turns out to be useful also in archaeological terms, especially in the situation when the old buildings were not preserved. Airborne laser scanning allows avoiding the problem of the penetration of high vegetation and shrub vegetation as well as ruderal vegetation into the area of fortifications. 3D modelling of objects or DTM / DSM allow the visualization without vegetation.

BIBLIOGRAPHY

Bogdanowski, J., 1993. *Krajobraz warowny XIX/XX w. Dzieje i rewaloryzacja*, Politechnika Krakowska im. Tadeusza Kościuszki.

Molski, P., 2012. *Ochrona i zagospodarowanie wybranych zespołów fortyfikacji nowszej w Polsce. Seria Architektura*, Prace Naukowe Politechniki Warszawskiej.

Środulska-Wielgus, J., 2005. *Atlas Twierdzy* Kraków, Tom 4, Urząd Miasta Krakowa, Wydział Kultury i Dziedzictwa Narodowego, Oddział Ochrony Zabytków Kraków.

Vatan, M., Oguz, M., Bayram, B., 2009. The use of 3D laser scanning technology in preservation of historical structures, *Concervation News*, 26/2009.

Wężyk, P., 2006. Wprowadzenie do technologii skaningu laserowego, Lidar w leśnictwie. *Roczniki Geomatyki*, pp.119-132.

Wężyk, P, 2008. Modelowanie cloud of points ze skaningu laserowego w obszarze koron drzew. Geoinformacja obrazowa w świetle aktualnych potrzeb. *Archiwum Fotogrametrii, Kartografii i Teledetekcji*, pp. 685-695.

Wężyk, P., Solecki, K., 2008. Określanie wysokości drzewostanów nadleśnictwa Chojna w oparciu o lotniczy skaning laserowy (ALS). Geoinformacja obrazowa w świetle aktualnych potrzeb. Archiwum Fotogrametrii, Kartografii i Teledetekcji, pp. 663-672.